STANLEY GIBBONS STAMP COLLECTING SERIES

STAMP COLLECTING

A Guide To Modern Philately

STANLEY PHILLIPS

Revised by John Holman

STANLEY GIBBONS PUBLICATIONS LTD
399 Strand, London WC2R 0LX

By Appointment to H.M. The Queen
Stanley Gibbons Ltd, London
Philatelists

Stamp Collecting was first published in 1932
First edition in this form 1983

Also in this series:
Stamp Collecting – How to Start
Stamp Collecting – How to Identify Stamps
Stamp Collecting – Collecting by Theme
Stamp Collecting – How to Arrange and Write-Up a Stamp Collection
Stamp Collecting – Philatelic Terms Illustrated

Designed by Julia Lilauwala

Printed in Great Britain by BAS Printers Limited,
Over Wallop, Hampshire

ISBN 0 85259 047 4
Item No. 2764

Preface

When published in 1932 Stanley Phillips's *Stamp Collecting* quickly became a standard reference work for all collectors who wished to take their philatelic knowledge beyond the bare essentials. At least two generations of philatelists were indebted to Mr Phillips for providing the foundations for their collecting. A second edition appeared in 1936 and there were six further editions, the last of which was published in 1965. Each new edition was revised by Phillips or a senior member of the Gibbons staff including the late C.P. Rang, James Watson and the present Editor of *Gibbons Stamp Monthly* Russell Bennett.

Phillips was a man of high ideals and strong views. He was convinced there was a proper way of doing things and that he—as a Managing Director of Stanley Gibbons—had a responsibility to set out for collectors a guide to the accepted ways of stamp collecting. Hence the predecessor of this book was born. Since then stamp collecting has developed and achieved a popularity even Phillips would have found surprising and areas of collecting scorned or neglected in the 1930s have now gained respectability. Changes too have taken place both in the operations of the postal service and in the physical charactersitics of stamps themselves.

There was thus a considerable need for extensive revisions to the book. Editorial work on a ninth edition of *Stamp Collecting* was begun in 1979. Later it was decided to completely modernise and update Mr Phillips's book and this work was completed in 1982 by John Holman, a newcomer to the Gibbons Publications team, working under the supervision of Russell Bennett. Extensive rewriting has taken place throughout, in particular the sections on Different Types of Stamps, Postmarks, Ways of Collecting, the Stamp World and Stamp Literature. The chapters on Cinderella Philately and Postal History—very much minority interests in Mr Phillips's day—are entirely the work of Mr Holman.

Phillips expressed strong views in his book and it has been our aim not to expunge these opinions where they are still relevant to modern collecting. However, today's collector is perhaps a more tolerant and sophisticated creature than his predecessor of fifty years ago and we hope this book reflects this change. It is our hope that this work will—together with the other books in the *Stanley Gibbons Stamp Collecting Series*—provide a readable but comprehensive guide for those new to philately and for the established collector who wants to take a broader view of the hobby enjoyed, in Mr Phillips's words, by a 'great army throughout the world'.

Stanley Gibbons Publications Ltd.

Contents

Introduction

If we peer into the dim recesses of the past, we find that primitive man, lurking in caves and thickets, was both Maker and Hunter. At home he fashioned stone or flint into axes or arrow-heads, and when he went abroad he hunted either the animals which he needed for food, or on special occasions perhaps a woman for wife or an enemy who trespassed on his domain.

As the mind of man unfolded and purely utilitarian considerations ceased to hold absolute sway, we find the Maker setting his hand to rude efforts at artistic creation, carvings on bone or pictorial scratchings on the rock, and we may imagine that the Hunter, too, occasionally turned aside from the search for food and gradually accumulated in his lair a pile of pebbles or lumps of gaily coloured rock which may have caught his wandering fancy.

The child is father of the man, and if we look around us today, we see the Maker and Hunter still at their tasks, though the making is now usually done by machinery, and the search of the Hunter be for fuel rather than for food.

So, too, when we consider the hobbies of the world, the absorbing pursuits to which men and women turn as a relief from the strain of life and work in this most strenuous modern world, we find once more the Maker and the Hunter; on the one hand the Woodworker, the Artist, the Photographer, the Modeller; on the other, the vast body of Collectors.

The individual who decides to make collecting of one sort or another his choice as an amusement for leisure hours, finds, when he comes to make inquiries, that there is one hobby which stands out above all others. It overrides the barriers of race and class and age, linking black and white, and king with schoolboy. It appeals to nearly every type of mind, and is within the reach of every purse. It has, without a shadow of a doubt, the largest number of followers that any collecting hobby can claim. Around and about it has sprung up a world press and a world trade, which in the operation of the law of supply and demand has created out of nothing a stable value of many millions of pounds, and gives regular employment to several thousand people. While other hobbies have waxed and waned in popular favour, this has gone from strength to strength, and is now perhaps more highly and widely esteemed than ever before.

This hobby is postage stamp collecting. The use of the word 'philately' instead of the more familiar term 'stamp collecting' is often very slipshod, little distinction being made between them. The more erudite word, not too carefully coined by some early collector from the Greek, means roughly 'love of exemption from taxation', a feeling which is surely so widely shared as to have ensured the world-wide popularity of the hobby, if its title were truly descriptive! Actually the intended meaning of the word is 'love of that which exempts from taxation', a description which might apply, on rare occasions, even to a Chancellor of the Exchequer, but does not apply to every kind of postage stamp.

We find in practice that the word 'philately' is sometimes used by collectors too snobbish to adopt the simpler term and by journalists in search of a synonym for stamp-collecting. The use of the derived adjective 'philatelic' is almost inevitable as there is no equivalent to be drawn from 'stamp-collecting'.

In its present sense, as used by serious collectors, a stamp collector is one who just collects, without any specific aim or purpose, while a philatelist is a student of what he collects, more particularly in the sense of the admirable definition given by the late A. J. Sefi in his book *An Introduction to Advanced Philately*:

> 'Modern Philately may be said to comprise the study of stamps from every possible angle of historical and philatelic interest. It includes inquiries into the reasons and circumstances leading up to an issue, and researches as to the essays and proofs for the stamps thereof; studies of all the different processes and methods of production used, and of any resultant varieties on the stamps themselves and, finally, inquiries into all the uses or misuses to which the stamps, once issued, might be subject.'

Within this definition is comprised the whole field of study which lies open to the collector who wishes to earn, in one way or another, the right to be called a serious philatelist. He need not attempt to cover it all, even in the case of one particular country or issue, but may deal with only one or two of the possible angles. Stamp collecting—its basis, inception and growth, and the varied attractions which have raised it to its present position, are described in this volume, together with the practical methods by which the collector may best approach his enjoyable task. It is hoped that the work here presented may be of real value to many who are already enthusiasts, and that its perusal may be the means of introducing many more to the pleasures now enjoyed by the great army of stamp collectors throughout the world.

PART ONE
Posts and the Postage Stamp

CHAPTER ONE
The Story of the Post

To appreciate fully the pleasures of stamp collecting it is necessary to realise that the postage stamp is merely the symbol of the working of the postal systems of the world. A postage stamp, as a single item in a collection, may, as we shall see, have intrinsic features of interest, but these are nothing compared with the fact that behind the postage stamp lies the post, that means of communication by which messages of commerce and friendship pass from one end of the world to the other, using every known means of transport, and sometimes in the most difficult circumstances.

The story of the post goes back to the rulers of ancient empires who, for the preservation of themselves and their dominions, were forced to establish courier services by which messages might be carried surely and rapidly, over great roads adequately provided with relay stations, whence untiring man or beast set forth on stage after stage of a journey which might take the ruler's message hundreds or even thousands of miles.

If such posts had not existed, and even in some cases where they did, the emperor might find himself dispossessed of an outlying province either by invasion or revolt before his central authority could take steps to meet the emergency. Letters impressed on clay tablets and in some cases enclosed in clay 'envelopes', have come down to us from Babylon, and Cyrus the Great is credited by the early historians with the horse-relays, a system which was taken up by the Romans and remained the basis of many postal systems until comparatively modern times. Egypt, too, had its postal system, but all these organisations were, of course, for the carriage of official mails alone, and in most cases the government couriers were strictly forbidden to carry private messages, and were severely punished if they broke the rule.

Private correspondence had to depend for transport on the servants of the writers, or, for more distant journeys, letters were entrusted to the hands of traders or seafarers who, in the dangerous conditions of those early days, might, or might not, arrive safely at their destination.

It is not possible to divide the history of the world's posts into periods according to the means of transport employed, for some of the most primitive methods of transportation are still in use in backward parts of the globe, but the letter-carrier who walked gave place to the running courier in those official postal systems where speed was of the greatest consequence and he, in his turn, was replaced by the mounted man. Then came the horse-drawn chariot or other vehicle, followed, after many centuries, by the railway locomotive and the motor-car.

On water, the vessel driven by paddles or oars was succeeded by the sailing ship and later by the steamship. In the air, the pigeon holds pride of place, for this useful bird carried messages for the early Greeks and Romans, and possibly even before their time. Again a long interval, and we find the balloon being used as a mail carrier in exceptional circumstances, often with very uncertain results. Today we have a world-wide network of air routes across continents and oceans; rocket posts have been tested and may eventually find a place among systems of rapid communication.

Stamp collectors are not particularly concerned with the telegraph, but here again, a definite progression may be noted from the primitive use of smoke and drum telegraph, the warning beacons of history, and the semaphore systems of later times, to the telegraph, radio and television of our own day.

Carriage of mail by bicycle and ship

Carriage of mail on foot and by pack mule

Some of the elements of this progress may be found illustrated on postage stamps such as the 1895 issue of Mexico (*SG 218/30* and *0231/43*), which depicts the carriage of mail by foot, pack mule, coach and rail. The 1906 series of Bosnia and Herzegovina (*SG 186/201*) depicts pack animals on the 30h., a horsed wagon on the 40h. and an early postal motor-car on the 50h. value. The United States parcel series of 1912 (*SG P423/34*) shows eight different scenes connected with the delivery of the mails.

A similar series of later date comes from India (*1937, SG 251/8*) which depicts the runner, the bullock cart, the camel, train, steamer, lorry and aeroplane as postal carriers, representing all stages of progress in the carriage of mails, yet all in use at the present day in various parts of the country. Many more stamps illustrate the theme, notably the various 1974 issues for the centenary of the Universal Postal Union. The set issued by Grenada (*SG 628/ MS636*) depicts a wide range of subjects from an eighteenth-century mail coach to *Concorde*.

Transportation of mail by bullock cart

Camel post

King John set up a corps of royal messengers

Early U.S. mail train and Concorde

As the great monasteries and universities of the Middle Ages were the repositories of learning and therefore, apart from the rulers, the first to make frequent use of letter-writing as a means of communication, it is natural that we should be able to trace to them the beginnings of our present-day postal systems, by which not only official correspondence but the communications of the general public are carried.

Regular communication was kept between the various monasteries, and as these were often indebted to local noblemen for sundry favours, it may be supposed that the monastic couriers also carried their correspondence at times. Persons of lesser degree on the rare occasions when they wished to send letters entrusted their correspondence to the services of casual travellers.

The universities, too, whose pupils came from many lands, found it necessary to employ messengers, not least to carry letters from the students to their parents.

As trade and commerce increased their range from the purely local to the national and international fields, regular private services for letter-carrying were established, some of them growing up quite by chance, and others owing their existence to the efforts of wealthy trading communities, such as the merchants of the cities of the Hanseatic League of northern Germany.

Extraordinary journeys were made by some of the messengers of the Middle Ages, the routes extending as far as Venice in the south and into the interior of Russia in an easterly direction. We have to remember, too, that roads as we understand them today were practically non-existent, and for the most part the courier had to make his way across country in the face of risks of all kinds.

In England we find King John (*1199–1216*) maintaining a corps of royal messengers, but though there are indications that the Holy Roman Emperor Charlemagne (*800–814*) met with some success in reviving the old Roman posts, these decayed with the break-up of his empire, and we have to come down to the time of Louis XI (*1461–83*) to discover the royal messenger service which was the forerunner of the French postal system of today.

As might be expected, so wily a monarch as Louis XI fully appreciated the value of a quick and reliable official postal service, and he organised it on an elaborate scale. For a heavy fee his subjects were permitted to use the royal mails, but, trusting no one, the monarch insisted that all letters so carried should be censored.

Though they were of course used at a much later period than that of which we are speaking, the stamps of Thurn and Taxis recall the story of a family which from the fifteenth century down to quite modern times held a leading position as postal organisers in Europe. Counts of Thurn and Taxis covered the continent with a network of posts which, in spite of competition, the risks of war, and a host of other difficulties, did wonderful service, though in a gradually decreasing area, for something like five hundred years. Even as late as the mid-nineteenth century we find the Thurn and Taxis posts covering a territory of 25,000 square miles with a population of nearly four millions, and it was not until 1867 that Prussia bought out the last remaining rights and this great service disappeared.

Cardinal Richelieu

Queen Elizabeth I

Thurn and Taxis families on Belgian stamp

Their activities did not, however, touch France to any great extent, and that country was indebted for its first really public postal system to the vision of Cardinal Richelieu (*1585–1642*). He appointed a postmaster-general, who in course of time built up a courier system which functioned very efficiently and which even included provision for registered letters. The good work done by Richelieu was continued by Mazarin.

The most interesting French post, however, from the stamp collector's point of view, was that instituted in the city of Paris in 1653 by Comte De Villayer. With the royal authority these posts carried letters and parcels throughout Paris, and boxes were set up in various parts of the city where letters could be posted — the forerunners of our modern pillar boxes.

A most fascinating feature of the service consisted in the fact that De Villayer sold wrappers bearing a special mark, which when wrapped round the letter entitled it to be carried by his postal system. The wrappers were torn off by the officials of the post before the letter was delivered, so that they could not be used again. Here we have the earliest form of stamped postal wrapper, which eventually gave rise to the invention of the adhesive postage stamp.

The post of King John in England, to which we have already referred, consisted merely of a staff of couriers standing by to carry royal messages as and when required, and we have to pass on to the reign of Henry VIII (*1509–47*) to trace the establishment of relay stations for the royal service. Elizabeth I (*1558–1603*) laid down formal regulations for the conduct of the service and references have come down to us which show that a certain number of private letters were carried by the post.

The very elementary nature of the post, so far as outlying districts were concerned, is shown by the fact that while King James of Scotland received news of the death of Queen Elizabeth in three days, parts of Devon and Cornwall did not hear the news until after the court had ceased to wear mourning for her. The speed with which news travelled depended largely on the condition of the roads and how near a particular district was to the main routes of travel.

The period of the Stuarts was the birth era of the British post as we know it. The posts were thrown fully open to the public (those who could write and pay) in 1635, and the first Post Office Act was passed by Cromwell (1657) and confirmed by Charles II (1660).

Henry Bishop, the first Postmaster-General, appointed by Charles II introduced the first ever postal markings—usually known as 'Bishop Marks'. They are fully described in Chapter 21.

King James I

Charles II and stamp commemorating the General Letter Office

Henry Bishop – first Postmaster-General (*shown on 1960 stamp exhibition label*)

Dockwra postal marking

The posts were largely farmed out, and the system of rewarding court favourites by remunerative appointments meant that the postal services were often at the mercy of persons who were more concerned to line their own pockets than to give the public satisfactory transport for their correspondence.

Enterprising individuals worked out schemes for improvement, but had to fight the monopolists so that when a famous pioneer, William Dockwra, set up in 1680 an admirable penny post which covered the whole of London, he came into conflict with James, Duke of York, to whom Charles II had allotted the profits of the Government postal service, and the absurd attempts of Titus Oates to link the Dockwra post with the Popish Plot led to that organisation being taken from its creator and incorporated in the official postal system. Dockwra's post is of special interest to the collector, as he used postmarks which indicated the date, time and place of posting, very much as they are used today.

The carriage of mails was improved in the years that followed, but the cost of sending letters, which was calculated on distance, remained very high and it was not until inland penny postage was established in 1840 that the truly popular post could be said to have arrived. As an immediate result of the introduction of the new system, the number of letters carried was more than doubled and cheap postage, one of the great benefits of modern civilisation, had definitely arrived.

Mail by train

Postmen of the 1830s

Meanwhile, the posts of Europe had been improving with the building of new roads and the spread of learning, and the new worlds which were being opened up overseas were going through the primitive stages of their organisation. It is noticeable that, from the very beginning of history, it was always the most enlightened rulers and statesmen who gave attention to the subject of intercommunication. It only remained for the development of the railway locomotive, the motor-car and the aeroplane to bring the postal systems of the world to the high standard of the present day.

The collector who is content to look at his stamps as pieces of paper interesting merely because of their design or some technical detail or defect will undoubtedly derive much pleasure from his hobby, but the man of imagination, who sees behind every stamp the romantic story of the post, will have a background such as few other hobbies can offer.

Think of those early couriers struggling across Europe for weeks and months exposed to attack by robbers or wild animals, or to danger from the elements and the country they traversed. Look at the mail coaches rumbling over terrible roads, and often finding a resting place in the ditch, or relieved of their loads by highwaymen. Read the story of the early express services of the U.S.A., whose messengers covered a rapidly growing territory, and who for very small wages served their countrymen by carrying correspondence through hostile and dangerous country.

Turn to our own day, and think of the men who serve in the great postal systems of the modern world, the seamen and engineers who drive our mail-ships through all the dangers of the seven seas and the staffs of the airlines who cross the mighty Andes, or link Britain with Africa, India or Australia giving us the quickest postal service yet devised by man.

The post by air and sea

Development of the Australian postal service

The collector whose imagination is not fired by the romance of the mails is poorer for the fact, but he need not for that reason turn away from the hobby of stamp collecting. It has many other aspects of appeal.

CHAPTER TWO
The Advent of the Postage Stamp

The seals which were affixed to letters carried by the earliest royal courier services may perhaps be regarded as the germ of the postage stamp idea. True they did not show that postage had been paid, but as the sight of the royal seal ensured prompt attention to the forwarding of the letter, the seal had in effect the power of a frank. The development of this idea may be found in the practice of 'franking' letters by means of the signature of a person (such as a member of parliament) who had the privilege of having his letters carried free in the days prior to the establishment of the more modern postal service.

Until the arrival of the postage stamp, postage on letters carried by the services which the public could use was either prepaid in cash by the sender, or the sum due was collected on delivery. There are therefore many different kinds of mark to be found on correspondence carried in various countries prior to the advent of the adhesive stamp, to indicate that postage has been paid. These are of great interest, and a few of them are often found in a collection of adhesive postage stamps to serve as an introduction to the collection proper.

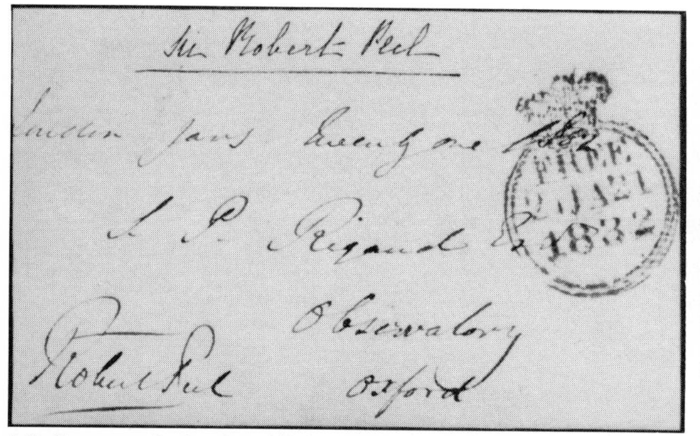

A Parliamentary frank – signed 'Robert Peel' (*Prime Minister 1834–35, 1841–46*)

Sir Rowland Hill

From 1835 onwards the subject of postal reform was being considered in England, and a committee was set up, which sat for three years, and issued numerous reports. Meanwhile Rowland Hill (*1795–1879*) had been at work, and in January 1837 he issued his famous pamphlet on Post Office Reform, the result of which was the formation of a larger committee to examine his proposals. The most important suggestions were for uniform penny postage and that all postage should be prepaid, and the natural corollary was the putting forward of a scheme for issuing stamped wrappers. Adhesive stamps were also referred to, but apparently without very much appreciation of how convenient they would be to the public, for they were mentioned as a possible alternative to the wrapper in the case of an illiterate person bringing an addressed letter to the post office, not enclosed in a stamped wrapper. The adhesive stamp could, in such cases, be stuck directly on the already addressed letter, and would thus obviate the necessity for re-writing the address on the stamped wrapper.

In spite of the opposition which is usually aroused by any reforms which spell progress, the advocates of penny postage won their battle and from 10 January 1840 anyone could send a half-ounce letter anywhere in the United Kingdom for a penny instead of at rates calculated by distance, which were so high as to render the use of the post too costly for the great mass of people. Penny postage, coupled with prepayment of postage, did away with the complications of collecting postal fees on delivery, and prevented the heavy loss of revenue caused by the carriage of letters by private persons in the attempt to avoid the heavy charges of the official post. This evasion was so general that Hill stated that though, from 1815 to 1825, the population had increased by about 30 per cent, there had been no corresponding increase in Post Office revenue. The final guarantee of success was afforded by the issue of the adhesive postage stamp.

In September 1839 the Treasury had invited suggestions 'as to the manner in which the stamp may best be brought into use', and prizes of £200 and £100 were offered for the most useful proposals. In the event four prizes of £100 each were awarded (over 2600 entries having been received), but the stamps that were issued in May 1840 were the work of Perkins, Bacon & Co., as the result of negotiations with Rowland Hill, who had been attached to the Treasury, and the designs for the wrappers and envelopes were the work of the artist William Mulready (*1786–1863*), who was invited to supply them. Thus the Treasury competition, though it produced some very helpful suggestions, and also provided Hill with a valuable assistant in the person of Mr (after Sir) Henry Cole (*1808–82*), one of the prize-winners, cannot be said to have been directly responsible for the issued stamps, letter sheets and envelopes.

Treasury Essay

The Penny Black

The 1d black and 2d blue adhesive stamps and the 'Mulreadys' (as they are usually called by collectors) came into use in May 1840. The 'Mulreadys' met with universal contempt and derision, so that within a week of their issue Rowland Hill was writing 'I fear we shall be obliged to substitute some other stamp for that designed by Mulready, which is abused and ridiculed on all sides'. In consequence the envelopes were withdrawn in 1841 and the letter sheets in 1844. The practical and beautiful adhesive stamps, however, found immediate favour with the public.

Mulready Envelope

So the adhesive postage stamp was born, and though its use is now being curtailed by the increasing employment of automatic franking devices, and the system of prepaying postage in bulk, it has such obvious advantages for private correspondence that we need not fear that it will disappear in our day.

It was not long before the success of the British experiment led to the issue of adhesive postage stamps in other countries, and it may be of interest to give a list of some of those pioneer countries, in the order in which their stamps appeared.

1843. Cantons of Zurich and Geneva (Switzerland) and Brazil.
1845. Canton of Basle (Switzerland).
1847. Trinidad (Lady McLeod local), United States of America and Mauritius.
1849. France, Belgium, Bavaria.

Early stamps of some Foreign countries (*Switzerland, Greece, Spain*)

Early stamps of some Empire countries (*New South Wales, South Australia, Turks Island, Trinidad*)

From 1850 onwards there were numerous accessions to the ranks of stamp-issuing countries and places, and although some of these no longer have their own stamps others have taken their place, and today there are more than two hundred territories which issue stamps for their postal services and for the interest and delectation of the collector.

CHAPTER THREE
Different Types of Stamps

Looking through an old-time stamp collection, we shall find that it contains many stamps (or labels that look like stamps) which are not mentioned in our modern stamp catalogues or collected by most present day philatelists.

The collectors of earlier days, like many juniors nowadays, placed in their albums everything they came across which bore the least resemblance to a postage stamp, and, in consequence we find there many labels which have little or no connexion with the post at all. Such items are usually classified under the generic title 'cinderella stamps' and the reader is referred to Chapter 12 for information about them.

Since the early years of this century, there has been a progressive reduction in the size of the field which the ordinary collector attempts to cover. This curtailment of the scope of a stamp collection has been due to the vast increase which has taken place in the number of stamps issued by all countries. As the number of adhesive stamps grew from year to year, collectors and dealers, finding their album and shelf space overtaxed, tended to discard non-adhesive and non-governmentally issued stamps. More recently cinderella items have become more popular although their appeal is still tiny compared to conventional stamp collecting. In this chapter we look at the main types of stamps issued by postal administrations for postal duty.

Before attempting to divide postage stamps into sub-groups, according to their various functions, the reader should note three terms, which are applicable to the whole group —definitive, commemorative and provisional. Definitives are the ordinary, everyday stamps in permanent use. Often these are used for long periods of time—for example the 'Wilding' definitives of Great Britain introduced in 1952–54 continued in use until 1967–68. The current 'Machin' design has been in use since 1967. Commemorative stamps issued for a particular event or purpose are normally on sale for a relatively short period of time—sometimes only a few weeks and rarely for longer than one year. This type of stamp is examined in Chapter 4. When, for any reason, a postal emergency arises, and stamps for a temporary use have to be produced in a hurry, the collector calls them *provisionals.*

Such stamps are frequently produced by overprinting or surcharging stamps already in existence, to make them suitable for the situation which has arisen, and this subject will be dealt with more fully in a later chapter.

Definitive stamps

Wilding and Machin definitives

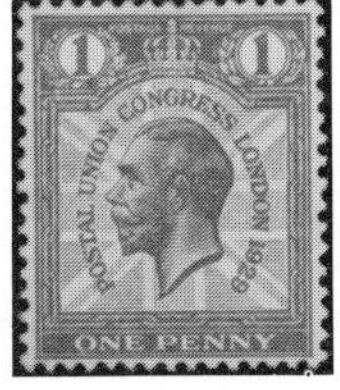

Commemorative stamps

Provisional stamps – new country names or uprating stamp denominations

Postage stamps proper are usually considered to be those which are used for franking ordinary correspondence. In many countries there is only one series of postage stamps, which serves for paying fees in connexion with every available postal service, and which can also be used on telegrams, or for revenue requirements. In other countries some of these functions will be dissociated from the general issue of postage stamps, and in such cases special stamps may be provided.

As ordinary postage stamps, which indicate that postage has been prepaid, are naturally the most numerous group we are not surprised to find that the next most important section is one which pays tribute to the innate forgetfulness or carelessness of the human race, and indicates that postage has not been paid. Such stamps, referred to as *postage due* or *unpaid letter* stamps, are affixed to understamped or unstamped correspondence by the postal authorities, to indicate to the postman and to the addressee the amount which is to be collected on delivery. In most countries the addressee is charged an additional small sum, for the cost of collecting the deficiency in postage, so that a postage due stamp represents not only the payment of a charge for carriage but also this extra fee.

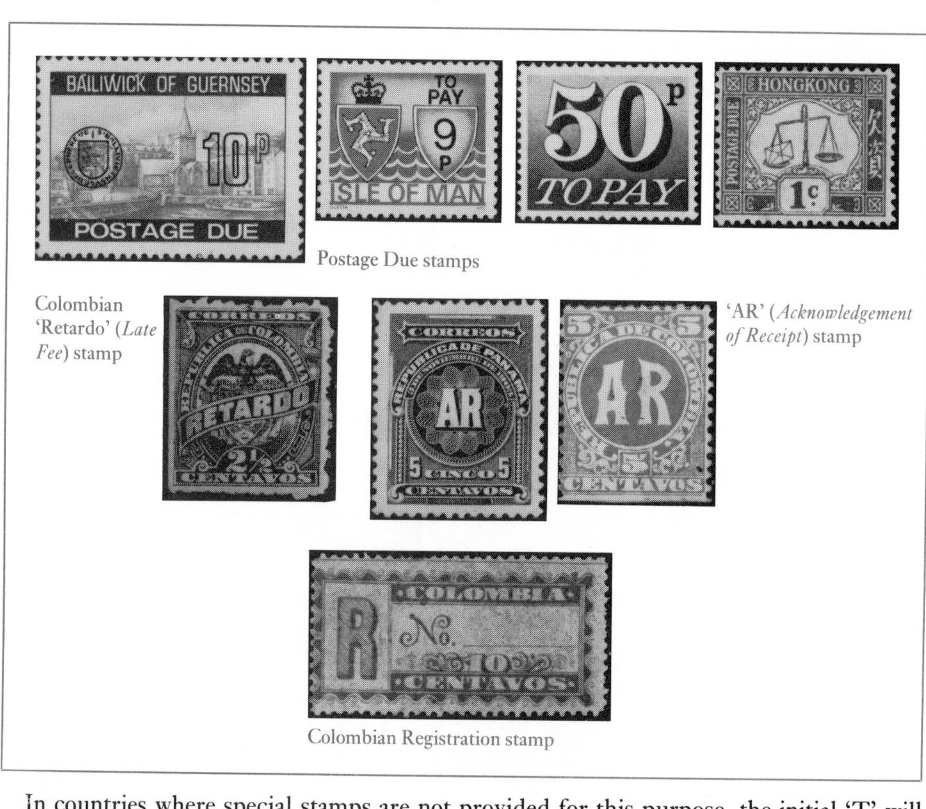

Postage Due stamps

Colombian 'Retardo' (*Late Fee*) stamp

'AR' (*Acknowledgement of Receipt*) stamp

Colombian Registration stamp

In countries where special stamps are not provided for this purpose, the initial 'T' will often be found stamped on letters accompanied by figures showing the amount due to be paid by the addressee. This letter stands for the French word *taxe* which is in international use in connexion with insufficiently stamped correspondence.

Human frailty is catered for more kindly by another class of stamp, the *too late* or *late fee* stamp. This represents an extra sum payable in order to catch a certain mail, after it has been closed down for correspondence posted in the normal course.

Another useful stamp is the *acknowledgement of receipt* stamp, which if bought, and attached to correspondence, ensures that the writer will receive, through the post office, a formal advice that the missive has reached its destination. Such stamps have not been very widely issued, the majority being found among the earlier issues of some of the South and Central American states. They often have the initials 'AR' as a prominent feature of their design, these standing for the Spanish words *aviso de recepción* (advice of receipt).

A service with which all are familiar is the registration of correspondence. An additional fee is paid, which ensures that extra care is taken in transit, and also entitles the correspondent, under specified circumstances, to compensation in the event of the contents of his letter going astray. Some countries have special stamps to indicate that the registration fee has been duly prepaid. They are often not unlike our own registration labels in Great Britain, except that they have the appearance of an oblong postage stamp with a rather more elaborate design than is usually associated with a label. In some countries a space is left on the registration stamp, in which the reference number of the letter it franks is written in ink by the postal clerk.

Express and 'Special Delivery' mail

Air mail stamps

In most countries it is possible to secure more speedy delivery of correspondence on payment of a special fee. Many countries have, at one time or another, provided *special delivery* or *express letter* stamps for this purpose, and in some cases the designs of such stamps have been selected to typify the rapidity (often fictitious) with which delivery could be made, such as a running postman, a motor-cycle, a van, or an aeroplane.

In the United States, stamps inscribed *Special Handling* have been issued. The use of these stamps and the payment of the special scale of fees which they represent, secured quicker handling of parcels. In Denmark, stamps overprinted or inscribed 'Gebyr', were used to indicate that certain fees had been paid, among which was one for the registration of letters too late to catch the normal registered post.

The rapid growth of mail-carrying by air in the 1920s brought into being another class of special service stamp, known to collectors as *air stamps*. They are not, in most countries, exclusively used on correspondence carried by air, but can also be used on ordinary correspondence, just as ordinary stamps can be used for airmail letters.

A set of six stamps and a miniature sheet (*SG 857a/MS857g*) were issued in 1938 by the republican side during the Spanish civil war for a submarine postal service between Barcelona and Menorca. Subterranean mail is represented in the stamp album by the special issues made for the pneumatic post in Italy.

Air mail stamps

Parcel post stamp

A 'jumbo-sized' U.S. Newspaper stamp

Stamps of distinctive designs are sometimes appropriated to specific classes of mail matter. *Newspaper stamps* are sometimes met with, and Austria has had special stamps for newspapers carried at express rates. The earlier newspaper stamps of Austria and Hungary, however, really represent a tax, collected by the post office, on foreign newspapers, but as the newspapers would not have been delivered without the appropriate tax stamps the latter can be regarded, in one sense, as postage stamps.

Parcels, too, have their own stamps in some countries, and Uruguay has issued a series of triangular stamps for use on farmers' parcels. The United States carried multiplicity of special stamps a stage further and issued distinct stamps for payment of postage due on understamped parcels.

It may be asked why these different stamps are issued by various countries, when other nations seem to get on very well with a single series for general use. It is, of course, a convenience for the postal clerk, who has to handle large quantities of mail very rapidly, to be able to tell, by a glance at the postage stamp, whether the item of mail is to be dealt with in any special way. This is why many of the stamps we have been discussing are issued in distinctive designs or colours, or, sometimes, in striking shapes or sizes.

In the days when practically all stamps were used for their legitimate postal purposes, and only very small numbers were taken by collectors, the use of special stamps was helpful for accountancy purposes in connexion with the cost of and receipts from various services. Now, however, collectors take so many stamps of every kind that may be issued, that the number of stamps sold for a particular service may be no indication at all of the number actually used for that service. Attempts have been made from time to time to maintain the principle, by refusing to sell stamps of certain classes to the public, but demand from collectors is usually so great that leakages nearly always occur. However, the issues for the International Court of Justice at The Hague and the O.H.M.S. overprints of Montserrat are examples of stamps which are not officially sold to the public in unused condition, although unused examples have appeared on the philatelic market.

The stamps issued by many countries, particularly in earlier days, for use by government departments (as for example, the *official* stamps of Great Britain and the *departmental* stamps of the U.S.A.) were for a similar purpose—that of checking the use made of the postal service by the various State offices. Overprinting of the ordinary postage stamps of a country with the name or initials of the department was often resorted to in this connexion, but some countries have issued stamps specifically for the purpose and others use stamps punctured with initials. They are known to collectors colloquially as *officials*, *departmentals*, or *service* stamps according to their function.

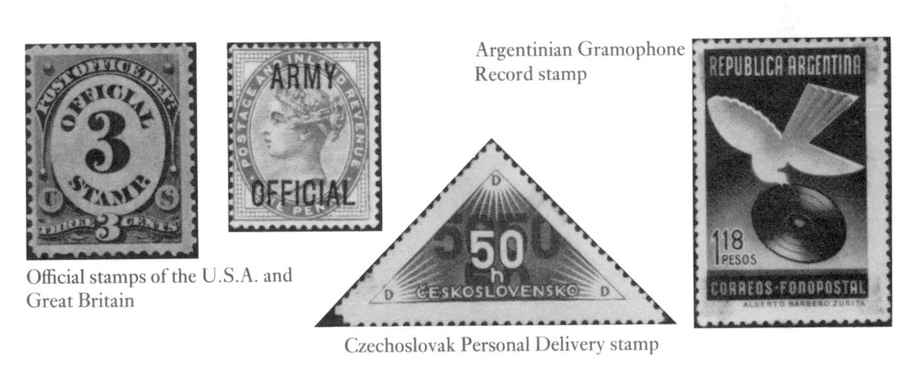

Official stamps of the U.S.A. and Great Britain

Argentinian Gramophone Record stamp

Czechoslovak Personal Delivery stamp

A very interesting, though not very numerous, class of stamps consists of those which, instead of indicating that postage has been paid, show that no postage is payable. These are known as *frank* stamps. They are found among the early issues of Spain, where we have two stamps which franked through the post copies of books which were considered of such public value that they were granted free transit. Similarly, Portugal has granted franking privileges at various times to the Red Cross Society, to civilian rifle clubs, and to the Geographical Society of Lisbon, each having its special stamps, while among the issues of France and other countries we find stamps specially overprinted or inscribed for use on soldiers' letters which were carried free.

In the Dominican Republic, in 1935, a special 25c stamp was issued, which had to be added on letters addressed to the President, while in 1937 Czechoslovakia introduced *personal delivery* stamps, which ensured delivery to the addressee only, a useful innovation for sweethearts!

Another novelty, this time from Argentina, was a service for the delivery of vocally recorded messages. In order that the public might have facilities for making these records, special mobile recording vans were employed. Special stamps were issued in connexion with this service. A gramophone record figures in the design of each.

Some stamps have a dual-purpose in that they can be used to prepay postage and can be used for the payment of a non-postal duty to the government. A stamp whose sole function is to pay a tax on a receipt, to frank a customs document, or to represent the stamp duty on a contract, does not come within the purview of the conventional collector, to whom it is known as a *fiscal* or *revenue*. These are dealt with in Chapter 12.

Where postage stamps can also be used for revenue purposes, the collector will try to find out by means of the postmark or some other feature, in which way the particular specimen before him has been used, and will exclude from his album stamps which (though also available for postal use) can be proved to have served a fiscal purpose.

A sub-group of postage stamps which is excluded from most European stamp catalogues, consists of stamps issued for use on telegrams. Why this group should now be disregarded it is a little hard to say, as the conveyance of a message by telegraph is not so very different from its transmission by letter, and the stamp performs the same office in relation to a telegram as it does in regard to a letter, with the exception that it cannot accompany it on its journey. Telegraph stamps have, on occasion, been used, with authority, for payment of postage, and when such use can be proved, they are collectable as postage stamps, under the name of *postal-telegraphs*.

Telegraph stamp

Postal Stationery – (*and opposite*) Victorian stamped postcards

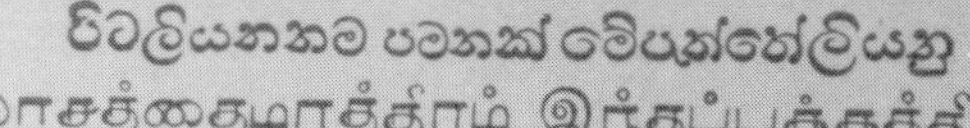

Postal Stationery 'Cut Outs'

Looking at the group of postage stamps themselves it will be noticed that these fall into two main sections: the adhesive stamps, which are printed separately from the postal packet which they are intended to frank, and the impressed stamps, which are printed or embossed on envelopes, postcards or wrappers before they are sold to the public. These impressed stamps, though of great interest and in many cases surpassing the adhesive stamps in beauty, are usually only collected by specialists and postal historians. Envelopes and other postal stationery bearing such impressed stamps are known colloquially to collectors as *entires*, to distinguish them from the impressed stamps cut from such stationery, which are called *cut-outs*.

The collector who comes across stamps of this class, either cut out, or in the complete piece of stationery, might well keep them, not in his main collection, but in a spare album. They may, on occasion, serve to elucidate problems in connexion with the adhesive stamps to which he is more particularly devoting his attention. Telegraph stamps may, for the same reason, find a place in this supplementary collection, and as fiscal stamps are often printed by the same firms as the postage stamps, and by the same processes, they also have a claim to be included.

Finally there is one other type of stamp which should be mentioned here—the local postage stamp—stamps whose validity is limited to a town, district, or route in a country or between particular seaports. Some representatives of this group have retained their places in the standard catalogues for a number of reasons—but the vast majority of old-time locals never come the way of the average stamp collector.

Local Stamp (*Ichang*)

Local stamps are historically interesting, as they often preceded the official government issues of their particular sphere. The fact that they were the product of more or less private individuals was the cause of their falling into disfavour with stamp collectors, for when stocks were exhausted and collector demand continued, the temptation to make reprints of them was, in many cases, too great to be resisted. The forger also took a hand in the game. Locals have a comparatively small, but dedicated, band of followers who have studied them intently and provided the necessary data for distinguishing between originals, reprints and forgeries. Some of the more frequently encountered local stamps are mentioned in Chapter 12.

Having examined the main types of official postage stamp the collector will encounter, we can now move on to look in more detail at one of the most popular of these—the commemorative or special stamp.

CHAPTER FOUR
Commemoratives and Special Issues

Whoever first had the idea of using postage stamps for commemorative purposes deserves both the acclaim and opprobrium of the philatelic world. On the positive side, he has added greatly to the pictorial and historical interest of the hobby, but from another angle he has done considerable harm, giving the countries of the world an excuse for issuing many more postage stamps than they might otherwise have done, and also opening up the way to one of the worst forms of exploiting stamp collectors: the speculative issue.

It was a natural suggestion that stamps, which are so widely circulated, and which travel far beyond the confines of the land which issues them, should be used to commemorate important events or anniversaries. A picture attracts the eye and tells its story quickly, and stamp pictures, which go everywhere and are seen by all, are particularly suitable for reminding the world of events which are worthy of its attention. When it was a question of commemorating an individual, there was the added factor, which carried some weight in less democratic days, that portrayal on postage stamps had originally been an honour reserved for kings and other rulers.

It is a curious fact that, though Britain did not for many years favour commemorative and special issues, it was a British postcard which was the seed from which sprang two of the most prolifically-issued types of stamps—commemoratives and charity stamps. This card, issued in 1890, commemorated the Jubilee of Penny Postage (and thus, of the postage stamp), and though the envelope containing it was only franked with a penny stamp, it was sold at sixpence, the surplus being devoted to a fund for postal servants. All very innocent and laudable, no doubt, but let us see what has grown out of this modest beginning.

No one can deny that a sovereign state has the right to use its postage stamps in any way it pleases, and it is natural that, when a nation is rejoicing over some great event, or celebrating an important anniversary, postage stamps should be pressed into service to do their part. In underdeveloped countries the postage stamp may thus become a valuable medium of education, particularly when it is desired to create, or revive, a national spirit and tradition in a country only recently enfranchised from a foreign yoke.

We must remember, however, that to many needy governments stamp collectors are of more importance than their own people, at least so far as stamps are concerned. A postage stamp can be attractively printed at a low cost. If sold to a member of the public for postal use, it carries with it a liability of the government to provide some form of postal service, to the franking value of the stamp; but when it is sold to a stamp collector, possibly at the other side of the world, the only cost to the country issuing it is the expense of printing it, and the liability to provide service need hardly enter into calculation.

1890 Penny Postage Jubilee card

The commemorative idea thus opened up the way to considerable abuses. Collectors became suspicious of a country which was always changing its definitive stamps, and thought that they were being exploited, but when a country labelled its new issue of stamps as an 'Independence Commemorative Series', and linked it with an historical event which had happened one hundred years before, there was, at first, a natural tendency to consider such an issue as justified, and, in fact, it often was. The excuse was, however, too good to be used only occasionally, and in course of time nearly every country that wanted to increase its postal revenue, started issuing commemorative stamps. Competition between nations for the money of the collector then became keen. Stamps had to attract his eye or appeal to his historical sense, or in some way specially impress themselves on his notice, if they were to stand out from the multitudes which claimed his attention. Thus all sorts of events came to be commemorated; many still, of course, on a purely national basis of genuine desire to issue such stamps for home consumption, but a large number mainly with the object of extracting money from the pockets of collectors.

Violent discussions have raged for many years as to whether the commemorative stamp has done harm to the hobby. It has certainly added greatly to the number of stamps to be collected, but against this must be set the fact that attractive stamps of topical interest are valuable recruiting agents for the hobby. The collector who is interested mainly in the designs and associations of postage stamps will not inquire too closely into the necessity of an issue if it throws light on some person or period hitherto unrepresented in his album, while the enthusiast who is studying the stamps of a country in their relationship to the postal services, may omit from his collection stamps which he considers to have fulfilled no particular function in such services.

If a test is needed as to the necessity or otherwise of a commemorative issue, we can hardly claim to judge it from the national point of view. An event or personage whom we, with our often very limited knowledge of foreign history, may never have heard of, may be an important figure in the story of the nation concerned. We can, however, assert with safety that a series of stamps, if it is to fulfil the purposes of a national commemoration, should be on sale at all the post offices in the country, at least concurrently with its ordinary postage stamps, if not in temporary replacement of them. When however, commemorative stamps are put on sale only at one or two special offices for a very limited period, most of the stamps often find their way into the hands of stamp dealers for sale to collectors. The inhabitants of the country then have hardly any opportunity of buying them or using them, and we may be sure that the motives of the postal authority concerned are far from national publicity.

The worst type issue of all, is, of course, the purely speculative one. Here the very lowest possible number of stamps is put on sale, in such a way that the public gets practically nothing, and the great bulk of stock is bought by a dealer on the spot for a sum which is agreed upon between him and the government. Then the stamps are available, from the local dealer, and at a price considerably in excess of their post office value. Alternatively, stocks are sold to dealers at wastepaper prices, and collectors who have paid full price lose their money.

In stamps, as elsewhere, however, the flock must not be judged by the black sheep, and the commemorative stamp is always interesting, whether necessary or not, for the very reason that the issuing government must link it with a particular person or event, thus adding, as the field of commemoration widens, to the ground covered by a stamp collection.

Commemoration of important events in the lives of rulers

Turning from the circumstances of their issue to the stamps themselves, we are faced with a most striking range of subjects which have been thought worthy of commemoration. Important dates in the lives of rulers and of nations are the most natural subjects for commemoration and celebration of all kinds. Such as the accession and coronation of kings, their jubilees, their weddings, the birth of an heir to the throne, the coming into power of a new president (or even, in the case of Ecuador, the triumph of a particular political party), and all sorts of minor events, some of which do not form the subject of a special commemoration, but are illustrated on the stamps issued as part of a royal wedding or jubilee series.

In the history of nations, the commemorations include the discovery of their land by one of the early explorers, the revolutions or other means by which they gained their independence, the adoption of a constitution and the setting up of a parliament. The patriots who were concerned in these struggles for liberty provide, with the anniversaries of their births or deaths, a natural excuse for further issues.

Stamps provide a very satisfactory and world-wide advertisement for those great international exhibitions which are now so often held and hardly one of these passes without its special issue.

There is one kind of commemoration which is most fittingly associated with postage

Independence and Self Rule

Canada's 1967 EXPO exhibition

stamps: the recording of events of importance in the postal history of a country. Anniversaries of such events as the establishment of the first postal service, entry into the Universal Postal Union, the issue of the earliest postage stamps, and the opening of new post offices, have been frequently commemorated by special stamps. Incidentally, in this group we find an example of how the commemorative 'habit' grows. Congresses of delegates from countries belonging to the Universal Postal Union are held at intervals of three or four years, each meeting being held in a different country. Because one country honoured the Congress by issuing special stamps when it met there, international courtesy has obliged the nation acting as host to each succeeding congress to follow the same example, and in 1929, for example, Great Britain, in spite of its official dislike for special stamp issues, had to follow suit.

The most prolific field for commemoration at the present day is found in the lives of famous individuals. Kings, presidents and patriots, have now given way to saints, poets, engineers, authors, painters, scientists, aviators, explorers, and others whom the world delights to honour. It is not surprising, in view of the importance now attached to sport, that a very large number of sporting sets have been issued, particularly in connexion with the Olympic Games. However, few stamps have featured individual sportsmen or women.

Postal service commemoration

G.B. 1929 Postal Union Congress stamp

In some countries, today, new postage stamps are an obligatory accompaniment of the opening of a railway, bridge, or public building. When there is no railway to be opened, a census will form the subject of special stamp issues, or perhaps an earthquake or hurricane will provide an excuse. Even football matches are commemorated!

Sport stamps

Pictorial stamps

Many so-called 'commemorative' issues do not in fact commemorate anything at all, and are therefore best described as 'special' or 'pictorial' issues. These are series depicting birds or animals, aircraft, cars, trains and many other thematic subjects. Many postal administrations issue such stamps, they are designed to show the 'way of life' of the country and so act as a form of publicity—chiefly on letters sent abroad. The British Post Office first issued such stamps in 1966—a set of four depicting landscapes—a Sussex scene (England), Rural landscape, Co. Antrim (Northern Ireland), Harlech Castle (Wales) and Cairngorm Mountains (Scotland). This was followed by a set depicting popular British birds and British technology. Others have featured flowers (1967, 1979), famous paintings (1967 and 1968), discoveries and inventions (1967), bridges (1968), ships (1969), architecture (1969, 1970, 1971, 1972, 1978), explorers (1972, 1973), trees (1973, 1974), medieval warriors (1974), sailing (1975), social reformers (1976), cultural traditions (1976), racket sports (1977), flora and fauna (1967, 1976, 1977, 1978, 1979, 1980), energy resources (1978), London landmarks (1980), British conductors (1980), sports (1980), folklore (1981), landscapes (1981), fishing industry (1981), British theatre (1982), maritime heritage (1982) and British textiles (1982).

British special (pictorial) stamps

In some cases these have been issued to coincide with anniversaries—*e.g.* the Rose stamps of 1976 celebrated the centenary of the Royal National Rose Society and the Racket stamps of 1977 the centenary of the Wimbledon lawn tennis championship—but no inscription explaining the anniversary or event commemorated appears on the stamp(s).

The American Post Office has issued considerable numbers of such stamps—celebrating famous Americans and portraying wildlife conservation, pollution control, the blood donor service, preservation of historic buildings, family planning, progress in electronics, mineral heritage, energy conservation, banking and commerce, American folk art, American dance, endangered flora, etc. The bold, colourful designs of these stamps ensures their appeal to both collectors of U.S. stamps and of thematic subjects.

U.S., French, Canadian and Australian pictorials

Other countries such as France—issue pictorial stamps to supplement the basic definitive issues. The French definitives show allegorical female figures (Sabine, Liberté, etc.), the pictorial issues which remain on sale for long periods of time feature French art and 'tourist' designs. The Australian Post Office has issued stamps featuring State Floral emblems, famous Australians, primary industries, national development, pioneer life, non-Olympic sports, education in Australia, etc. Canadian pictorials have featured Canadian industries, earth sciences, Canadian writers, endangered wildlife, etc.

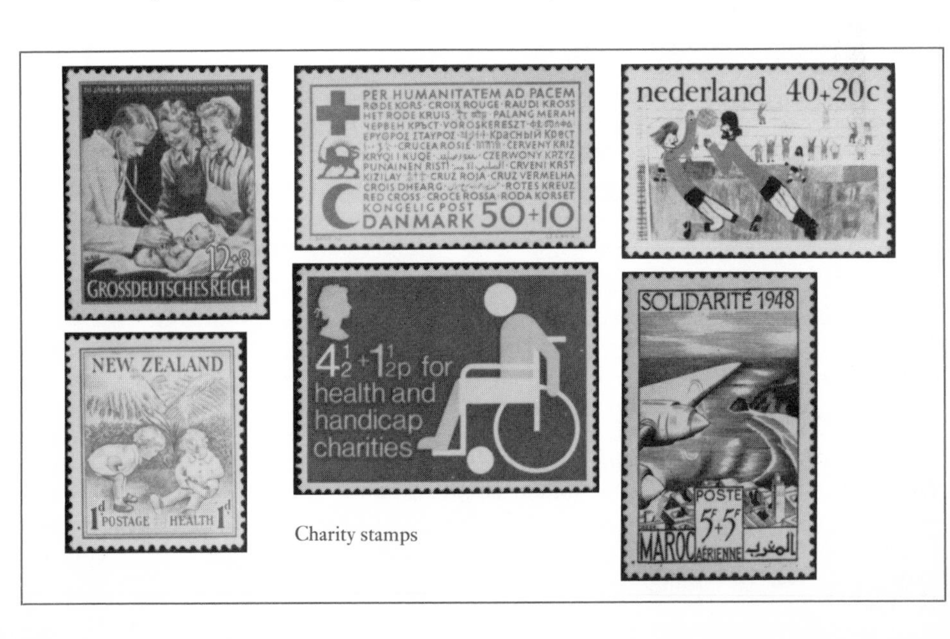

Charity stamps

Then there are charity stamps, which are sold to the public for a sum which is divided into two portions, one representing its postal value which carries a right to service, and the other being devoted to charitable purposes. Here again, we have no right to criticise a state which offers its own nationals this easy method of contributing to charity, which implies, of course, as in the case of commemorative and special issues, full distribution of supplies to all post offices and the willingness of the public to buy them.

But what of the country which issues charity stamps which are not easily available to its own people, and the greater part of which go to collectors? Here the collector is being doubly taxed, for he is paying for postal services, which he does not require, and is also contributing to a charity in which he may have no interest. It is not surprising, under these conditions, that unnecessary charity stamps are not popular, unless they have some special beauty to commend them, or when, by a combination of commemorative interest with the charity appeal, the attention of collectors can be otherwise aroused. A good illustration of this are the three miniature sheets of stamps issued by the British Post Office in 1978, 1979 and 1980. Each was sold at a premium over the face value of the stamps—used in the staging of the 1980 London International Stamp Exhibition.

British 1979 miniature sheet – sold in aid of the London 1980 stamp exhibition

A number of countries now have their regular series of charity stamps, and vie with one another in making them as beautiful as possible. In most of these countries, by far the larger part of the quite respectable sums realised for charity in this way comes from the pockets of stamp collectors at home and abroad, and very little postal use is made of them by the general public. One notable exception is Switzerland, which for many years has produced an annual set of charity stamps, the profit from which is devoted to child welfare work. At first these *Pro Juventute* stamps bore pictures of children in the picturesque dress of the various Swiss cantons. Later, the arms of the cantons formed the subject of the designs for many years, and more recently some really beautiful views of Swiss scenery have appeared followed by some pretty Swiss girls, Alpine flowers and insects. While large numbers of these stamps are sold to collectors each year, they also fulfil the proper purpose of a charity issue, for the Swiss take pride in using them for several weeks after they appear, in spite of their increased cost as compared with the ordinary postage stamps.

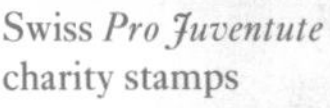
Swiss *Pro Juventute* charity stamps

Grenada War Tax stamp

Purse-strings being looser and hearts softer at Christmas, some of these annual charity issues appear in December—and the collector who, tempted by a pretty set, indulges in the purchase of stamps which he might regard as not strictly necessary can at least console himself with the thought that some of his money will be devoted to good works.

Charity stamps have been issued for a multiplicity of causes. During the First World War enormous sums must have been raised by their means for Red Cross and other work among the troops and on the Home front. After hostilities caused, both in 1918 and 1945, the claims of widows and orphans, war-invalids and returned prisoners were urged by many stamps, while there were also frequent issues of anti-tuberculosis and similar stamps. Child welfare work is always a popular draw, but the aged, the destitute, and sufferers from famine, earthquake, flood and hurricane, have all, to some extent, been relieved from the pockets of stamp collectors.

Mention of Red Cross stamps calls to mind the other groups of issues called into being by war. The term 'War Stamp', as loosely used by collectors, applies to any stamp issued mainly as a result of war-time exigencies. Thus war charity issues, stamps overprinted for use in occupied territory (sometimes called 'occupation stamps'), stamps used by the armed forces, and various temporary issues due to local vicissitudes, all come within this wide definition, together with another class called 'war-tax' stamps.

These latter owe their existence to the necessity for new revenue which was paramount during the war of 1914–18. Many countries raised their rates of postage, but some, in order to mark the fact that the change was only a war-time measure, issued distinctive stamps for prepayment of the special war tax, or else issued stamps at a price which combined the tax with the normal postal rate. The idea was not new as Spain had issued similar stamps as far back as 1874, but now, in addition to the tax on correspondence, the various governments could rely on a big sale of the new stamps to collectors throughout the world.

After 1918 new groups of stamps came into existence. The stamps of the new nations of Europe, and of the older ones during the post-war reconstruction period, were then the centre of interest, under the title 'New Europe' (which, by some was horribly abbreviated to 'Neurope'). Stamps issued in districts which decided their future nationality by referenda bore witness to their temporary independence, while the Great Powers busied themselves with preparing permanent stamps for the ex-German colonies for which they received mandates, which took the place of the temporary 'occupation' stamps of the war period.

Stamps of East Germany (*DDR*), West Germany (*Bundespost*) and West Berlin

Similar events took place after the Second World War when, for example, Germany herself was divided into four zones of occupation, British, American, French and Russian, while Berlin was placed under joint Allied control. Various stamps were issued by the joint Anglo-American, French and Russian Zones until 1948–49 when political events and new governments created the three stamp-issuing entities which exist in Germany today: West Berlin, West Germany (the German Federal Republic) and East Germany (the German Democratic Republic).

Apart from war tax stamps, other stamps have been issued from time to time, the use of which was made compulsory on certain dates, or for certain periods, in addition to the ordinary stamps. The taxes were for various purposes: to build a new post office, to help postal servants, or to raise funds for charity. It is a delicate question whether such stamps should be classed as postage stamps. They only paid a tax, but as correspondence could not be delivered unless they were affixed, they may be held to have served in some sense a postal function.

The reader has now been introduced to the main groups of postage stamps, though as he becomes more familiar with the hobby he may find, here and there, issues with still stranger uses than some of those which have been mentioned.

If, in connexion with commemorative and charity stamps, too much stress has been laid on unnecessary issues aimed at the pocket of the collector, it should be emphasised that unnecessary stamps still form only a relatively small fraction of the total number of stamps issued. They are often distinctly attractive and interesting in themselves, and any collector who does not think that interest and attraction worth paying for, is at liberty to draw his own line of demarcation, and to collect only those stamps of which he approves.

This may particularly apply to that phenomenon of commemorative stamps, the omnibus issue. In 1935 some 62 Commonwealth territories issued stamps marking one theme: the Silver Jubilee of King George V. This paved the way for other such comprehensive series: the Coronation in 1937, the 1948 Royal Silver Wedding, and the 75th anniversary of the Universal Postal Union in 1949. More recently, omnibus sets have appeared for the World Cup (1966), the Royal Silver Wedding (1972), the Silver Jubilee of the Queen's Accession (1977) and the wedding of the Prince of Wales (1981). Moving away from the Commonwealth, the annual series of *Europa* stamps issued by most European postal administrations are a similar case, and the former French and Portuguese colonies have issued omnibus sets with common or very similar designs. Some omnibus issues, such as the 1963 Red Cross and the 1974 centenary of the Universal Postal Union, have world-wide participation, and if one aims at completeness some omnibus series amount to many hundreds of stamps sometimes at very considerable cost.

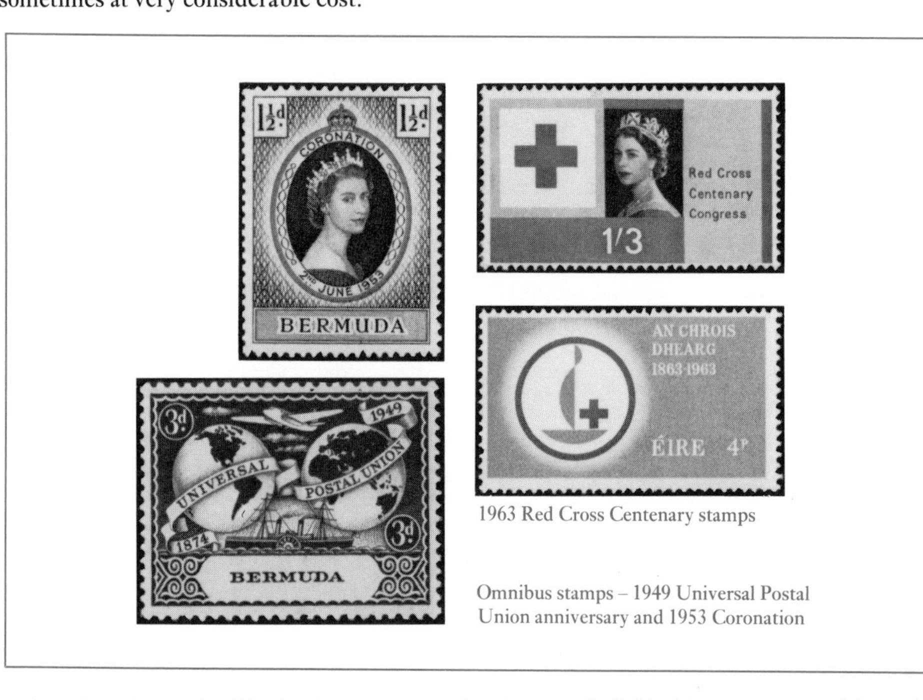

1963 Red Cross Centenary stamps

Omnibus stamps – 1949 Universal Postal Union anniversary and 1953 Coronation

Omnibus issues (and indeed commemorative issues of all kinds) occur now with such frequency that the majority of collectors confine their interests to one country or a group of countries. The days of the truly comprehensive general collector are well and truly in the past for all but the millionaires.

CHAPTER FIVE
The Anatomy of the Stamp

In this chapter we look at the production of postage stamps, and the interest which the various stages and processes have for the collector.

It is a curious thing that, even among the inner circle of advanced students of stamps, there is great ignorance of how stamps are produced, a tendency to discuss the effects of production methods, as seen in the stamps themselves, with no more than a very vague idea of the causes which have given rise to those effects. The majority of collectors vaguely assimilate the idea that any variation in a stamp or its design is of importance, or at least may affect its value. This belief is often based on a lack of knowledge about stamp production and the result has been the creation of a band of 'fly speck collectors' who worry themselves and the editors of stamp magazines with infinitesimal variations. This can bring our hobby into disrepute among those who do not know it at its best and sanest, since, when they are closely questioned, they are unable to explain the causes of the varieties they so avidly accumulate. When considered objectively it becomes clear that the only stamp variations which have any real significance are those which help us to build up the history of an issue, on the lines of A. J. Sefi's definition, quoted in the Introduction.

In order to place philatelic study clearly before the reader, let us follow a postage stamp rapidly through its life, regarding it, meanwhile from every point of view from which it can be of interest to the student.

In writing the biography of an individual, the author usually tries to give us some idea of the home into which he was born, and of the family background which may have influenced his early upbringing. Similarly, the collector who wishes to appreciate fully the stamp which he is going to study, will first try to gain some idea of the postal system and earlier postal history of the country from which it comes. There is nothing which can take the place of such knowledge, as an imaginative background to a stamp collection.

I remember being present once when a famous American collector was displaying a very highly specialised collection of stamps issued by a certain British Colony in the pioneer days. A large and attentive audience was looking at the stamps as they were passed round, but while they noted the various details which were of technical interest, the owner's description of the collection took them, with early settlers, along the trail of the gold rush, or conjured up visions of the hardy mail carriers struggling through snow and ice, or by crazy coasting steamer, to the end of their route. So near did the speaker bring us to the life of which the stamps and envelopes in his collection had formed part, that he was even able to tell us something about one or two of the early settlers to whom they had been addressed, many years before. A collection with a background like that will live in the memory of anyone with sufficient imagination to appreciate the romantic story which lies behind it.

Having acquired some background knowledge, we shall want to know the reason why the stamps we are studying were issued. If they were the earliest stamps of their country, the story may be fairly obvious but for the appearance of more modern stamps there may be 101 reasons. There may be a change in postal rates, a monarch may die, territory may pass from one nation to another, or a temporary shortage of stamps may give rise to a provisional issue. Commemorative and special stamps naturally owe their existence to the national celebration or the national need of the moment. At all events, there is a reason for the existence of every postage stamp, and the collector who wants to know will have to find out that reason.

Now we come to the actual preparation of the stamps. Having decided on an issue, the authorities are faced with the problem of obtaining designs. The work of preparing them may be committed to an artist of repute, or an open competition may be held in the hope of discovering unexpected talent. Sometimes an official may make suggestions or a rough sketch, leaving these to be worked up by an artist, or a member of staff at the printers.

The design will comprise the pictorial part of the stamp, any frame or border which is required, and space for essential information such as the country name, the cost of the stamp, designations of purpose ('Airmail' or 'Postage Due'), and possibly some wording describing the design or the event commemorated.

Rough sketch for stamp design
and the finished product

Having a general idea in his mind, the artist may make a rough sketch or series of sketches, on a large scale. He has a difficult task, for even the largest postage stamp is a small affair, and while he tries to preserve artistic balance, he must make the essential inscriptions fairly prominent, for practical reasons, and he must not overcrowd his drawing with fine lines, or the printer will find it difficult to reproduce. These artist's sketches do not often come the way of the collector, but are much prized when they do, as they give a very good idea of the evolution of the design in the artist's mind, and they often bear comments by officials, with suggestions for improvement, or notes by the artist to the engraver, pointing out essential details.

At this stage, essays may be prepared. An essay is an attempt to show what a stamp would actually look like, when printed. For example, an existing stamp may have its centre cut out and a photograph stuck in place of it, to show how a different portrait would look in the existing framework, or the artist may do some work with pen or brush, to indicate various ways in which a design might be improved upon. Many essays are very similar to issued stamps, as the artist has often gone so far as to have his design engraved and printed, in order to show clearly what it would look like. The term essay is, however, only applied to designs which are not finally adopted or are not adopted in that particular form and without alteration. A collection which starts with the essays for an issue, may continue with proofs (in black and in colour) and a range of colour trials.

Designs by Andrew Restall for 1965 Battle of Britain issue and the issued 9d stamp

It is a curious fact that the adopted design nearly always seems inferior to many of the essays and sketches, and that the adopted colours are often bettered in the series of colour trials. Possibly familiarity with the issued stamps has bred contempt for them in the mind of the collector.

The materials of which a postage stamp is composed are the paper, the ink (which gives us the colour and design), and the gum (if any). Stamp collectors do not usually make any intensive study of the nature of the inks with which stamps are printed, so that we need not pay particular attention to this subject, which is highly technical. Metallic inks are occasionally used to give a striking effect as, for example, in some of the stamps of Greece and Iran, while silver and gold inks have been used for overprints to make them stand out from the basic stamps. The subject of ink as it appears to the collector's eye, that is, as colour, is the source of much controversy within the stamp world. This is easily explained, as colour is a very subjective thing, and what appears red to one collector may appear orange to another! Colour and shades of colour are very important in philately for they can enable a collector to allot a specimen to a particular period or printing, and they can act as a guide or an additional point of comparison in trying to decide whether a particular stamp is genuine or forged or to detect whether an item has been tampered with in some way.

The principal difficulty in connexion with colours is that there is no mechanism available to the average collector for measuring stamp colour scientifically and the majority of collectors have to rely on their own eyes. One's own appreciation of colour may vary, according to one's state of health and the condition of one's eyes. Even to a normal eye the colour of a particular stamp will appear different according to the conditions under which it is viewed. It will appear one colour or shade in sunlight, another in a duller light, and perhaps something entirely different under artificial light. In particular, fluorescent strip lighting can seriously distort the colour of stamps.

Nor must the capacity of the eye for mixing colours be overlooked. Colour is only light, and light rays reaching the eye from various coloured surfaces naturally mingle. Thus stamps should be compared with one another under exactly the same conditions. Stamps printed in the same colour and shade will appear different if viewed against backgrounds of different colours. Similarly, in the case of stamps printed in two or more colours, you cannot assess one colour properly without isolating it from the others. Stamps heavily postmarked appear darker in shade than unused or lightly postmarked copies, for the eye mixes the black of the postmark with the colour of the stamp.

Apart from distinct colours, the methods by which stamps are printed can give rise to variations within the same printing or even within the same sheet. Lithography is particularly prone to such differences of shade, and litho shades are usually regarded as relatively insignificant. Owing to inconsistency in the composition of the ink, or to unsuitable conditions of either temperature or humidity when the printed sheets are drying, misleading shades can be produced. On the other hand, for certain stamps, such as the typographed issues of Great Britain for King Edward VII, shades have a very important significance in separating different printings and the work of three different printers.

The collector has also to be on his guard against changes which can occur *after* a stamp is printed. These may be due to fading, caused by exposure to bright sunlight, or they may occur when stamps are kept in a hot, moist climate. The paper upon which the stamps are printed can yellow with age, with consequent alteration to the apparent colour of the stamps, while deterioration of the gum may also have an effect as time goes on. And who is to say what reactions will take place in time between some modern stamps and the fluorescent and phosphorescent coatings which they receive?

Another great drawback with colours is that there has never been, within the hobby, a single recognised standard for naming them. Philatelic literature, including stamp catalogues from different publishers, is notoriously inconsistent. The collector nowadays does have one invaluable tool, the *Stanley Gibbons Stamp Colour Key*, first published in 1970. The 200 colours in the key incorporate the 100 colours in the standard *Gibbons Colour Guide* (first published in 1921) but the additional 100 shades enable more specialised collectors to match shades with a greater degree of accuracy. It is the policy of Stanley Gibbons Publications Ltd. to use this key for all additions to the Gibbons catalogue, be they new issues or rewritten sections. As this Colour Key becomes established, British collectors, at least, will have a consistent standard to go by.

Stanley Gibbons Colour Key

The majority of stamps have gum on the back, in order that they may easily be stuck on correspondence. Quite a few early stamps were, however, issued ungummed. The same practice was followed from time to time in some countries of hot moist climate, where the stamps were likely to stick together in the post office; pots of gum or paste were provided at post office counters for public use. The modern issues of China (until 1974) and North Korea are sometimes without gum. Special tropical gums are used for some countries, while others store their stamp supplies with paper interleaving or talcum powder between the sheets.

As the paper on which stamps are printed is often gummed before it is passed through the press, a type of mucilage is required which will not cause the paper to curl. The majority of sheets of stamps do curl, however, as the collector will find to his cost if he has to deal with them. The 'ripple' gum, adopted by Germany for her stamps at one period, employed the principle of breaking up the gum, to give a non-curling effect. Some countries use different gum for stamps issued in winter and in summer, in order that climatic conditions may be allowed for.

Generally speaking, the authorities responsible for the issue of stamps will want a gum that is fully adhesive, tasteless, and probably colourless. From the collector's point of view, an examination of the gum is only important when the fact that it is yellow or white, shiny or dull, crackly or smooth, enables him to distinguish between stamps printed at one period and those produced later, or between genuine and forged stamps or originals and reprints. In the case of forgeries and reprints, the gum is often the most difficult thing to imitate correctly, and it thus provides a very useful test.

The subject of paper has been more scientifically studied by philatelists than gum or printing ink and, indeed, the processes of paper-making are of great interest. They need not, however, be described in detail here. From the point of view of the authorities, the paper provided for stamps must be suitable for the printer's purposes; it must not be too thick for convenient use by the public; and it should provide as much protection as possible against the work of forgers wishing to make imitations of the stamps or of anyone attempting to clean off the postmark, so that the stamps can be used again, with the intention of defrauding the Post Office.

Paper may be divided into two main classes, hand-made, which is produced sheet by sheet, and machine-made, which is turned out in continuous rolls by machinery. Hand-made paper was used for printing some of the earlier postage stamps of various countries. Its production being the result of manual skill, there is often variation in the thickness of a paper, even in the same sheet.

The kinds of paper which the collector will have to distinguish with the greatest frequency are *wove* and *laid*. Wove paper has a plain, even mesh, and is the normal paper employed for books, newspapers and similar work. Laid paper is watermarked with parallel lines, close together, so that, by transparency, a stamp printed on this paper shows light and dark lines in the paper alternately. When the lines run from top to bottom the paper is described as 'vertically laid' and when they run across the stamp as 'horizontally laid'. A distinction is drawn between laid paper, with its close lines, and *bâtonné*, which is watermarked with straight parallel lines some distance apart. The paper is described as wove *bâtonné*, or laid *bâtonné*, according as the spaces between these lines show the characteristics already described. Paper watermarked with crossed lines, making it appear to be covered with small squares, is called *quadrillé*.

Laid batonné paper; Curacao stamp printed on laid paper

Stamp printed on granite paper

Granite paper has coloured fibres in its texture, while ribbed paper has close parallel ridges on the surface of the paper, often not intentional, but arising out of some part of the process of manufacture or printing. Paper ruled with faint coloured lines has been used on occasion for printing postage stamps, for example Latvian issues of 1919. Various makeshift papers were used for stamp-printing after the First World War. In addition to its ruled paper Latvia employed the backs of German staff maps, cigarette paper and bank notes, while Lithuania used a greyish paper, formerly employed for making ration-coupons.

The thickness of paper is often taken into account in catalogues or books describing postage stamps, but as the terms used are usually the vague 'thick', 'thin', or 'medium' without any accurate basis, the collector is often puzzled. It is not necessary, however, in most cases, to draw any close distinctions, as only very marked differences in thickness have any serious importance. The thinnest paper used for stamp printing is the tissue paper employed for some Afghanistan stamps (1891–92). This type of paper is sometimes erroneously called 'pelure', but in its correct philatelic application, pelure paper, though very thin, is hard and tough. At the other end of the scale we find carton paper, a thick semi-card paper.

For the general collector there is no need to enter into a distinction between the papers made by different manufacturers, where these occur in the same issue of postage stamps. Sometimes, as in the stamps of Norway, a distinction can be made by the watermark, or, as in the Basted Mills, Cowan and Waterlow papers of New Zealand, by their texture and general character. It is only the advanced philatelist who need enter into such refinement of detail and, in fact, other collectors may disregard paper differences with little loss, when it is merely a matter of thickness or texture.

One special paper which is worth mentioning is the Dickinson silk-thread paper, on which the Mulready envelopes and wrappers of Great Britain were printed. In this paper, a silk thread is embedded in its substance, during manufacture. The embossed 10d and 1s postage stamps of Great Britain of 1847–48 were also printed on this paper, but the stamps most likely to come the way of the tyro are some of the earlier Swiss issues, for which a similar paper was used.

The Dickinson paper was the first of a long range of stamp papers intended to provide protection against frauds on the revenue. In the early days of the postage stamp, the authorities were in constant dread of the forger being able to imitate their postal labels as, if such imitations were turned out in large quantities, considerable loss would result. The early postage stamps of many countries were successfully imitated by rogues; more recently it has been more profitable to imitate the stamps for which collectors will pay good money, than to produce forgeries of stamps in daily use.

The use of special papers was one of the means adopted for defeating the forger, and many ingenious suggestions have been put forward from time to time for papers which it would be extremely difficult for the forger to procure or imitate, and for papers which would render it near impossible to clean off postmarks or pen-cancellations without damaging the stamp.

The protective paper most frequently met with is known to collectors as 'chalky' or 'chalk-surfaced'. 'Enamel' paper belongs to the same class of coated papers, all of which have a specially prepared surface which is supposed to show at once the effect of any attempt to clean off the cancellation. In recent years chalk-coated paper has been used as this produces a sharper printed impression, thus improving the overall appearance of the stamp. The rogue who removes pen-marks or postmarks so that the stamps may be used again, or else sold to collectors as unused, has found means of doing his work and leaving very little trace behind, though, as we shall see later, science has come to the collector's aid, and traces which the eye cannot see are now easily revealed by the ultra-violet lamp.

As an example of ingenious protective papers which never came into general use, we may instance the 'double paper' of the U.S.A. The face of this paper was thin and porous (another type had narrow slits cut in it) and it was backed by a layer of firmer paper. Any attempt to remove the postmark caused the thin paper to vanish and with it the design of the stamp, which was then rendered useless. Supplies of these stamps were used experimentally, and the collector may occasionally come across one among the early issues of the U.S.A.

The colour of paper now remains to be considered. The vast majority of postage stamps are printed on paper approximately white, but where a long series of stamps has to be produced in the same design, coloured papers are sometimes used to give a wider range of colour distinction than can be given by varying the colour of the design alone. The issues of many former British colonies provide examples of this practice, and yellow, green, blue and red papers were employed for certain denominations. These papers were usually coloured right through, but France, for some of her own stamps and for many of those of her colonies, used to use surface-coloured paper, not dyed, but with the colour printed on the surface of the paper.

The term 'blued paper', for which the French *bleuté* is sometimes substituted, is applied to paper that has unintentionally been turned a bluish colour by something used in its manufacture, or in making the ink with which the stamp is printed. The early stamps of Great Britain provide examples of very vivid blueing of the paper, while later stamps, such as the 1897 issue of Barbados, show a fainter blueing.

An apparently surface-coloured paper which is a source of much trouble to inexperienced collectors, is often produced when stamps are being printed from engraved plates. These plates, as we shall see later, should be thoroughly wiped after they are inked, but if this is not carefully done, ink will remain on the flat portion of the plate and will be transferred to the surface of the paper, which will thus appear coloured. Such variations are of little importance to the collector; nor should attention be paid to stamps accidentally stained at some time after issue.

In recent times several postal authorities have introduced sophisticated machinery to help speed-up the job of sorting mail. These machines require the use of stamps printed on special papers with a luminescent coating either incorporated in the paper or applied on top of it in the form of overprinted bands. Details of these papers are given in Chapter 6 (Stamp Printing).

A method of protecting stamps against imitation is to print on paper watermarked with a special device. To make special paper calls for larger resources than the forger can usually command, and with very careful checking of the quantity of paper handed over to the printer and actually used by him, any chance of the correct paper coming into wrong hands can be avoided.

Paper is made from pulp which, in the machine-made variety, is run, in its liquid state, on to an endless 'web', and at one stage in its progress, and before the paper is fully formed, it comes under the pressure of a revolving cylinder known as the 'dandy roll'. This cylinder is covered with wire cloth, and if the wire is interwoven like cloth, the result is a 'wove' paper, while a dandy roll whose wire is in parallel lines will give 'laid' paper.

To produce the watermark which is really a thinning in the paper, devices made of wire, or cut out of brass, are attached to the dandy roll at the desired intervals and, being pressed into the wet paper as it passes, reproduce these devices as thinner portions in its texture, which can be seen by transparency when the paper is held up to the light. Most watermarks can be seen in this way, but where the thinning is less pronounced the watermark can be detected by placing the stamp face downwards on a black surface. If even this is not sufficient, a drop of benzine (*not benzene*) poured on to the stamp will usually emphasise the watermark, and black trays or tiles, recessed to hold the benzine, are available for this purpose. Do not use benzine on modern stamps printed in photogravure, as the ink may run. Electric (battery or mains) watermark detectors are available; these are based on the use of small coloured filters. The stamp is placed on a slide and inserted into an illuminated box—the various filters are then rotated until the colour of the stamp is matched by that of the filter, so that the colours are 'neutralised' and the watermark should appear in clear relief. The Morley-Bright watermark detector has been devised to produce a permanent print of a stamp's watermark which can be mounted alongside the stamp in the album.

It must not be supposed that all stamps have watermarks, indeed nowadays most countries use unwatermarked paper for stamp printing. Where the watermark is present it may take one of several forms:

(1) *A paper-maker's watermark*, which is just the normal watermark indicating the maker and (perhaps) the class of paper which is used. It may be a name, a number or a device, but it has no postal significance, and is often disregarded by collectors, though it will be appreciated that if two or more makers have been supplying paper for stamp-printing, their distinctive watermarks may supply valuable data for deciding to which printing particular stamps belong. Many paper-makers' watermarks only occupy a very small proportion of the area of the paper so that most stamps printed on such paper are without watermarks, and for practical purposes the issue would be described in stamp catalogues as having no watermark.

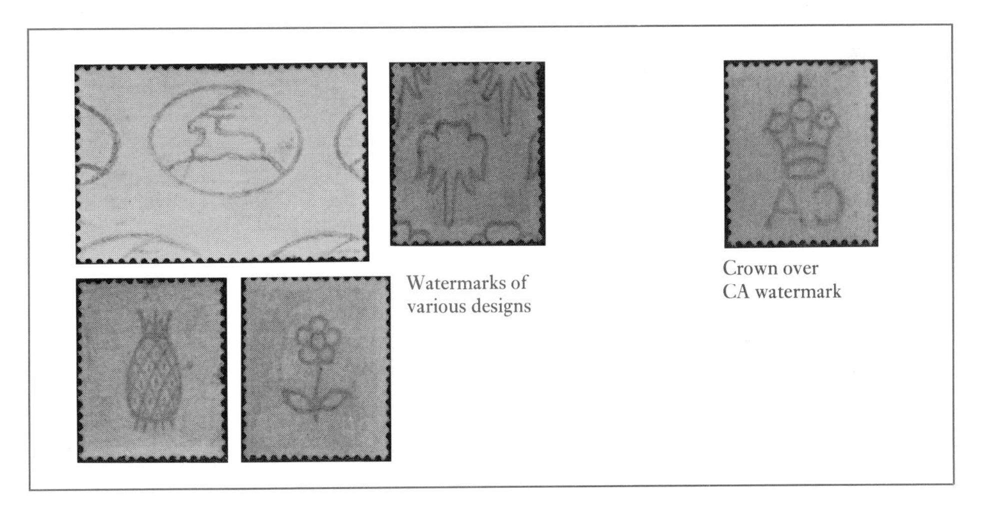

Watermarks of various designs

Crown over CA watermark

(2) A single device, covering more or less of the surface of the paper, but in many cases leaving a proportion of the stamps in the sheet without watermark. The distinction between such devices, which are known to collectors as *sheet watermarks*, and the paper-makers' watermarks (apart from the fact that the latter may be repeated several times in the paper of a single sheet of stamps) is that the sheet watermarks are of postal origin, that is, they represent the arms of the country, or some other device, which gives a definitely postal status and use to the paper. An example is the 'arms' watermark of the 1854 issue of India.

(3) *Single watermarks.* Here small watermark devices are so arranged in the paper that, if properly printed, each stamp in the sheet will have its own watermark. The 'Crown over CC' and 'Crown over CA' watermarks of many former British colonies are examples.

(4) *Multiple watermarks.* Here the device is repeated at close intervals throughout the sheet of paper, so that each stamp may show a portion of several devices. A minor distinction may be drawn between a watermarked device and a watermarked inscription (such as some

of the watermarks of Brazilian stamps), as the latter may be of such size that only one or two letters or portions of letters will be identifiable on each stamp, while the 'Multiple Script CA' watermark of the British colonies and other small devices are usually identifiable in their entirety from a single stamp, or at most one or two stamps, owing to their smaller size.

It is not always possible to secure properly watermarked paper for stamp printing, and in one or two instances a 'false' watermark has been printed faintly on the paper, to give the same protection which a real watermark would afford. An instance will be found in the 2c, 5c, and 20c stamps issued by Argentina, in 1922, during a temporary shortage of the normal paper.

Multiple Script CA watermark

'Watermark' printed on back of stamp

Other methods of so-called watermarking have been adopted by Switzerland (1862 issue), where the watermark is actually impressed in the paper, a kind of reversed embossing which can easily be seen, and by Czechoslovakia, which, in the anniversary series of 1923, arranged that a protective device should appear in the gum of the stamps. It is, of course, not a watermark at all, and does not look like one but it serves the same purpose.

Another question which has to be considered by the authorities in connexion with paper, is the size of the sheets which are to be printed, and this is intimately connected with the size of the stamps, the space which is to be left between each row of stamps, and the number of stamps which have to be printed on each sheet of paper. It may be noted here that the size of the 'printer's sheet' may be larger than that of the 'post office sheet', that is, the sheet as sold over the post office counter, for printers often turn out two or more post office sheets on one piece of paper and these are cut up before being distributed for sale.

The size of the stamps will, naturally, be determined at an early stage in the proceedings, and the numbers of stamps in the sheet will usually have some connexion with the currency of the country, so countries with a decimal currency usually have sheets made up of 100 stamps, or multiples of 100; Great Britain used to have sheets of 240 stamps for ease of accounting, so that, for example, a sheet of 7d stamps would be worth exactly £7. Since decimalisation, definitive stamps are printed in sheets of 200. Commemorative stamps are normally printed in sheets of 100 because of their large size, previously in sheets of 120.

Some stamps are printed in small sheets containing as few as ten, six or even four stamps. One reason for this may be that the postal administrations issuing the stamps hope that collectors will buy them in whole sheets, although counter clerks will sell the stamps singly if requested. Such small sheets (or *sheetlets* as they are sometimes called) should not be confused with *miniature sheets* which contain one or more different stamps, usually with a decorative border, and are sold intact by postal administrations.

The space between the stamps in a sheet has to be calculated in relation to the question of the perforations, or means of separation of the stamps, with which we shall deal in a moment. The division of a sheet of stamps into smaller sections, by means of blank margins, will be considered in Chapter 9.

Miniature sheet commemorating the 21st birthday of Prince Albert of Monaco (*1979*)

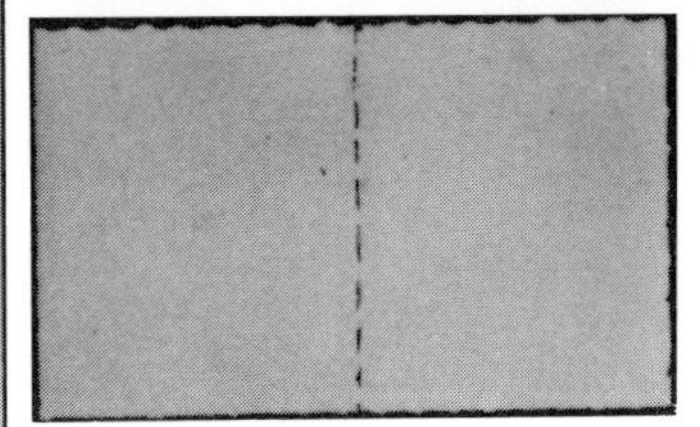

Rouletted stamps (*front & back*)

Serpentine roulette on early stamp of Finland

Having the design, his gummed paper, and his ink, and having decided on the general make-up of his sheet of stamps, the printer then considers the actual printing—dealt with in Chapter 6. Jumping this stage, we now deal with the various means adopted for separating stamps from one another easily and expeditiously.

The earlier stamps, both of Great Britain and of many other countries, were *imperforate*, and that is to say the paper was not weakened in any way between the rows of stamps, and the post office clerks and the public had to use scissors to separate them. This system was found so inconvenient that various methods of facilitating the separation of stamp from stamp were experimented with and some of them adopted by various countries, that which is known to collectors as *perforation* being now the standard method. Stamps are now issued imperforate only in an emergency, or to create extra varieties for sale to collectors, or to give a special character to a particular issue.

A system of separation which is now almost obsolete is that known as *rouletting*. This is done with a small wheel or series of wheels, with small points on their circumference, something like a spur. Where the cuts made by these points in the paper between the stamps are in short straight lines, the simple term 'rouletted' applies (or the French alternative *percé en lignes* is employed). Rouletted stamps, when separated, show a straight edge, corresponding with the length of the roulette cut, with a small projection between each cut.

In some cases curved cuts are made (arc roulette, or *percé en arc*) and when two stamps are torn apart, the edge of one will show a series of arched projections, nearly touching each other, while the other will show corresponding indentations. Another type has the slits cut in a zigzag fishion, and the edge of the stamp after separation looks like a saw (zigzag roulette, or *percé en scie*). Early stamps of Finland have a curious serpentine roulette-which produces long 'teeth' when the stamps are separated.

Rouletting in colour, such as is found in some of the stamps of Thurn and Taxis and elsewhere, which show each roulette slit coloured, is not true rouletting. The slits, in such cases are produced during printing, by the use of thin strips of metal with sharp edges, which project higher than the blocks from which the stamp designs are printed and thus cut the paper and colour the edges of the cuts at the same time.

Rouletting is distinct from perforation, in that it does not remove any paper from the sheet, but merely makes holes or slits in it, while a perforating machine punches circles of paper right out of the sheet. Sharp pins are sometimes used to produce a method of separation which while called pin-perforation, is really a roulette, as the pins do not remove any paper. Sewing machines have on occasions been used to produce a crude form of perforation.

Turning to perforation proper, with which the modern collector is more frequently concerned, this is done by rows of punches which remove circular pieces of paper from the sheet. The lozenge perforation of some Bulgarian postage dues is an exception, though. The simplest form of perforating machine has a single line of punches, which makes one row of holes at a time. The sheet has therefore to be moved as the space between each pair of rows of stamps is dealt with to produce the vertical lines of holes and then the sheet is turned round so that the horizontal rows of perforations can be made. A machine such as this is called a 'single-line' or 'guillotine' machine, and the perforation produced by it is known as 'single-line' or 'line' perforation. A 'harrow' machine is so called from its resemblance to the agricultural implement of that name, for the lines of punches are so arranged that they perforate the vertical and horizontal intervals of a sheet of stamps at one blow. Single-line and harrow machines are not very much used at the present day.

The great difficulty which is met with in perforating stamps is that of ensuring that the lines of holes fall in their proper place between the stamps and do not cut into the stamp design. The spaces between the stamps are naturally small, as otherwise the stamps would have wide margins of paper around them and would look unsightly; and when millions of stamps are being printed the extra space would mean larger sheets, larger plates and more paper, all of which would involve waste of money and material. Time has also to be considered and it is obvious that, though the single-line perforator has its advantages, as giving more opportunities for accurate adjustment, it necessitates each sheet of stamps being put through the perforator twice, once for the horizontal rows of holes and once for the vertical, with a number of movements in each direction.

The type of perforator which has now come into general use is called a 'comb' machine. This has the punches so arranged that there is one long line equivalent to the length between two rows of stamps, and shorter lines projecting at right angles, at intervals equivalent to the width of the stamp. Such a machine, therefore, perforates the space between two rows of stamps and the spaces between the individual stamps of one row, at a single blow, and as the sheet moves along it thus completes both horizontal and vertical perforations without any necessity for turning the sheet round. In producing recent British stamps a 'multiple comb' perforator has been used, which perforates several rows entirely and three sides of the next row.

In deciding as to the space between the punches in a perforating machine, consideration has to be given to the strength of the paper and its resistance to tearing. The perforation holes should be so spaced that, when an attempt is made to tear the stamps apart, the tear follows the line of holes and does not cut across the paper of the stamp. If the holes are close together, separation of the stamps will be easier than if they were more widely spaced, but the mesh of the paper, and the way it runs, may make it necessary to space the holes differently in the horizontal and vertical rows. To the collector, this spacing is not very important, unless it provides him with evidence that certain stamps were the work of a particular printer or period, and stamp catalogues differentiate between the various 'gauges' of perforation. The yardstick of perforation measurement is the number of holes in a distance of two centimetres, ascertained by using a 'perforation gauge'. These have rows of dots inscribed on them—the dots correspond to the holes perforated on a stamp and each row is numbered with the appropriate measurement, *e.g.* 14 (14 holes in a 2cm measure). If the stamps has the same perforation gauge on all four sides it is expressed in the form: 'Perf.14' or 'P.14'. Some stamps have a different perforation gauge along the top and bottom and sides—for example 15 holes along the top and bottom rows and 14 down each side—this is a compound perforation and is expressed in the form 'Perf.15 × 14' or 'P.15 × 14', the horizontal measure being given first.

The description 'Perf. compound of 11 and 12' indicates that the stamp has mixed perforations—some gauge 11 some gauge 12, but the opposite sides do not necessarily have the same gauge, *i.e.* there might be three sides perf.11 and only one side perf.12. 'Perf.12½,13' (note the comma) describes a perforation which actually gauges between 12½ and 13, sometimes cited as 12¾. Some perforation gauges do not measure in quarters; the Gibbons Catalogue normally refers to perforations only in whole and half units.

The description 'Perf.12½–13' or '12½ to 13' indicates that the pins were spaced irregularly in the perforating machine, with the result that the space between the perforation holes is erratic—thus you might get part of a line of perforations gauging 12½ and just beyond it a section which measures 13. Some specialist collectors require measurement of perforations to the nearest decimal point so as to distinguish between stamps of different printings but for the ordinary collector this is unnecessary.

The use of automatic machines for the sale of stamps has given rise to various special kinds of perforation, having as their object the holding of the stamps safely in the machine, or the prevention of the delivery of two stamps for one coin. Some of the experimental 'automatic-machine perforations' consist of large holes of various shapes, pierced for the pegs, etc. by which the machine grips them, but they also fulfill the ordinary function of perforations in making it possible to separate the stamps from those adjoining them. The best known of these perforations are those used by the Netherlands in modern times.

CHAPTER SIX
Stamp Printing

There are four main processes of printing of which the collector must have some idea, but before we consider them in more detail it will be advisable to summarise their main characteristics which are indeed, very easy to remember. The names given to them are Line-engraving (or Intaglio or Recess-printing), Typography (or Surface-printing), Lithography and Photogravure.

In Line-engraving the design of the stamp is cut into metal, the lines of the design being represented by miniature troughs. Before printing, the ink is forced into these troughs, but it is wiped off the flat surface of the remainder of the plate. The paper on which the design is to be printed, usually after being damped, though a dry process is now used by some printers, is forced against the engraved plate and into the cuts representing the design, which are full of ink. The ink is picked up by the paper, where it stands up in microscopic ridges, visible as such in many cases to the naked eye when the stamp is held edgeways between the observer and the light, and often to be felt by the finger.

Fine line-engraved stamps

Typographed stamps

Surface-printing, or Typography, shows us the reverse of this method, for here the engraving is done so that the lines of the design stand up on the plate in ridges of metal, and the uncoloured parts of the stamp to be are represented by depressions on the plate. When the plate is inked only the ridges receive the ink, and from them it is transferred directly to the paper to form the design of the stamp. If too much pressure is used in printing, the ridges of the plate will be represented by corresponding ridges on the back of the stamp, but in good printing such ridges are often only present in a microscopic degree.

In the process named Lithography, we find the mean between Line-engraving and Surface-printing, for here there is no engraving, the design being drawn, or otherwise produced, on a perfectly flat stone or plate of a special character, which is so treated that, when the inking roller is passed over it, only the actual lines of the design drawn on it will pick up any ink, the rest of its surface remaining free from ink. On the finished stamp there are no depressions or ridges on the paper, the print being quite flat.

The photogravure process entails the design image being laid on a copper plate or cylinder and etched. The resulting hollows on the plate are inked and the normal printing follows by what is called rotary photogravure (or rotogravure).

Litho-printed stamps

Early and modern photogravure stamps

This is as far as some readers will want to go in this chapter, but the majority will find in the following description of the various stages of these processes many things which will help them to appreciate differences which they will notice in their stamps. In what follows, only the elements of a single method of printing by each of these processes are analysed, but numerous variations in method are employed by various firms and at various times.

In *Line-engraving*, the first stage is the engraving of the design in recessed lines on a small, flat plate of softened metal, which is the original, or 'master die'. On this die, the design is in reverse, looking to the eye as the design of the stamp itself would look if viewed in a looking glass.

After this die has been hardened, a soft steel roller is rocked backwards and forwards across it and receives a positive impression of the design, which, in its turn, is hardened. By a reversal of the process, the rocking of the roller, under pressure, on the surface of a softened steel plate, the design is transferred (as a negative impression, this time) to the plate. This process is repeated until the metal plate has received as many negative impressions of the design as the printed sheet of stamps is to contain, and when the plate has been hardened it is ready to print from, the impressions on the paper, from the negative designs on the plate, being of course, positive.

It is obvious that everything that appears on the master die will be reproduced on each of the impressions of the design on the printing plate and also on the stamps, unless the engraver makes a deliberate alteration to the plate, which he can do by softening it, scraping off any lines he may wish to alter, and *re-engraving* them as he wishes. The scraping-off of the surface metal naturally leaves a dent in the plate, and this is hammered up from behind until the whole surface is level. If the plate is damaged, so that some of the lines of the design are blurred or removed, similar work may be done, which is called *retouching*. With all his skill, it is very difficult for the engraver to repeat the damaged lines exactly, and if one design on a plate has been retouched, it will probably differ slightly from the others, which are exact reproductions of the die.

Retouch

Another variation which sometimes arises during the making of plates by the process we are considering, is the *re-entry*. When the roller-die is rocked over the plate under pressure, to transfer its impressions of the design to the plate, it is obviously important that these impressions should be very accurately positioned. Between them, in the printed sheet, the perforation holes will come, and if they are too close together there will be no room for the holes.

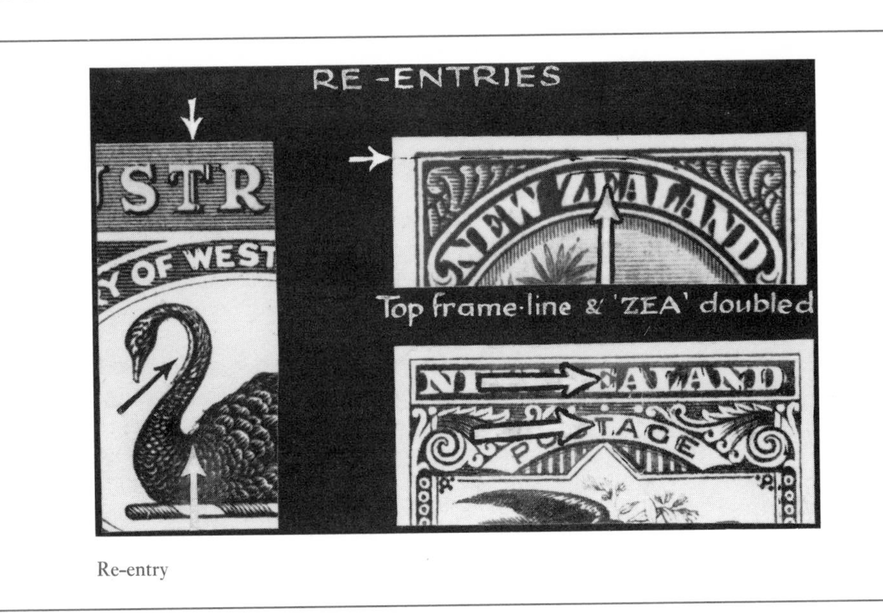

Re-entry

It sometimes happens that in entering an impression on the plate from the roller-die, the latter is rocked on the plate in a slightly wrong position, a little too high, or to one side. If the mistake is disregarded by the plate maker, the printed sheet will show one stamp similarly out of position, as is frequently seen among the earlier postage stamps of various countries. A careful worker will, however, note his error, scrape off the badly placed impression, and re-enter (that is to say, rock again) the roller on the plate in the correct position.

Suppose, however, that he does not erase very carefully every line of the first, incorrect impression, any lines that he leaves on the plate will take up the ink and reproduce themselves on the paper. They are lines similar to those of the correct impression, but as they are in the wrong position of the first impression, they will be found beside, above, or below the lines of the correct complete impression, and on the stamp it will appear as if portions of the design are doubled. This appearance, when resulting from the re-entering of the die, as described, is called by collectors a *re-entry*, but not every doubling of this kind seen in stamps is caused in this way. Re-entries are often detectable as a doubling of the frameline of a stamp, though sometimes an inner portion of the design will be doubled, and cases are known, as in the 1½d New Zealand stamp issued to commemorate the South African War, where one stamp in the sheet has the greater part of the design doubled.

When a sheet of stamps was printed in two or more colours, separate plates were prepared for printing those parts of the design which appeared in each colour. In the case of some earlier issues of British colonies printed in standard designs, but not always in two colours, an economical system was adopted by which the same plates could be used for printing the portrait and other parts of the design which were common to the stamps of the various colonies while separate plates were provided for the part of the design which included the name of the colony and the denomination of the stamp. The plates which printed the portrait were called 'head plates', while the others were known as 'duty plates'.

In preparing for the printing of stamps by the *typographic* (letterpress) process, the engraving of the die is again the first stage, but in this case the design is engraved *en épargne*, that is to say, the lines of the design stand up as ridges of metal, instead of being minute troughs as in the line-engraved (or intaglio) plate. This is, of course, negative, and from it, in the process known as *stereotyping*, a mould is taken, which is used for the casting of as many separate reproductions in metal (called clichés) as there are to be stamps in the printed sheet. When these are suitably locked together at the correct intervals, they form the equivalent of our engraved printing plate, but with the design in relief instead of in recess.

If electrotyping is employed to secure reproductions of the die, the latter is first used to make a wax mould. On this a thin shell of copper is deposited electrically, which, when removed, is found to reproduce faithfully the lines and ridges of the die. When as many of these reproductions as necessary have been made, they are suitably strengthened and can be locked or joined together to make one printing plate.

Coming to the third printing process, *lithography*, we have here, instead of a plate with the design in recess or in relief, a plate of zinc or other suitable metal (in early days a flat stone) on which the design is drawn or transferred in flat lines on its surface. The surface of the stone or metal is prepared in such a way that only the lines of the design pick up the ink, and from them it is transferred to the paper. The 'offset' process of printing is a modern variant of lithography, in which the design is not printed immediately on the paper, but is transferred from the plate to a rubber roller and thence to the paper. A special photo-litho process involving the use of fine screens has been introduced for stamp production in recent years. (The word 'offset' is also applied by collectors to an accidental reversed impression of the design which has found its way to the back or front of a sheet of stamps.)

In recent times, photography has played its part in the production of postage stamps, the process mainly employed being known as *photogravure*. The distinguishing characteristic of stamps printed by this method is that the design, under a magnifying glass, is seen to be broken up into a series of dots.

In photogravure the design subject, usually a combination of photograph and drawing permitting subtle gradations of colour, is photographed, the resulting negative being used to make what is termed a multipositive plate (the equivalent in size of a sheet or pane of stamps). The multiple design is then printed down on to a specially prepared sheet of carbon tissue, the surface of which has been photographically superimposed with a fine grid or screen. It is this screen which breaks up the design into fine dots. The tissue, now containing positive impressions, is wrapped round the copper cylinder for etching. Subsequently, the cylinder is made ready for printing, the recessed design first contacting ink rollers, then paper, in the rotary printing press.

Most British stamps since the mid-1930s have been printed in photogravure by Harrison & Sons Ltd, who started as printers in *c.* 1750 when James Harrison set up a press. From 1910, when the company was awarded a contract to print British stamps, Harrisons used the letterpress process, but in 1924 it was decided to install the special plant and equipment required for photogravure at their works at St. Martin's Lane, London. In 1933, when the company again secured the contract to print British stamps, suitable premises were acquired at High Wycombe in Buckinghamshire, now the firm's headquarters for postage stamp security printing. The first British definitive stamps printed in photogravure were issued in 1934, the first commemoratives (George V Silver Jubilee) the following year. In 1972, Harrisons installed a sophisticated rotary printing press—the 'Jumelle'—named from the French for 'twin'. This giant machine combines recess and gravure printing, and the two processes can be employed together on the same stamps, or independently on different issues with both units working simultaneously if needed. The recess image is impressed on the cylinder by an automatic transfer machine, and seven gravure colours combined with three *intaglio* colours can be printed in one pass through the machine. A rotary perforator is built-in, and the 'Jumelle' can also be used for printing stamps for coils (or rolls) and booklets from the same cylinders. Two issues have been printed in both photogravure and recess—the Sailing stamps of 1975 and the Maritime Heritage Year set of 1982.

Recess printing is no longer regularly used for British stamps—although high value stamps continued to be printed by this method until 1977. The 50p stamp commemorating the London 1980 international stamp exhibition was recess printed. Following the switch to photogravure in 1934, only Postage Due stamps continued to be printed by the typographic process; these too switched to photogravure in 1968. Occasionally stamps have been printed in a combination of typography and lithography—the 1973 Inigo Jones and Parliamentary Conference stamps for example. In recent years the British Post Office have contracted for several issues to be printed in lithography—1969 P.O. Technology, 1970 Commonwealth Games, 1980 Sports, 1981 Duke of Edinburgh Award and 1982 Motor Cars. Several definitive and regional values have also been printed by this method.

Stamp printed by two printing processes – recess and photogravure

Embossed stamps

Embossing was used in earlier times for producing stamps and beautiful examples are provided by Gambia, Great Britain, Heligoland, Portugal and other countries. The relief effect in embossing is achieved by the use of two dies, one engraved in relief and the other in recess, between which the paper is pressed. Various methods have been adopted to provide the coloured part of the design. In recent times the Queen's silhouette on some British commemoratives has been embossed in gold (1968 Paintings) or printed in gold or silver and then embossed (various issues 1968–72 and 1976).

We need not discuss in detail the actual mechanism of printing, which, in itself, calls for just as much skill and experience as the stages of the work already described. The important factors which the printers have to consider, and which may affect the appearance of the stamps, are the mixing of the ink to the correct shade and consistency and the use of it under the proper conditions of temperature and humidity; the proper 'registering' of the sheet as it passes through the press, so that the stamp designs fall in their proper position in relation to the edges of the paper; the application of the correct quantity of ink to the plate (and, in the case of line-engraving and photogravure, the proper wiping of the surface of the plate or cylinder, leaving the ink only in the recessed lines of the design); and the passing of the sheet through the press in such a way that it receives the design evenly and with only the requisite amount of pressure over all its surface.

Spoilt sheets will result if the sheet goes crookedly through the press, or if the paper gets creased or folded, or if the ink on the freshly printed sheet gets smudged. Such sheets will normally be destroyed, but occasionally they leak out and come into the hands of collectors, often in an unfinished condition. Such sheets are called 'printer's waste', and are of very little philatelic significance unless they tell us something about methods of production which we cannot learn from the finished stamps.

A modern development—the 'facing' and sorting of letters by sophisticated machines—has brought about the use of specially treated paper for stamps. These issues are of great interest to collectors and some background information about them will not be out of place here. Letters bearing such stamps are faced and segregated by electronic scanning devices, considerably easing the manual task of facing and sorting. Britain pioneered these experiments with graphite-lined stamps in 1957. These comprised thin ($\frac{1}{32}$″ wide) black lines printed vertically on the back of stamps (beneath the gum) and were used in electronic machines to sort first class and second class (printed paper rate) mail at the Southampton Head Post Office. Initially only the ½d, 1d, 1½d, 2d, 2½d and 3d values were so treated, later the 4d and 4½d stamps were added. This graphite material was electrically conductive and the machinery could distinguish first class mail bearing stamps with two graphite lines from second class mail—stamps bearing one line only. The stamps are sometimes referred to as 'Napthadag' stamps—this being the scientific name of the graphite substance used. However, the use of these stamps was not an unqualified success as failures were caused by metallic paper fasteners and damp mail.

Graphite-lined stamp

Experiments then began with luminescent coding—the use of phosphor overprints on ordinary stamps or the printing of stamps on fluorescent or phosphorescent papers.

In November 1959 existing graphite stamps were overprinted on the face with phosphor lines which when exposed to ultra-violet light releases energy in the form of visible light—the sophisticated machinery 'reading' the light emitted—again two phosphor lines (or bands) for first class mail, one line for 'printed papers'. The phosphor lines on these stamps can clearly be seen—they have a slightly brownish tinge to them.

This was followed by stamps overprinted with phosphor lines only—in June 1960 (½d, 1d, 1½d, 2½d, 3d, 4d, 6d, 1s 3d 2 lines, 2d 1 line). When the second class postal rate increased from 2d to 2½d in 1961 a new 2½d 1 line stamp was issued and the 2d was overprinted with two lines. Further values were added later—4½d, 5d, 7d, 8d, 9d, 10d, 1s and 1s 6d. The lines on these are not as clearly visible as the phosphor-graphite stamps and it is usually necessary to hold the stamps up to the light at eye level when they become visible as broad bands down the sides of the stamps (left side only on some 2d, 2½d and 3d stamps, later printings of the 3d had one band down the centre of the stamp).

Collectors of G.B. stamps may see references to 'green', 'blue' and 'violet' phosphors. Very simply these adjectives describe the three different chemicals used on the stamps—Lettalite B1, B2 and B3. The phosphor-graphite and early phosphor issues were Lettalite B1 ('Green' phosphor), later the chemicals were improved—B2 (1961–65) and B3 (1965 onwards). Green, Blue and Violet refer to the colours that the lines glow after exposure to ultra-violet light. These differences are of little consequence to the average collector, but specialists like to obtain specimens of each type. Obviously an ultra-violet lamp is required to distinguish the stamps. Some are very scarce—for example the 2d 1 line blue phosphor. On early printings the phosphor lines were 8mm wide, later 9·5mm. These variations are not listed in the general Stanley Gibbons catalogues, collectors interested in learning more about them are referred to the *Stanley Gibbons Great Britain Specialised Catalogue, Volume 3*.

The use of phosphor lines continued with the Machin stamps first introduced in June 1967. However, the use of lines was not always satisfactory and in 1969 some 1s 6d stamps were issued on an experimental 'phosphorised paper'—the phosphor being incorporated into the chalk-coating (see above) of the stamp. Phosphorised paper is also referred to as 'Phosphor-Coated Paper' (P.C.P.). Further experiments took place—now on decimal Machin stamps—in 1974 and 1976 and in 1979 phosphorised paper was introduced for all stamps which formerly had two phosphor lines (the one line stamps for second class mail remained). For a short while in 1979 some values (1p, 2p and 10p) were printed on paper which had a phosphor band printed across its entire width before the stamp design was printed on top. These phosphor underprints are referred to in the Stanley Gibbons catalogues as 'All-over phosphor' stamps. They are referred to elsewhere as 'Phosphor Pre-treated Paper' or 'Printed Phosphor Paper (P.P.P.) stamps. These variations are included in the standard catalogues and are usually collected by the average as well as the specialist collector. Slight variations in phosphorised paper stamps (referred to as PCPO, PCP1 and PCP2) are not included in the catalogues and are normally only required by the advanced collector. Decimal stamps having one band printed down the left or right hand side of the stamp (½p, 2½p pink, 6½p, 7p, 8p, 10, 11½p, 12½p) or down the centre (½p, 1p) were issued in stamp books and coils, not in sheets. Some other values having two lines (2½p rose, 3p, 12p, 14p, 15½p) were also only issued in booklets—the sheet stamp equivalents being on phosphorised paper. A listing of the basic types is given in both the Stanley Gibbons *Part 1* and *Elizabethan* catalogues, details of variations of interest to the specialist are to be found in the *Great Britain Specialised Catalogue, Volume 4*.

Commemorative stamps have also been produced overprinted with phosphor lines printed on phosphorised paper. Some of the early issues (1962–63) were printed in very small quantities and are consequently scarce and priced considerably more than the ordinary (non-phosphor) stamps.

Other countries adopted similar mail sorting machinery as Britain and stamps with phosphor lines or bands have been issued in Canada, France, Portugal, Israel, Japan, South Africa, the U.S.A. and Yugoslavia.

The Canadian Post Office introduced facer-cancelling machines at Winnipeg in 1962 which were activated by phosphor bands on the stamps. These bands are visible to the naked eye and the stamps listed in the standard (*Part 1*) catalogue. In 1971 new sorting machines were installed in the Ottawa area which were activated by stamps bearing fluorescent bands. These are hardly visible to the naked eye and are not listed in the *Part 1* catalogue but details can be found in the *Elizabethan Specialised Catalogue*.

The French P.O. issued certain definitive stamps with phosphor bands in March 1970 for use on mail handled by the Clermont-Ferrand P.O. The sale of these stamps was later extended. Commemorative stamps have not yet been issued with phosphor bands. Phosphor bands have been printed on certain Portuguese definitive and commemorative issues since 1975. Most Israeli stamps have phosphor overprints since 1975. Certain Japanese definitive stamps with a 'phosphor frame' were issued in 1966. South African stamps were printed with a phosphor frame from 1964, this was dropped in 1971 in favour of phosphorescent (phosphorised) paper which cannot be distinguished from non-phosphor stamps without the ultra-violet lamp. Since 1972 all stamps have been printed on phosphorised paper.

In America, starting in August 1963, printings of some postage, air and commemorative stamps were made coated all over with phosphor on the front in connexion with mail sorting machines. These are impossible to distinguish without the aid of an ultra-violet lamp and so are not afforded separate catalogue recognition. However the Gibbons catalogue does indicate which stamps exist with this phosphor overprint. From 1972 to 1978 some stamps have a phosphor band instead of all-over phosphor—at first the band was a narrow strip in the centre of the design; on later issues it was broader and covered most of the design, leaving a narrow non-phosphorescent frame. Since 1978, all photogravure-printed stamps have the phosphor in a block covering the design area but leaving a narrow, non-phosphorescent frame.

Phosphor lines have been printed on certain Yugoslav stamps since 1973.

A number of countries have issued stamps printed on phosphorescent or fluorescent paper rather than stamps overprinted with phosphor lines. These serve much the same purpose as the phosphor-lined stamps. The difference between fluorescence and phosphorescence will not concern many collectors although the more scientifically-minded philatelist may like to read up about this and there have been quite a few specialised articles on this subject in the philatelic press in recent years. Stamps printed on fluorescent paper have been issued by the following countries (dates of first issues in brackets): Canada (1971), Denmark (1962), West Germany (1960), Italy (1968), Netherlands (1961), Russia (1969). Not all stamps have been printed on this paper, the Gibbons catalogue indicates those which have. Where stamps are produced on both ordinary and fluorescent paper this is noted but the fluorescent paper variation is not separately listed, since to the naked eye there is no difference between the two stamps, the difference can only be detected under ultra-violet light. Normally fluorescent stamps give a yellow reaction under U.V. light.

Stamps printed on phosphorescent paper (normally reacting green under U.V. light) have been issued by the following countries: Argentina (1971), Australia (1963), Brazil (1972), Finland (1972), Lebanon (1973), Mexico (1962), Netherlands (1967), Norway (1962), South Africa (1971), Sweden (1967) and Switzerland (1963). The Swiss stamps can easily be distinguished by having violet fibres in the paper; they are given separate catalogue recognition.

In Australia, the experiments with phosphorescent coding have been going on since 1963 using a substance known commercially as helecon, one of the zinc sulphide group. Helecon has been incorporated in stamps in two ways, either in the ink with which the stamps are printed, or included in the surface coating of the stamp paper. Such stamps are not given separate listings in the Gibbons catalogues as they can only be distinguished under U.V. light. Specialists will, of course, require copies for their collections.

We have looked, albeit briefly, in this chapter at the four main processes used to print stamps and at the coding systems used in recent years to aid postal mechanisation. However well intentioned and managed a printing works is, errors will occur from time to time—either in the printing of a complete run of stamps or sporadically on a single sheet or small number of sheets. Errors and varieties are of very great interest and fascination to some collectors and the following chapter explains their occurrence and their philatelic significance.

CHAPTER SEVEN

Errors and Varieties

It is a curious trait of the stamp-collector that, while other people consider a commodity which has been defectively manufactured to be of less value than the perfect article, he insists on regarding a postage stamp which shows the results of some mistake as being, in most cases, of greater interest than a correctly printed specimen. Naturally, if proper care is exercised, incorrect stamps will be less plentiful than correct ones, and as they are regarded as collectable they often have a greater value. All kinds of mistakes can happen during the complicated process of stamp production, and it will be as well to review these in detail, especially in regard to the relative importance attached to each class by collectors, as there is no very consistent basis of appraisal. It is true that the terms 'errors', 'major variety', and 'minor variety' are used to indicate very roughly certain grades of importance, but they are loosely employed.

The first possibility of mistake arises when the artist is drawing his sketch. he may be wrong in some essential detail of his picture, as when he put one of the Union Jacks on the 2½d Jamaica, of 1921, upside down, or he may go wrong in the lettering of the inscription,

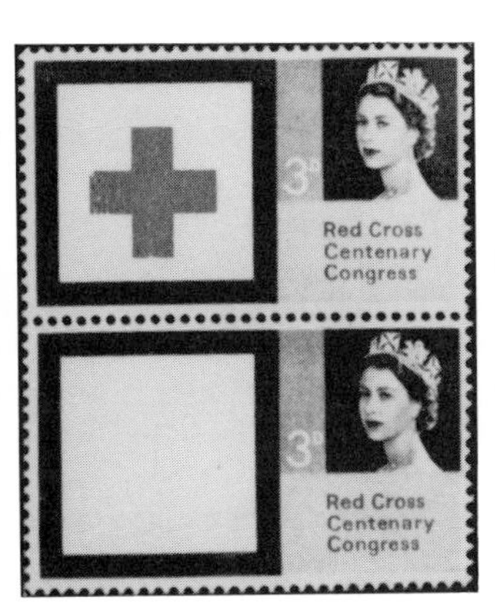

Jamaica Union Jack error of design (error at top, corrected stamp below); modern British errors – missing Red Cross (*1963*), missing value, Geographical Congress stamp (*1964*) and missing P.O. Tower (*1965*)

mis-spelling a word or making one letter look like another. If the engraver of the die follows the artist faithfully, he will copy his mistakes and these will appear on the plate and in the designs of the finished stamps. Mistakes of this kind hardly come within the definition of the word 'error', for every stamp is alike, and the collector employs the word more often to signify a variation from the normal run of a particular stamp.

In the next stage of preparing a line-engraved plate, we have already seen how retouches and re-entries occur. The importance attached to these by collectors varies in proportion to their prominence, but a really clear retouch or re-entry will be keenly sought. So also will be stamps which show evidence of serious damage to the plate, particularly if stamps printed at a later date prove that retouching has been effected to repair the damage.

A scratch on an engraved plate, or accidental damage to a typographic plate, may result in one particular stamp in the printed sheet having a word wrongly spelt, as for example, the first British 1½d stamp of King George V, where the words 'THREE-HALFPENCE' appeared on one stamp of a certain plate as 'THREE-HALFPENCF'. Mistakes of this kind, which have a certain appeal to the eye and to the imagination, are popular with collectors, and often attain considerable value though, logically, they are of no more importance than similar damage which does not alter a letter, or any essential of the pictorial design.

G.B. HALFPENCF, variety

The use of the two dies to produce plates for printing a particular stamp is very likely to result in the issue of stamps differing slightly in detail, unless purely mechanical means of reproducing the one from the other are adopted. Sometimes, a second die is intentionally different from the original one, with the object of improving the general appearance or some particular detail, but often, with hand-engraved dies, the second die will not be an exact replica of the first, and there will be unintentional differences in the design of the resulting stamp. In the catalogues, stamps or issues resulting from the use of a noticeably different new die are said to be in a 'redrawn design'. Good examples of pairs of dies differing slightly in minor details are to be found in the Queen Victoria portrait used by Cyprus, St.Lucia and other colonies in the 1880s and the head-plate of the familiar King George V colonial 'tablet' type.

Differences caused by the use of different dies are perhaps better described as variations rather than varieties as the stamps are considered normal and acceptable by both printers and postal authorities. The term *variety* is nowadays normally reserved for a stamp having a fault—either trivial or major.

It sometimes happens that one die is smaller than another which is otherwise similar, and the resulting stamps are consequently of two different sizes, but a variation in size does not always betoken the existence of a different die, as many collectors seem to think. One very frequent cause of varying stamp sizes is paper shrinkage.

In printing from line-engraved plates, the paper, as we have seen, is usually dampenedbefore the actual printing takes place. If the paper is always of exactly the same characterand the dampening is done under the same conditions, the shrinkage of the paper when drying will be practically constant and all the stamps will be of equal size. If, however, the shrinking varies for any reason, the stamp designs will shrink more or less, as the case may be, and you will get stamps of different sizes. Varieties caused by paper shrinkage have no interest or importance for the collector.

Some printers now use a process in which the paper is not dampened. When this dry process is employed for stamps previously printed by the wet process, a change of size is likely to occur and may then be of value as indicating the adoption of the new method.

In some cases it occurs from the method of manufacture that a number of 'types' differing only slightly in detail may be identified among the stamps in a sheet. For example, a design may be transferred to a lithographic 'stone' by 'laying down' a certain number of reproductions at one operation, and repeating this operation until the number of reproductions required for printing a sheet of the desired size is obtained. If the unit of transfer to the 'stone' is six reproductions of the design, each of these six will probably differ in some small detail, and the stamps will show the same differences, and thus, in the printed sheet, we shall find six 'types', which, to a specialist, are collectable.

Following out the lithographic process, it is possible that, after some sheets have been printed from the 'stone', one of the designs on it may receive a scratch or other damage, or the transfer may be folded or creased when first laid down on the stone. The resulting damaged or folded transfer is interesting to the specialist. Let us suppose that, for purposes of reference, he calls the 'type' of which one of the transfers has become damaged, Type C, to distinguish it in his own mind from the other five types which he finds on the printed sheet. In later printings from the 'stone', he notes that the variation caused by the damaged transfer has disappeared, and that, in the position it previously occupied in the sheet, there is now a stamp of Type B. Here he has evidence of a 'substituted transfer', *i.e.* the replacement of one transfer by erasure from the 'stone' and the laying down of another.

Again, the collector might notice that in some sheets his six types are arranged in rows of six, A B C D E F, repeated down the sheet. In other sheets, he finds that, though the same types are present, they appear in groups of six placed side by side, thus

A B C A B C

D E F D E F

Obviously, though the same types of transfer have been used, they have been laid down afresh on the 'stone', and the resultant re-arrangement of the types in the sheet is called a new 'setting', a term which is applied to any particular grouping of types in a sheet of stamps, whether they be of the stamps themselves or of a surcharge or overprint.

It sometimes happens that, in making a printing plate, or in laying down the designs on a 'stone', one stereo is inserted, or one design laid down, upside down in relation to its fellows. If the printed sheet of stamps showing the results of such a mistake were cut or torn up into units, every stamp would still look exactly the same, but if the inverted stamp is retained in a pair with one of its fellows we have that much-sought-for error a *tête-bêche* pair. Some classic examples of such errors are found among the early stamps of France.

There is another way in which *tête-bêche* pairs may be created, which has not the same importance. Large sheets of stamps may be printed from two or more plates, or a single plate may be used to print half the sheet at one operation, the blank half of the paper being then brought beneath the plate to receive the impression in its turn. If, in the first case, the two plates are printed simultaneously, so that all the impressions from one are upside down in relation to those printed from the other, it will be possible to get *tête-bêche* pairs consisting of one stamp from the inner row of each section of the sheet, usually with more unprinted paper between them than there would be between adjacent stamps in the same section of the sheet. In the other case, the same thing would happen if the sheet of paper were turned round before receiving the second impression from a single plate.

Tête-bêche

Double printing

Turning to the actual printing of the stamps, we find that several mistakes are possible in the passing of the sheet of paper through the press. If, through inadvertence, it goes through twice, the design will be doubled, and the greater the distance between the two impressions, the more highly will it be prized by collectors. A slight doubling of the design may also be caused by the slipping of the paper as it goes through the press but such variation has not anything like the same importance.

If the sheet is put through the press twice, once face upwards, and then face downward, it will have the design on both sides, and both designs will be positive. Such a true 'printed on both sides' variety is regarded as being a first-class error, while there is another rather similar, and much more plentiful kind of variety which is of less importance to collectors.

When the printing press is running, a sheet of paper should be fed through it at each revolution of its mechanism. If this is not done, the plate is inked and makes the movement which would normally bring it into contact with the paper, and the latter being absent, an inked impression of the plate is transferred to the roller or flat bed on which the paper would rest when receiving the impression from the plate. When the next sheet of paper is fed through the press, it receives a positive impression on its surface, in the ordinary way, but it also receives a reversed impression on the back, from the bed on which it is resting. Such impressions are called 'offsets' or 'blanket prints' according to the circumstances under which they occur.

Another type of offset, still a reversed impression, is due to sheets being piled on one another while they are still wet, so that the back of one picks up the ink from the surface of the one below it. A similar happening, but with the face of one sheet coming in contact with the face of another, might produce the appearance of a double print, one print being reversed, but none of these varieties are of philatelic importance.

Offset variety

Many collectors will only be concerned with modern photogravure-printed stamps. Stamps printed by this method are usually produced in vast quantities and minor varieties abound.

Retouches are probably the most frequently encountered photogravure varieties. Cylinders are carefully inspected before printing commences and any major flaws which would appear as conspicuous streaks or patches on the printed stamps are made good. The consequent retouch is evident on the stamp as a cluster of coloured dots forming a distinguishable patch. Some retouches are small and not easily seen, others are massive and easily recognised; the retoucher uses a burin (engraving tool) to make minute, pin-point indentations on the faulty patch which will be inked in the course of printing.

Even more interesting are the flaws which pass unnoticed and appear on the printed stamps and which may, at a later stage, be retouched on the cylinder before it is used again, providing collectors with examples of the two states: before and after retouching.

Random white patches may occur on stamps during printing, due to various causes, one of which is a form of *dry printing*, when the ink thickens slightly in the trough and tends to strip off the stamps as they are printed. Similarly, foreign matter may adhere to the printing cylinder and appear as spots, blobs and dashes of colour on the stamps. Sometimes these extraneous dabs are given picturesque descriptions, such as 'Wart on nose' or 'Flying saucer'.

The numerous white dots and flecks inherent in the photogravure process inevitably occur amongst the fine detail of certain stamps, notably the emblems surrounding the Queen's head on the G.B. 'Wilding' ½d, 1d, 1½d and 2d stamps; the Queen's jewellery pearl earrings and necklace and the diadem on the 'Machin' definitives and decimal 'country' (regional) issues. The Scottish lion and the Welsh dragon especially seem prone to such varieties.

Machin variety – large blob on diadem

Fine lines and letters do not reproduce well by photogravure, and this is especially noticeable in certain issues, such as the 'British Paintings' issue of 1973, and the 'Roses' set of 1976, both of which employed a finely printed, cursive style of type in the inscriptions—resulting in faint impressions or joined letters.

Similarly the tiny imprints recording the names of artists or printers at the foot of certain G.B. commemorative stamps are extremely fickle, sometimes faint or only partially printed and often having broken letters. In certain instances the imprints have been so weak that they have been engraved by hand on the cylinder—examples can be identified by the crude and uneven capital letters. The 9d. 'Aberfeldy Bridge' stamp of 1968 (*S.G. 764*) is known (and listed) with both imprints—'HARRISON' and 'RESTALL'—on adjoining stamps (R.18/3 and 4) redrawn by hand. Broken imprints are also commonly found on the photogravure-printed stamps of South Africa. These varieties are normally found on one particular stamp within each sheet and where the printing of an issue is bad many stamps within the sheet will show varieties. In a particularly bad case almost all stamps will have a variety of some description although most will probably be trivial and of very little interest to the majority of collectors. It is important to identify the location of the variety stamp in the sheet and this is usually referred to by the row of the sheet followed by the number of the stamp in the row—*e.g.* R1/4 = the first horizontal row of stamp, the fourth stamp from the left.

Normally such varieties are collected in pairs or small blocks showing some normal stamps alongside the one with a variety. These are referred to as positional blocks. Varieties are not usually collected on used stamps but where used copies are kept they should have postmarks well clear of the variety.

As a rule of thumb, varieties which will be of significance to collectors and will deserve a place in a varieties catalogue will be those which are clearly visible to the naked eye, those which need powerful magnification to be seen are not so likely to be sought-after.

So far we have been considering mostly stamps printed in one colour, but when two or more colours are employed, the possibility of the creation of 'errors' is increased, for the sheet of paper has to go through the press as many times as there are colours to be printed. Here correct 'registration' of the various colours is very important, that is to say, each time the sheet goes through the press, it has to occupy exactly the same position in relation to the printing plate, otherwise the parts of the design in the various colours will not dovetail accurately. Taking the simplest example, a stamp printed with the centre in one colour and the frame design in another, incorrect registration will give us the centre misplaced to right or left or up or down. Slight misplacements are not regarded as of any importance by collectors, but a striking difference of position would be highly collectable.

Colour shifts

It is, however, a slight displacement which causes most trouble to the inexperienced collector, where there is normally practically no white space between the portions of the design in different colours. The slight difference of position, and the overlapping of the colours, which will make part of the design indistinct, or even invisible, causes many collectors, keen to make discoveries, to think that they have found evidences of the use of a new die. In fact they have only found one of the most ordinary happenings as far as two-colour stamps are concerned.

The printers of the 'King as Admiral' stamps of Rhodesia, on which George V's head was printed in black or another colour and the frame in a second colour, did not destroy sheets of stamps in which the registration was poor, but filled in the gap between centre and frame with a wash of colour applied by hand, which effectively concealed the slight defect. These stamps, though only curiosities, are keenly sought for by specialists in Rhodesian issues, but they can, of course, be easily faked.

If a sheet of stamps with the frame already printed in one colour is passed through the press wrong end first when the centre is to be printed, the resulting sheet will consist of stamps with centre inverted, an extremely popular class of error, and one in which great rarities are found.

Centre inverted error

If the sheet of paper is passed through the press twice, when either colour is being printed, we get stamps with centre double, or frame double, as the case may be, while through forgetting the printing of one colour we obtain specimens with frame or centre omitted. It is possible, also, to have a sheet of stamps with the frame printed on one side of the paper and the centre printed on the other. Such varieties are so easily noticed, however, that stamps showing any of those described above, save inverted centres or centres slightly misplaced, are nearly always from 'printers' waste', *i.e.* spoiled sheets, which have leaked out of the printing works when they should have been destroyed.

Printers' waste has little importance, to the purist who requires his errors and varieties to have been accidentally issued over a post office counter, though it is not always easy to ascertain whether 'errors' of any kind have been the result of a genuine accident, and have got into circulation in the ordinary way through an oversight on the part of the checkers or allowed to leak out through lack of proper control.

Now let us look at the printing ink, and see what mistakes the printer can make in this connexion. The most serious is, of course, that he should use an entirely wrong colour for printing a sheet or sheets of stamps; producing a brown stamp, for example, where the normal is green. Such 'errors of colour', where due to printing accidents, are as keenly sought for as inverted centres, but the collector must exercise some care in accepting discoveries, for as will be shown later, it is possible for colours to change through exposure to moisture or sunlight, even to fumes in the air.

Stamps coming from a certain part of Iran were found to be in curious colours, and on inquiry it was discovered that the change was caused by the fumes from the oil wells which were a feature of the district. As we shall see in Chapter 12 that it is easy for unscrupulous persons to change the colours of stamps by the use of chemicals so that, before buying any so-called errors of colour, it is advisable to see first whether they are catalogued, and even if they are it is best to consult an expert, as to whether the colour may have been changed, as a mere 'colour changeling', even if accidental, is of interest only as a curiosity.

Variations in the mixing of the ink and in the temperature and humidity of the atmosphere during printing and drying will result in variations in 'shade' or tone. Marked shades are attractive to collectors, because they hit the eye, but their importance from the research point of view is limited to those occasions when they indicate, or serve to identify, stamps from separate printings. Heavy or light inking of the plate or cylinder will also produce shades, and so will any variation in the amount of pressure. In stamps printed by primitive methods, or where proper care is not taken, it is possible to find several shades in one sheet of stamps, due to varying pressure on different parts during printing.

Sometimes blobs or lines of colour are found on stamps which do not form part of the normal design. These may be due to defects on the plate or cylinder as already noted, but frequently they are the result of dirt or other extraneous matter getting on to the plate. If a sheet of paper is fed through the machine with another piece, perhaps quite small, adhering to its surface, the latter will pick up the ink from the plate and will receive part of the design. If, then, this piece of paper is detached later, it takes with it part of the design, leaving a blank space on the sheet, which may be a small portion of one stamp, or parts of several. None of the varieties mentioned in this paragraph, though often striking in appearance, are of philatelic importance. They are merely 'freaks', and should be treated as such. Nevertheless they are popular with many collectors.

Inking varieties are prolific on photogravure-printed stamps. One common occurrence is the white or coloured hairline running across the surface of such stamps. In the course of photogravure printing, surface ink is removed from the face of the cylinder by a flexible steel blade known as the *doctor blade*. The lines on the stamps are caused when a particle of grit becomes wedged between the moving blade and the revolving cylinder. The 'missing colours' on some photogravure-printed stamps are due to the gradual slowing down of the multicolour press (for adjustment, etc), when one colour (*i.e.* one inking roller) ceases to be applied before the others run down. Strictly, this also is printers' waste and should be rejected. Far more interesting on photogravure stamps is the evidence of weak impressions and subsequently retouching.

Errors and varieties connected with the paper on which the stamps are printed are not of many kinds, if we leave watermarks aside for a moment. The most important errors of paper are due to the use of a wrong kind (*e.g.* laid for wove) or of a wrong colour.

As already stated, variations in the thickness of the paper are not of any great interest unless thereby identifying stamps as belonging to different printings, or distinguishing between originals and reprints, but specimens showing any very marked difference should be kept. Occasionally one finds a local thickening in a sheet of paper, due, perhaps, to a lump of some foreign substance getting into the pulp during manufacture, or to some slight defect in the making of the particular sheet. The actual effect, in the printed sheet, will be that the colour will be deeper in the design printed on the thicker part of the paper, as the thickening will cause heavier pressure at that spot.

Curious things happen when sheets are printed on paper which is folded or creased. If a concertina crease is opened up after the sheet has been printed, there will be a wide, white gap across the stamps affected by the crease. If a corner of the sheet is turned over during printing, part, or all, of the design of some of the stamps will be missing. Freaks of this kind, which only occur in a single sheet, and are never twice alike, must be classed with the other oddities mentioned in connexion with colour.

Errors and varieties of perforation are also popular, and there are one or two groups which come in the 'major variety' class. The first of these consists of stamps intended to be issued perforated, but of which a sheet or sheets has not been perforated at all. Some of the sheets from which imperforate stamps come are probably proof or trial sheets which the printer did not trouble to perforate, and which have afterwards got into philatelic circulation.

The collector should exercise very special caution in regard to stamps offered to him as imperforate errors, or even as specimens of a normally imperforate issue, where the same stamp was also issued perforated. Some stamps are printed with very wide margins around them. This was particularly the case with many of the older stamps, and it is therefore quite an easy matter to create imperforate 'varieties' with a pair of scissors. No stamp which exists perforated should be accepted as imperforate unless it has so much margin on each side that it is larger than the largest possible stamp that could be produced by trimming the perforations off a perforated stamp. Even the presence of part of the design of the adjacent stamp, with an imperforate margin between, is not sufficient evidence, as a stamp with perforations so badly misplaced as to cut into the next design may have been trimmed. There are, of course, special indications such as colour or other details, which enable some imperforate stamps to be identified regardless of the extent of their margins, but expert knowledge is required in most cases, and naturally, in the case of imperforate 'errors' the characteristics of the perforated and imperforate stamps will be the same. Most collectors adopt 'safety first' tactics and collect imperf stamps in pairs.

(*top left*) *Doctor Blade* flaw on G. B. 1971 7½p Ulster Paintings stamp
(*top right*) Misplaced perforation variety
(*bottom left*) Imperf block of four – a major error

Next we come to varieties caused when the sheet is fed through the machine but the perforating process is not completed. If a single-line perforator is being used, and it misses one stroke, there will be an imperforate space between two rows of stamps and the result will be pairs of stamps 'imperforate between', that is, perforated all round their outer edges, but not at their line of junction. Though the cause, in each case, is only the omission of a single stroke of the perforator, stamps from the outer edge of the sheet with one side imperforate are not popular, while pairs imperforate between are generally keenly sought after. Perhaps the lack of attention paid to stamps from a sheet with an outer edge accidentally imperforate is due to the fact that some countries have intentionally issued their stamp sheets with the outer edges not perforated. This means that the corner stamps of the sheet will have two adjacent sides imperforate while the other outer stamps will have one side imperforate. Many examples will be found among the stamps of Canada and the U.S.A. and the resulting partly perforated stamps—known as 'straight edges'—are denied access to many collections as being defective specimens, though in actual fact they are just as they were printed and issued, and are really scarcer—though owing to the lack of demand, less valuable—than the stamps perforated all round.

Stamps with these 'straight edges' must not be confused with stamps normally issued with two *opposite* sides imperforate, such as are issued for use in coils by many countries.

When a comb machine misses a stroke, the effect is different, for it will be remembered that the comb perforates three sides of the stamps in a row at one blow. A mistake of this kind will therefore give us stamps imperforate on three sides, unless the stroke of the perforator is that in which the 'teeth' are engaged in perforating the marginal paper of the sheet, while the 'back' of the comb, the long line of pins, is perforating the outer margin of a row of stamps. In this case we shall get stamps with only one side imperforate.

It is a curious example of the fickle nature of philatelic taste that whereas double prints, double centres and double overprints and surcharges are regarded as highly interesting, a double perforation receives less attention. Where the second blow of the perforator has descended alongside the first rows of holes fall in the same line, and the holes do not quite coincide, the effect when the stamps are separated, may be to make them appear as if they had been finely rouletted, one set of holes having cut into the other so that the resulting perforations seem quite small. Examples of this may be found on early British stamps.

If the pins of the perforator become blunt, the resulting holes will not be so sharply defined as those made by sharp pins. We thus get 'clean-cut' and 'rough' perforations.

Imperfectly perforated stamps – of little significance

Wing margin on G.B. Victorian stamp

Where the pins are so blunt, or the strike of the perforator is so badly adjusted, that the holes are not punched out, we get a series of circular depressions instead of perforations, and these are called 'blind perforations'. Since the introduction of the 'Jumelle' press by Harrisons in 1972 for the printing of British definitive and commemorative stamps, a number of 'part-perforated' varieties have been discovered. It is believed that these occur when the operation of the Kampf perforator attached to the press is interrupted. Such sheets often show a number of 'blind' perforations (where the pins have failed to cut completely through the paper) as well as portions completely imperforate. Only when the mis-perforation produces completely imperforate pairs of stamps are these 'freaks' noteworthy.

As we have seen in an earlier chapter, the differing 'gauges' of perforation are due to various spacings of the perforating pins, while perforations showing large or small holes naturally result from the use of pins of large or small section. Neither gauge nor size of holes is of any philatelic importance except when it enables us to distinguish between one printing and another, or between genuine, forged or reprinted stamps, but where a number of different perforating machines have been used for an issue, many collectors will try to secure specimens with every possible gauge of perforation.

It is not an easy matter to ensure that the lines of perforation holes always fall in the narrow spaces between the rows of stamps. Even if the distances of the printing plate and perforating machine exactly agree, it may happen that the paper itself may shrink in one direction or another during the process of printing (this frequently happens when printing from line-engraved plates on paper which has been dampened) so that the intervals become not quite accurate.

Whether the cause be inaccurate placing of the sheet of stamps in the perforating machine, inaccurate adjustment of that machine, or paper shrinkage, the result will be similar—instead of the line of perforation holes lying dead in the centre of the space between two rows of stamps, it will be nearer to one row or the other, and may even cut into the design of the stamp. Extreme cases of this are found among British Penny Reds, sometimes one comes across a stamp which is so badly perforated that it is actually made up of the right half of one stamp design and the left half of the adjacent design.

The usual result of inaccurate perforating is to make single stamps, when severed from the sheet, appear 'badly centred', *i.e.* the design of the stamp does not lie centrally in the space bounded by the perforations. If the perforations cut into the design of a stamp, it may well be refused a place in the album, and even a specimen which looks particularly lop-sided owing to bad centring may be eschewed, but only the most fastidious collector would refuse a place to every stamp whose design is not mathematically in the centre of the perforations. Extreme fussiness of this kind is not far removed from eccentricity.

Among the early surface-printed stamps of Great Britain and some of her colonies will be found some which have the marginal paper between the design and perforations on one side very wide. This is due to the fact that the white 'gutter' or margin between the panes only received one row of perforation, so that the margin became part of the stamps. Such stamps—usually called 'wing margin' copies—are not always popular because of their lop-sided appearance, though they are exactly as issued. Fakers have been known to buy the stamps with wide margins cheaply, trim them down to normal, and provide them with faked perforations. It is, however, possible to detect this fraudulent practice, as stamps with certain check letters always had wing margins, so copies of these without such margins must have been tampered with.

Misplaced perforations, however curious the results of them may appear, can only be classified as 'freaks'. The same applies to varieties, less frequently met with, where a sheet has been torn or damaged before perforating, patched with adhesive paper, and then put through the perforator, proof of this being afforded by the fact that the adhesive paper is perforated as well as the sheets of stamps. Creased or folded sheets give some very curious perforation effects when the folds are opened out, but these too can only be reckoned as freaks.

'Mixed' perforations, some of which are given catalogue status (*e.g.* the pictorial issues of New Zealand), are found in sheets which were first perforated with a machine of a particular gauge, and then found to be inaccurately or incompletely perforated. The defect was remedied by patching them on the back with strips of paper, and the defective parts were then re-perforated with a machine of another gauge.

Errors and varieties of watermark must next claim our attention. Their causes are in most cases very similar to those we have noted in connexion with the printing of stamps in two colours, but here instead of two parts of the design, we have the watermark in the substance of the paper, and the design which is printed on it, and it is the relation of these which gives us our errors.

The normal position of a watermark (unless it is of so symmetrical a design that it cannot be said to have a 'right way up') is usually with its top and bottom at the top and bottom of the stamp design, respectively, and with the design or lettering reversed when looked at from the back of the stamp. Catalogues usually show the watermark designs as they appear from the front of the stamp, but the collector normally looks at the back of the stamp (or through it when he holds it up to the light) in order to see the watermark, and in that case a normal watermark, say of words or letters, would read or appear backwards as in a looking-glass.

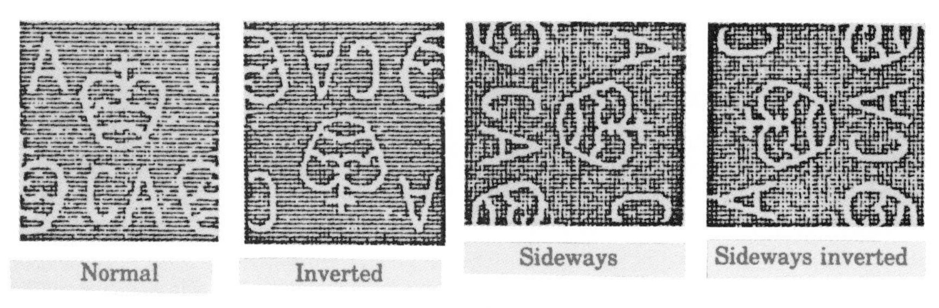

Watermark variations (*as seen from front of stamp*)

If, however, the printing is done on the wrong side of the sheet of paper, the watermark will read normally when looked at from the back of the stamp, which is then said to have the watermark reversed.

If the sheet is fed through the press wrong end first, the watermark will be inverted, *i.e.* its foot will be at the top of the stamp, and if the sheet goes through sideways, the watermark will be sideways. Some sideways watermarks are normal for their particular issues, however, sheets of paper having been printed on in a certain direction in order to accommodate the stamps of, perhaps, a different size from those for which the paper was originally intended.

A combination of printing on the back of the paper and with the sheet fed in the wrong end first will give us a watermark which is inverted and reversed, that is to say that the watermark lettering or design will appear positive (not looking-glass way) from the back of the stamp, and will also be upside down in relation to the design of the stamp.

Double watermarks may occasionally be found, but these are merely freaks, the second being a 'ghost' taken up by pressure from another sheet at some stage during manufacture or storage.

In some British stamp booklets, half of each printing used to contain stamps with inverted watermarks (or, if the booklet was made up with stamps with sideways watermarks, half of each printing would contain stamps with sideways-inverted watermarks). This was not due to errors in printing, but to the special sheets printed for making up into booklets. Similarly, special printings for rolls for coil machines sometimes had sideways watermarks. Since the vast majority of these issues normally had upright watermarks (that is, from ordinary Post Office sheets), these variations are often quite scarce, commanding substantial premiums over the normal stamps.

In certain issues, such as the middle issues of some of the Australian States, so little care was taken as to which end of the sheets went first through the press, that inverted watermarks are so common as to have hardly the interest of abnormality. Some watermark varieties find a place in general collections; specialised collections of course include them.

As far as major watermark errors are concerned, the principal of these is when a stamp is printed on paper which has the watermark allotted to another issue. A striking example of this is provided by the 1d scarlet Edward VII stamp of Transvaal issued in 1905, which is found normally on paper with 'Multiple Crown CA' watermark, but which is also known on the Cape of Good Hope paper, with watermark anchor (*S.G. 274, 274a*).

In the same way, it may happen that a sheet of unwatermarked paper is used for a stamp which should be printed on watermarked paper. Where whole sheets of stamps are issued without watermark when they should normally have one, the result is obviously an error of major importance.

There is another class of stamps which miss the watermark, which is of comparatively minor interest. In many cases sheets of stamps, as printed, show blank, unprinted paper round their edges, and sometimes between the different sub-divisions ('panes') of the sheet. This marginal paper may have the same watermark as the stamps (inadvisable, as it could then be used by the forger for his products), it may be watermarked with some appropriate inscription ('POSTAGE' or 'POSTAGE AND REVENUE', or the name of the country) or it may have no watermark at all. Even if there are watermarked inscriptions on this marginal paper, there may be intervals which are unwatermarked. If the sheet of paper, is put through the press rather too much to one side or the other, the impression printed from the plate will fall to a greater or less extent on this marginal paper, and thus we get stamps from the margins of the sheet which either have no watermark at all, or show portions of the letters of the marginal inscription as their watermark. These tend to confuse the ordinary collector as they are never mentioned in the stamp catalogues, being purely fortuitous varieties. They may be kept as curiosities but have no particular value. To distinguish stamps from a sheet with no watermark, from those (much less important), which have merely been printed on unwatermarked sheet margins, it is necessary to have so many stamps joined together as will serve to prove that they come from a sheet without watermark. Usually a block of four will suffice, and sometimes even a pair, as sheet margins are narrow and it is unusual to get more than a single stamp printed on the marginal paper.

One final variation may be looked for in watermarks. This consists in omissions from the lettering or design of the watermark, due to damage to one of the metal devices on the dandy roll. Instances are met with among British stamps with the various 'GvR' monogram watermarks, but the most interesting modern example is connected with the Multiple Script CA watermark formerly used by the Crown Agents. Here the crown fell off two different dandy rolls and stamps are to be found with the watermark showing a blank space. In correcting one of these mistakes a completely different type of crown was put in instead, resulting in yet another interesting variety for the keen-eyed collector.

In Chapter 6 details were given of the graphite and phosphor lines found on British stamps. Varieties of course occur—some sheets being found with the phosphor lines omitted or partially printed, others have the bands misplaced so that a stamp which should have had a narrow line down each side of the stamp has just one broad line down one side. Some stamps with the phosphor lines completely missing are scarce and command high prices, minor misplacements are of minimal value although major shifts are keenly sought after and sometimes attract high prices. Phosphor omitted and major misplacements are listed in the *Stanley Gibbons Great Britain Specialised Stamp Catalogue (Volumes 3 & 4)*.

While the outsider may smile at the idea of collectors prizing so highly the results of mistakes in printing, the enthusiast knows that stamp collecting would not be nearly so enthralling if it were not for the chance it holds out at every turn of making finds of scarce errors among the less valuable normal stamps. It is, however, necessary to keep a sense of proportion and to concentrate mainly on the errors and varieties which have been indicated as being of major importance, otherwise the collection will come to be a hotch-potch of minor freaks and curiosities, which have little interest and still less value.

CHAPTER EIGHT
Overprints and Surcharges

When stamps came into general use, it often happened that some sudden alteration was required which did not allow the necessary time for the complicated processes of engraving a fresh die and making new plates, much less ordering supplies of the stamps from a source outside the country of issue, and many stamps for countries overseas were then printed in Britain or in the U.S.A.

A way out of the difficulty was found by taking existing stamps and making the necessary alteration by printing it across them, the overprint being applied either from ordinary printer's type, from a stereotyped plate, or in some cases from a lithographic stone. Such an addition to the stamps is described by collectors as an overprint, when it does not affect the face value of the stamp, and as a surcharge when it confirms or alters the face value.

The most frequent occasion for an emergency issue of stamps of this nature was a sudden demand for a stamp of a particular denomination, perhaps due to a change in the postal rates, which caused an unexpected shortage, or even a call for an entirely new denomination. Surcharging was then resorted to, and the resulting stamp, supposing a six cent stamp had been surcharged with the words 'Five Cents', would be described by collectors as '5c on 6c' or 'the provisional 5c on 6c'.

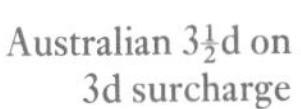
Australian 3$\frac{1}{2}$d on 3d surcharge

British stamp overprinted for use in the Irish Free State

Again it has sometimes been decided to issue stamps for a particular country or colony, at a date by which it would be impossible to have distinctly designed stamps ready. In this event, overprinting might be resorted to, the name of the new recruit being printed across the stamps of the mother country, or, as in the case of Gibraltar, in 1886, on the totally unrelated issue of Bermuda (*S.G. 1–7*).

Another function of the overprint is to convert a stamp from one use to another, as, for example, when postage stamps are overprinted in a special way, to convert them into postage due, or express, or air stamps, or whatever it may be.

Sometimes it may happen that a stock of stamps may be stolen from a post office or central store, and it becomes a matter of urgency to prevent those stamps being used for postal purposes in order to avoid grave loss to the revenue of the country concerned. In such cases, the practice is sometimes adopted of overprinting a device or inscription on the remaining stocks of stamps, and forbidding the use of any stamps which are not so overprinted. Overprints of this kind are called 'control marks' or 'control overprints' (not 'controls', a word which is usually applied to the letters and figures on the margins of sheets of certain British stamps). Examples of such control marks will be found on some of the issues of Persia whose stamps were frequently looted.

In the 1920s the stamps of the U.S.A. were specially overprinted with the abbreviated names of the states of Kansas and Nebraska, owing to a number of raids on post offices in those districts. Stamps with the names of these states on them could not be used in any other state and thus the chance of thieves being able to profit by their sale was minimised.

When political changes took place, such as a change of ruler or government, the application of an overprint to the existing stamps was often the quickest way of meeting the situation. Thus when Fiji was ceded to Britain, in October 1874, the stamps of the native King Cakobau, which bore his initials 'C.R.', were quickly overprinted 'V.R.' and the world knew at once what had happened (*S.G. 16–21*).

In El Salvador, where presidents used to come and go with great and often painful rapidity, a certain General Ezeta ordered the usual annual set of stamps from the U.S.A., but by the time they were ready (1895) the General was, at least politically if not actually, no more. The Ezeta portrait issue was then overprinted with the arms of the country, so effectively that only very faint traces of the portrait can be seen (*S.G. 95–106*).

When Yugoslavia became a state (1918), the only stamps available in certain parts of the country were those of Hungary, but on them appeared the portrait of the Emperor Charles and the Iron Crown of Hungary, the wearer of which was *ipso facto* king of Hungary. In this case the crown, as the symbol of rule, was blotted out by an overprint, but the portrait of the Emperor was allowed to remain visible (*S.G. 74–76*).

At the present time there are few purposes for which stamps have been issued, which have not also had their distinctive overprints or surcharges. We have war and occupation overprints as well as stamps, for it was naturally a great satisfaction to a conqueror to sprawl his mark across his opponents' stamps, pending the issue of a special victory series. Thus we find stamps of the German colonies overprinted with the inscriptions of the countries who captured them from her in 1914–18, and stamps of the Allied powers overprinted for use by the German Armies of Occupation. There were many similar happenings during the Second World War. Then there are a host of charity and commemorative overprints, in connexion with events and anniversaries in all parts of the world.

Overprinting is economical but is not very popular with philatelists. Collectors may be tempted by the pictorial designs of a commemorative series but they do not find a commemorative overprint very attractive. The demand, is, therefore, much less than for distinctive issues of stamps of this nature.

Stamps overprinted 'SPECIMEN' or 'CANCELLED' are normally sample stamps for official record purposes, for issue to the press, or for distribution to the various postal authorities of the world through the U.P.U. International Bureau at Berne, Switzerland for their official collections. The overprint is intended to prevent such sample stamps being used for postage. Such stamps now enjoy greater popularity than formerly. They are in most cases numerically rarer than those without the overprint, as usually only small quantities are overprinted, and in some cases it was not intended they should ever come onto the philatelic market.

El Salvador – General Ezeta's portrait obliterated by coat of arms

Specimen stamps

A major stamp error – incorrect surcharge (*bottom stamp*)

Inverted surcharge and doubled overprint

In recent years some postal authorities have made large quantities of specimen stamps available to the publishers of philatelic magazines to give as free gifts to the readers.

Some countries have made available specimen copies of their high value stamps at considerably less than face value. These are intended for sale to younger collectors who if they had to pay face value for the stamps would be unable to complete their sets.

Looking at overprints and surcharges from the point of view of philatelic study, it will be obvious that, as these are printed by the methods already described when dealing with the production of postage stamps, they present similar problems. Thus, in the case of lithographed overprints, we may distinguish flaws, substituted transfers and other typical varieties, while typographic overprints provide us with evidence of damaged plates and stereos.

When overprints are printed by letterpress from printer's type, which consists of loose units 'locked up' in some kind of framework, there is an additional possibility: that the type may work loose and that letters may either become misplaced during the printing, or may fall out altogether and fail to print.

Major errors of overprint or surcharge are caused in the same way as are the errors we have considered in the case of stamps. A sheet which is put twice through the overprinting press will bear a 'double overprint' (or surcharge).

If put in face downwards, it will be overprinted on the back, or it may, by some freak of fortune, be overprinted on the front and on the back. Fed into the press the wrong way round, the sheet will have an inverted overprint, and in the case of double overprints, if the second overprinting is done with the sheet the wrong way round, we shall have the overprint 'double, one inverted', as the stamp catalogues describe it. Triple and quadruple overprints are known, but when one reaches this stage suspicion of deliberate intent on the part of the printer begins to approach to certainty. Even the simpler errors are often the result of deliberate mistakes on the part of some wanting to make money out of collectors, but there are naturally many instances of errors occuring through genuine human error.

Another important class of overprint or surcharge error is that in which the new inscription or device is applied to a sheet of the wrong stamps. This is a not-infrequent happening nor is it a rare occurrence to find an overprint applied in ink of the wrong colour.

If a sheet of stamps is put through the press for overprinting, and care is not taken to 'register' it correctly in relation to the overprint plate or type, we get the kind of variety known as a 'misplaced overprint'.

If the misplacement is in the horizontal direction, we shall find the overprint falling either towards one side of the stamp instead of in the centre, or perhaps even on the junction of two stamps, so that, instead of each stamp bearing a complete overprint, it is provided with two halves of an overprint. Such varieties, due to sideways misplacement, come in the 'freak' class, and will be keenly sought by some collectors.

Similar misplacement in an upward or downward direction, which results in the overprint being out of position, or partly on one stamp and partly on another, produces other 'freak' varieties. If, however, we have a two-line overprint, reading, for example, 'WAR' in the upper line and 'TAX' in the lower, and this is misplaced vertically to a certain degree, we shall find that there are stamps in which the word 'TAX' is above the word 'WAR'. Such varieties receive rather more attention than the other misplacements already noted, but are still not as important as the misplacements resulting in one row of stamps missing the overprint altogether. Pairs of stamps one with the overprint, and the other without are regarded as important, and often valuable varieties. They may be caused either by vertical or by horizontal misplacement, and in such cases there will usually be a superfluous overprint on the marginal paper at the end of the sheet opposite to that which has the row of unoverprinted stamps.

'Offsets' or 'blanket prints' of overprints are also found, and these sometimes produce the effect of a double overprint, but their character can usually be detected because of a lack of clarity and detail in the offset overprint.

We must devote a few words to type-set surcharges or overprints, for comparatively few stamps have been printed from loose type, whereas quite a number of overprints and surcharges have been applied in this way. In setting up sufficient repetitions of an overprint or surcharge for a sheet of, say, 100 stamps, it is likely that mistakes will occur. The order of letters may be transposed, a wrong letter or an extra letter may be inserted, or a wrong figure may be put in in the case of a date or surcharge. Such errors are worth looking for, and one is never quite sure what will turn up, for even if one has seen a complete sheet with a type-set overprint, and has been convinced that it contains no important errors or variations, it does not follow that there are not any errors in that particular overprint. The sheet inspected may have been one of the earliest of the printing. At a later stage the type may have worked loose, and one or two letters have dropped out of some of the overprints, or stamps may be found with various letters of the overprint widely spaced. Later still, the printer notices the loosening of the type and, stopping the machine, he tries to put things right. The letters which have fallen out he can replace, but he may replace them by the wrong letter, or he may lock up without replacing them, giving rise to fresh errors or to new defective spacings. There is thus an infinity of variation possible in type-set overprints, and even where overprinting is done from a stereotyped plate, the stereotyping may have been done from handset type showing errors of various kinds which will, unless rectified on the plate, be repeated throughout the printing. Letters which are merely out of alignment are not regarded as important variations, nor are minor differences of spacing.

The point to bear in mind in regard to surcharge and overprint varieties is that letters showing damage or breakage are of no special importance or value, unless they enable a setting to be 'plated' or divided into its types, with a view to ascertaining the original arrangement, or, more important still, when they enable us to distinguish between genuine overprints and forgeries, a matter in which the collector will also be assisted considerably by the colour and sheen of the ink used.

Perfin stamps of Straits Settlements and Australia

Another method of converting stamps to fresh uses consists in puncturing them with lines of holes to form devices or letters. These stamps are known as 'perfins'. Thus the stamps of the Australian Commonwealth have been perforated 'o s' for official use, British stamps perforated 'B T' were used by the Board of Trade, and there are many other instances.

Not all initials of this kind are of public bodies. Some firms still perforate their stamps with their own initials in order to prevent theft from their post rooms. For the same reason, overprints—known as security endorsements—have been applied to stamps, perhaps the most frequently met with being the word 'CAVE' on the stamps of Ceylon. At one time 'perfins' and security-endorsed stamps were regarded as worthless. Nowadays many collectors find them of interest and there is a flourishing society of collectors studying such material

CHAPTER NINE
Stamp Sheets, Booklets and Coils

The average stamp collector does not collect complete sheets of stamps but will be well aware that there are points of interest to be noted in connexion with these larger units.

As has already been said, stamps are printed in sheets, the number of stamps in which usually bears some relation to the coinage of the country of issue, and usually a multiple of ten. For various reasons, these sheets are often subdivided into small sections, either by leaving blank, unprinted paper between each section, or by printing on the intervening paper some distinctive pattern or device. Each sub-division of a sheet of stamps are called 'panes', the intervening spaces 'gutters', and those round the outer edge of the sheet are known as margins.

The work of the stamp printer is a complex task, and he has found, in these margins, a very convenient place for making notes, while the postal authorities have also made use of the available space for various purposes. As the purposes of both printer and postal controller have to do with the printed sheet of stamps, each of them has had recourse to the method of making these notes on the printing plate or cylinder, so that they are reproduced on each sheet of stamps that is printed. Thus the margins of sheets of early British stamps give particulars as to the cost of a single stamp or of a row of them, and remarks about the gum, which is described as 'cement'. The printer has added a 'plate number' on the marginal paper, this indicating the numerical order of the plate in the series made to print stamps of that particular denomination.

The plate number on the margins of the sheet must not be confused with the plate numbers for which collectors search, and which are incorporated in the design of each stamp of many of the earlier British issues. Colonial stamps printed from standard key-plates also have plate-numbers in the margins, and it is thus possible to ascertain when a new plate has been brought into use for a particular stamp, when no detail of the stamps themselves is changed.

'Serial' or 'Sheet numbers', usually printed in black, run continuously through a printing, succeeding sheets being numbered in sequence. These numbers are sometimes useful in determining a sequence of shades, but have no special value in themselves.

Numbers are not always used to indicate a different plate, for in some countries arbitrary signs are employed for this purpose, and in other cases dots or nicks are made in the marginal rule on the plate. These marginal rules—sometimes called 'jubilee lines' because they were first noted by British collectors on the stamps of the 'Jubilee' issue of 1887–92—are intended to take the shock of the inking rollers, and raise them to the level of the printing surface of the plate. Without such a protection, the edges of the stamp designs on the outer edge of the plate will have to do the lifting, and will wear away more quickly as a result. These lines appear on the sheet of stamps as lines of colour running parallel to the outer edges of the stamps. Where they run right round the sheet without a break, or with perhaps a small break at the corners of the sheet, they are termed 'continuous', but when they are broken into short lengths, equal to the length of the side of the adjacent stamp, they are called 'co-extensive'. On the printing plate, the lines are, of course, ridges of metal, so that the printer can conveniently mark them with dots or scratches to convey to himself any message he likes concerning the plate and its history, a message which is often quite unintelligible to the collector.

Marginal inscription on sheets of German stamps
Plate numbers on sheets of Ceylon 2c and modern G.B. litho-printed stamps

(*above*) Sheet serial number
(*right*) Jubilee line (marginal rule) on Victorian 4½d stamp

When the Stamping Department at Somerset House took over some of the plates for printing the British King Edward VII stamps from De La Rue, the jubilee lines on the sheets printed by them showed mysterious markings which greatly intrigued collectors. These marks indicated approximate years of printing and in some cases there were also month cuts under the appropriate stamp.

Coloured dots are often printed on the margins of stamp sheets in order to facilitate registration of the paper in its correct position in relation to the plate. These dots are so placed that, when projections or pins on the machine pierce them, the sheet is known to be correctly placed.

(*above*) Control number
(*left*) Five cylinder numbers on modern commemorative stamp

The letters, or figures and letters, which appeared on the sheet margins of many British stamps until 1947, were known as 'control numbers' or more briefly 'controls'. These numbers were placed there for accountancy purposes, the figures having reference to the year and are prefixed by an index letter. Starting in 1884, only the ½d and 1d of the Victorian and Edwardian issues have 'controls', but in the later reigns all values to the 1s had them. They are collected either as single stamps with margin bearing the control attached, or in strips of three, or blocks of six, with bottom and side margin. The small figures on the margins of sheets of British photogravure stamps indicate the cylinder from which the sheets were printed and are known as 'cylinder numbers'.

They are nearly always collected in blocks of six (2×3) for definitive stamps. Sheets of definitive stamps are normally printed in horizontal pairs, the two panes being split before despatch to post offices. Both have the same cylinder number but to differentiate the right from the left-hand pane, a small dot or stop appears after the cylinder number on the right-hand pane (*e.g.* 4.). Specialist collectors usually require blocks from each pane.

For commemorative stamps the block should be large enough to include all numbers. For multicoloured stamps, a separate cylinder is used for each colour, each cylinder having its own number—for example the Great Britain 1979 13p Christmas stamp depicting Mary and Joseph was printed from five cylinders—2A (*black*), 1B (*brown*), 1C (*blue*), 1D (*red*) and 1E (*gold*). Cylinder numbers are highly popular for a number of reasons—mainly because they can be used to identify stamps with particular shades. Each new cylinder will normally produce stamps of a slightly different shade to its predecessor—sometimes these are sufficiently pronounced to achieve catalogue listing—for example the Great Britain 1s Machin stamp from Cylinder 11 (pale bluish-violet) which is listed in the *Elizabethan Specialised Catalogue*.

If the cylinder proves unsatisfactory it will have a very short life and the number of sheets released will not be large. In some instances sheets from a particular cylinder will only be distributed to post offices in a certain area of the country (say the North East) and so may not be easy to obtain. For these two reasons the price of some cylinder blocks are many times the combined value of the stamps they contain. Instances are known of less than a dozen blocks of a particular cylinder surviving.

Somewhat akin to cylinder numbers are check dots—often known as 'traffic lights' which first appeared on the 1962 National Productivity Year stamps. They are used to check sheets for missing colours. 'Traffic light' blocks are now almost as popular with collectors as cylinder blocks and indeed make a very colourful addition to the album page 'Traffic lights' are of course only found on sheets printed in two or more colours hence they are only rarely encountered on sheets of definitive stamps—currently only the high value £1, £2 and £5 stamps. Also in the margins of sheets of stamps printed in two or more colours are found 'Autotron' scanner and other registration check marks—normally these are of relatively minor interest to collectors.

'Traffic Lights' Gutter Pair
'Traffic Lights'
Printer's imprint on sheet margin

Some printers place their name below the design of each stamp in the sheets, and here also the name of the designer or engraver may sometimes be found. Other firms print their name on the sheet margins, when it is known as a *printer's imprint*.

While the separation of a large sheet into panes facilitates the work of the post office clerk, enabling him to divide the sheet into quarters or halves, as required, many countries provide him with additional indications on the margins of the sheets. These may take the form of arrows or other marks, showing where the sheet has to be divided in order to obtain a desired fraction of it, or figures may be printed opposite each row of stamps, indicating the total cost of the stamps in the portion of the sheet if it is divided at that point. Blocks of U.S. stamps with marginal arrow are known as 'arrow blocks' while a block from the centre of a sheet, showing the intersection of vertical and horizontal dividing lines, is called a 'centre line block'.

If the number of stamps to be printed did not occupy the whole of the central surface of the sheet of paper used, it was customary to print on the blank portion some device which prevented the paper being used by forgers. The high values of the Russian arms types of the later Tsarist and early revolutionary periods have the intervals of the sheets printed with interlocking 'V's'. Austria filled in gaps in her early sheets with a cross, and these crosses, even unattached to the stamp, have a certain value in that country; while in Britain, in the days when a halfpenny was charged for the privilege of buying stamps in booklets, one stamp of that value was omitted from the book, and replaced by a piece of paper of the same size, printed with a cross—known as the 'kiss' stamp.

Design used to fill blank space on printed sheet

Mixed value booklet pane

This mention of booklets brings us to another method of distributing stamps to the public. The great convenience of having stamps available in books containing a number of each of the denominations in most frequent use is now widely recognised, and many countries issue stamps in this way. Very often the booklet stamps are printed from special plates or cylinders arranged so that the resulting sheets may be cut up into panes and bound mechanically, to give the desired number of stamps of each kind. In order to make up a booklet of the required total, it is sometimes necessary to have an extra stamp of a particular denomination, and we find booklet panes from which we may detach a pair of stamps, one of which is in one colour and of one denomination and the other totally different.

Sometimes odd spaces are filled with advertisements or a printed device, as already mentioned. The special requirements of booklet printing often make it necessary that some of the stamps should be placed *tête-bêche* in the special sheets, but usually booklet *tête-bêche* pairs are the result of the deliberate placing on sale of sheets printed for booklets but not made up (as in the case of the first Union of South Africa 1½d *têtes-bêches*), or of the leakage of booklet sheets from the printing works or stamp store (as happened with some British issues). It is this *tête-bêche* printing of sections of the booklet *sheets* (not panes) which gave rise to the inverted watermarks in some British booklets, as mentioned in Chapter 7.

Another way in which stamps are issued to the public is through the medium of automatic machines. Here the stamps have to be in coils or rolls, and at first these rolls were made up by joining together by hand strips of stamps taken from ordinary sheets. In early rolls, the overlapping joins may be noted, but nowadays the stamps for issue in rolls are printed in long strips and joining is not necessary. Where the rolls are sold at a post office, they are normally wrapped round with paper—known as the 'leader', which is attached to the stamp at the outer end. Details of the contents and price of the roll are printed on this leader paper.

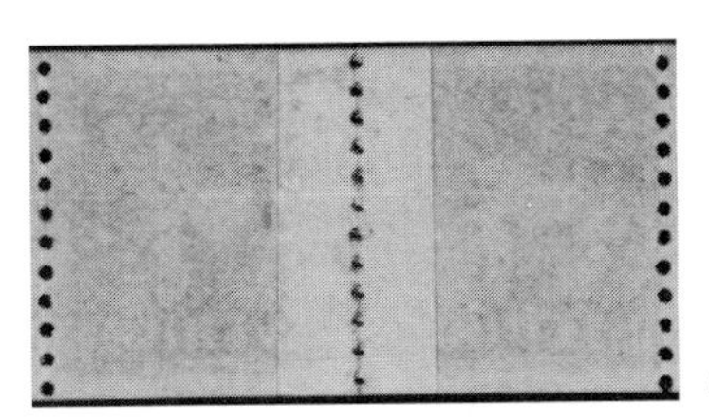

Coil Join

Complete sheets, particularly of the early issues of many countries, are of great interest, as they convey much information which cannot be gathered from a single stamp. Collecting in sheets is, however, a rich man's hobby, and the ordinary collector can only include such items when they come his way at a low cost.

In Germany during the inflation period of 1922–23, the margins of the stamp sheets were sold to business firms, who had the privilege of having their announcements printed on them, a novel form of publicity which gives such sheets a curious interest. A similar practice was adopted in South Africa but there the announcements are usually of a national character. Advertisements also appear in the margins of the panes of French stamp booklets.

CHAPTER TEN

The Other Side of the Stamp

We have already mentioned two characteristic features of a postage stamp, for which the collector has to examine its back (the gum and the watermark) while the paper is also best scrutinised from the unprinted side.

The back of the stamp is sometimes well worth attention, however, apart from any question of paper, gum and watermark. Look at the back of any stamp of the St. Anthony of Padua commemorative series issued by Portugal in 1895, and you will find a Latin prayer printed on it. Fiume has also printed inscriptions or designs on the back of stamps, the words 'POSTA DI FIUME' on the back of the issue of May 1919, and the snake and stars badge of D'Annunzio's 'Arditi' on the back of the higher values of the 'Reggenza Italiana del Carnaro' series of 1920. In such cases, the printing on the back of the stamps is probably an attempt to provide a substitute for a watermark, and would necessitate an additional operation by the forger before he could produce stamps of a convincing nature.

Sometimes there is a definite attempt to imitate a watermark by a printed device, as in the case of certain New Zealand stamps of 1925. Experiments were being made with papers of various kinds and, in a temporary emergency, stamps normally printed on paper watermarked 'NZ and Star' were issued on paper with the same device faintly lithographed on the back.

Portuguese stamp with Latin prayer printed on back

Advertisements on reverse of New Zealand stamps

Another purpose for which stamp backs have been employed is advertising. In Great Britain the idea never went beyond the experimental stage, but those who like curiosities may still find unused $\frac{1}{2}$d and 1d Victorian stamps with the words 'PEARS' SOAP' printed on the back. In New Zealand stamp advertisements were actually permitted for some time, and the Queen's portrait series of 1882–97 may be found with a variety of advertisements on the backs of its stamps, some of them even being illustrated.

While on this subject, mention may be made of other ways in which advertising has been brought into contact with stamps. In Italy a scheme was put into practice of issuing certain postage stamps to which was attached an advertisement, which may be said to have formed an integral part of the stamp as there was no perforation between stamp and announcement. The idea was soon dropped, as it met with the objection which has wrecked most of these postal advertising schemes, whether by stamp or by postmark, that a manufacturer or business man might find his correspondence going out franked or postmarked with publicity for a rival firm. Belgium has also experimented with stamps with advertisements attached, and in British stamp booklets there have been stamp-size labels bearing advertisments.

Pears Soap advertisement on British Victorian stamp

Latvian stamps printed on old German military maps and banknotes

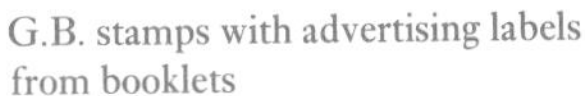

G.B. stamps with advertising labels from booklets

Returning to the backs of our stamps, we find that, in times of stress and difficulty, materials quite out of the normal have been used to print stamps on. Thus, as already mentioned, the first stamps of Latvia were printed on the backs of a large stock of German military maps, owing to a shortage of paper. Cigarette paper was also used for one issue, also Bolshevik banknotes with inscriptions calling on the proletariat of the world to unite. But stamps printed on wallpaper and on jam-jar labels are the result of an attempt to exploit the popularity of the war-map issue, and are not official productions.

In Lithuania, under similar conditions, the paper used during the war for ration tickets was employed for stamp printing, while in Oaxaca, Mexico, during a revolution (1914) post office receipt forms were printed on (*S.G. XI–6*).

Perhaps the most bizarre case was that in which the back of a stamp became the front. From 1910 to about 1912, Nicaragua was hard put to it to maintain supplies of stamps. Presumably funds were not available to pay for printing a new issue in the U.S.A. or in Britain, whence previous definitive issues had come, and for a time fiscal stamps were provided with surcharges which converted them into postage stamps. When supplies of these failed, the authorities turned out a stock of railway stamps and considered how they could convert these for postal use, the difficulty being that they already bore a surcharge converting them to fiscal use, on the front. But the Nicaraguan mind was by that time fertile in expedients, so a postal surcharge was added to the back of the stamp, which had thus been in turn a railway stamp, a fiscal, and a postage stamp.

Nicaragua 'back and front' stamp

Among the stamps of Russia listed in the catalogues under dates between 1915 and 1917 are some which are printed on card paper, and with an inscription on the back (*S.G. 165–167, 172–176*). These are actually paper coins, rather than stamps, for they were intended for use as small change, though the designs on the face of them are similar to those of the postage stamps in use at the time. A few have been found used on letters, but it is doubtful whether they have any right to be regarded as postage stamps. Stamps, enclosed in small containers with transparent sides, were used as coins in France and other countries during the 1914–18 war. Rhodesian stamps were also once used for money, in a time of emergency, being stuck on cards bearing the fiat of the local authorities that they should be accepted as change.

If the backs of stamps are always examined with the same care as is given to their faces, it will be found that there are other interesting points to be noted from time to time. A stamp whose back is of special interest should not be hinged to the album page, but enclosed in a transparent mount.

However, the vast majority of stamps do not have any interesting printing on the back—they bear only gum. Until very recently collectors did not pay much attention to gum—except that is to check that most of it was there in the case of unused stamps. In the late 1960s collectors became more concerned that their stamps should be unhinged and thus be in the state they were supplied by the printer to the post office and sold over the counter. Many of the older stamps are now rarely encountered in unmounted mint condition and such is their scarcity that they can command many times the price of a similar but mounted stamp. Each collector will decide what he is prepared to pay but should one day the unmounted mint craze come to an end collectors who paid very high premiums for their unmounted copies may feel very sorry for themselves. Of course recent issues are easy to obtain unmounted and should normally be collected in this condition.

Increased interest in the gum amongst British collectors coincided with the change in the type of gum used on British stamps. By the end of the 1960s, supplies of the traditionally-used *gum arabic* became more difficult to obtain and printers looked for man-made alternatives. As a result British stamps bearing a synthetic gum—polyvinyl alcohol—were introduced in 1968. Stamps printed on paper coated with both types of gum can easily be told apart—gum arabic is shiny, P.V.A. is matt and colourless. As a result a colouring agent was added but still some customers thought they were buying stamps without gum. Slight differences in the colour of P.V.A. gum (white, cream, pale brown) are sought by certain collectors but for most collectors such differences are rather too esoteric. These differences are not listed in the standard catalogues.

In 1973 the printer added a substance known as dextrin to the P.V.A. gum—this was required for technical reasons associated with the introduction of new machinery. Collectors refer to this type of gum as P.V.A.D. or simply as 'dextrin'. This gum appears 'green' as opposed to 'yellow' for ordinary P.V.A. (P.V.A.D. stamps are only listed in the *Great Britain Specialised Catalogue.)*

The subject of gum is not one to excite many collectors, for most it is sufficient to remember that some stamps exist with different types of gum and that one may be much scarcer (and therefore more expensive) than the others and that nowadays it is inadvisable to use stamp hinges on unmounted mint stamps as this will seriously (if illogically) affect their future value.

CHAPTER ELEVEN
Postmarks and Covers

Postmarks

A *postmark* is any mark struck on mail passing through the post. A mark employed for defacing stamps on mail is more properly termed an *obliteration*. The term *cancellation* is frequently used to mean an obliteration but a cancellation need not necessarily be an obliteration, as the term includes any kind of mark or defacement applied to a stamp to prevent its being used (or re-used) for its original purpose. Thus a fiscal penmark, the 'SPECIMEN' overprint, the 'cancelled to order' bars of Labuan and Borneo, and the bars printed across, or holes punched in the stamps of Spain, are equally cancellations (they prevent the stamp being used or reused for postal purposes) while none of them are either postmarks or obliterations (*i.e.* used on mail travelling through the post).

Labuan stamp with 'cancelled to order' bars

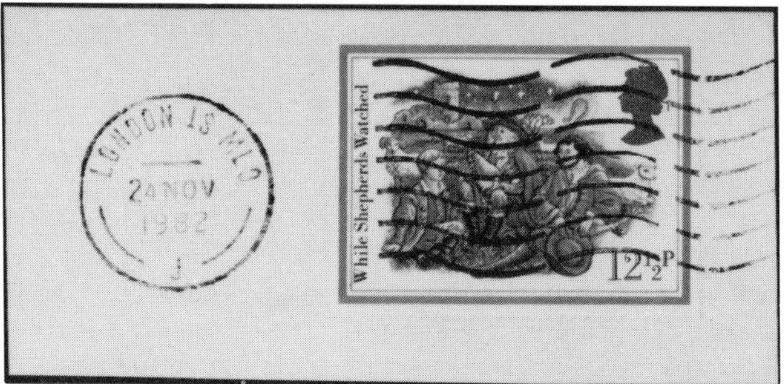

British first and second class mail postmarks (*first class shows time of posting as well as date*)

Postmarks of various kinds were in use long before the adhesive stamp was thought of. They may tell the place of origin and the destination of a letter; they may indicate the route or method by which a postal packet is to be carried; they may have reference to the weight of it, or to the amount chargeable for carrying it, or as a postage due if a proper sum has not been prepaid and, most important of all to the stamp collector, they may tell the date on which the letter was despatched.

Putting on one side the various marks which convey general information, let us consider for a moment the two essentials of the modern postmark and their value to the collector. These features are date and the place of origin of the letter, and if, in addition to the postmark of departure, there is an arrival postmark giving the destination and the date on which it was reached, the student can ask for little more in the way of valuable evidence as to the use of that individual stamp. An envelope with an arrival postmark on the back is said to be 'backstamped'.

The date is usually given quite clearly in the average postmark, sometimes with the hour of the particular mail in addition. (The British P.O. postmark first class mail with the time of posting, second class mail is given only the date of posting.) Even where no date is given, however, the format or size of the particular mark employed may be given an approximate dating, if research has proved that such a mark was not in use until a certain period.

The place of posting may be indicated clearly in words, or it may be shown by a code in which figures or letters stand for a particular office. Such were the early postmarks of Great Britain with their figures, or letters and figures, in a frame of bars. For a time some of these obliterations were assigned to British post offices in overseas colonies and in foreign countries and this has given rise to the study of British stamps 'used abroad', these being identified by the postmark. It should be noted that at a later period some of the obliterators which had been used abroad were re-allotted to offices at home, so that it is only when they are found on certain issues that their overseas use can be proved.

'32' Numerical postmark (*32* = Putney)
U.S. 'Killer' handstamp

Single and double-ring handstamps

In some postmarks, the portion which obliterates the stamp contains the details of place and date, while in others, there are two sections, an obliteration (or 'killer'), either of bars or some other suitable pattern, and a portion, intended to fall on the envelope, and therefore be more legible, which will give the place and date of posting. There are, however, many types of postmark which are solely obliterations.

There is an infinite range of variety in the patterns both of obliterations and place-and-date marks, and some collectors pay more attention to the study of these than they do to actual stamps. Where there is a series of numbered postmarks indicating the various post offices of a country, it is quite an interesting study to try to find out to which offices the various numbers were allotted, and then to try to complete the series of numbers on stamps or entire covers. If documentary evidence is not available, then the information must be acquired gradually from the envelopes and letters themselves.

Early cancellations are also collected for their quaint form, while there is a bias, even among stamp-collectors, in favour of postmarks and cancellations in colours not normally used. Thus a collector will pay more for a red postmark of a type which was usually applied in black even though the fact that a clerk happened to use the wrong ink pad does not really have any particular significance.

To the philatelist, who is studying stamps, or postal history, the postmark is valuable as evidence. If he does not know the date of issue of a stamp, he is always on the lookout for dated postmarks, and if he finds an 'early date' earlier than any yet known, he can add to philatelic knowledge. Absolute reliance cannot be placed on a single dated copy, however, for the dates in most postmarks are composed of loose pieces of type inserted into the handstamp used for cancelling, and it is quite easy for mistakes of transposition to occur. If there is a postmark of the place of arrival (and this is usually found on the back of the envelope) this will serve as a check on that of departure. It will also indicate the length of time taken on the voyage, while, if postmarks of intermediate places are also present, it is possible to work out the route followed by the particular mail.

All this information is very helpful to a student who is trying to build up the history of a stamp issue, and to find out the conditions under which it was used. Postal markings giving information other than place and date of posting are also extremely helpful on occasion, and it is this informative value which was the chief cause of the relatively recent cult for collecting entire covers, though, as in other directions, the zeal of the collector sometimes outruns discretion, and he includes with covers of real value others which tell him practically nothing.

A close study of postmarks is very helpful to the expert. Some rare errors were only used at a particular place so that all copies that are genuine must have the postmark of that place, a fact which the forger often does not know. On other occasions he ignores the fact that at the time when a certain stamp was in use, a particular type of postmark had not yet been introduced, so that he frequently produces fakes with a cancellation which immediately betrays the fraud to the collector who has studied postmarks.

Another opportunity is provided for the stamp detective when the forger has tried to apply an overprint or surcharge to a used stamp. His overprinting will naturally lie over the postmark; not always an easy thing to see, but when seen, a definite proof of faking, as, in the life-story of any respectable stamp, overprinting always *precedes* postmarking.

Stamp collectors are often creatures of fixed ideas, and in spite of all that can be written in the philatelic press, certain opinions persist from generation to generation. One of these is that a violet postmark or cancellation is necessarily a proof that a stamp has been used fiscally (*i.e.* on a bill, or other legal or commercial document, and not on correspondence). As a matter of fact, many countries, particularly in south and central America, use violet ink regularly for postal cancellations and it must therefore be clearly understood that it is the form and not the colour of the postmark that matters, though violet ink is used so frequently for fiscal markings, that its presence on a stamp may certainly afford a warning.

In the same way, the practice of writing across stamps used on receipts and similar documents has given rise to the belief that *all* stamps in any way penmarked are fiscally used. Here again, the collector is wrong, for in several countries there was a period when postmarking was done with pen and ink—for example on the early issues of Venezuela. Even now, in times of emergency, handwritten cancellations are resorted to, and these are naturally of special interest.

It is necessary to be quite clear on this subject of fiscal versus postally used stamps. There is a good deal to be said for the point of view that a stamp of dual usage, is collectable as a postage stamp only when it can clearly be seen to have been used postally (or in unused condition—in which state it is *potentially* a postage stamp), and it is this attitude which is responsible for the rejection of fiscally-used stamps by the majority of collectors. However some stamps, quite beyond the reach of most collectors in unused or postally used condition, are more easily obtainable with some form of fiscal cancellation. It is probably better to take these as space-fillers, rather than to have a blank space in the album, for at least they will show what the missing stamp looks like, and an honest footnote 'fiscally used' will save the owner from any charge of ignorance or intent to deceive. On the other hand it is not worth including common stamps fiscally used, as sooner or later these will turn up in postally used or unused condition.

Some collectors are also prejudiced against stamps used telegraphically, that is, those which are stuck on telegraph forms or receipts for telegraphic fees instead of on a letter or parcel. However, many of these bear ordinary postmarks, and are indistinguishable from stamps which have paid for other postal services, but in some cases a distinction can be drawn, by means of the shape or wording of the cancellation. There is no logical reason why any prejudice should exist against stamps used on telegrams. A telegram is a message just as much as a letter, and its transmission is an entirely postal service. The collector should be aware when he is admitting telegraphically-used stamps into his collection, but, apart from being able to recognise them, he can reasonably include them in his collection as postally used specimens.

There is another class of cancellation about which the collector should be aware and which has been the subject of intense controversy over the years—cancelled-to-order (usually referred to as C.T.O.). C.T.O. stamps are those which have been obliterated, not in the ordinary course of post, but in bulk, either because the purchaser wishes to have them in used condition, or in order to prevent them being used for postage.

It sometimes happens, though now, fortunately, less frequently than of old, that a government decides to sell its surplus stocks of stamps withdrawn from circulation. The natural outlet is the stamp collector, the natural channel the dealer. It may not be convenient for the postal authorities of the country concerned to invalidate the supplies of these stamps held by the public, yet if they sell their stamp 'remainders' at less than their face value, while they are still available for postage, they are simply going to lose revenue, for the stamps will be used to pay postage instead of going comfortably out of the way into the albums of collectors. It is often the practice, therefore, to cancel the stamps in some way, usually with some form of postmark, before handing them over to the dealer who buys them.

Cancellations of this nature may be easily recognised as in the case of some issues of North Borneo (*c*. 1888–1909) and Labuan (*c*. 1894–1902) where a cancellation of bars was used which, though employed as a proper obliterator in earlier times, was not in *general* use during the currency of the issues to whose remainders it was applied. On the other hand, when the authorities decided to sell remainders of certain issues of Rhodesia (*c*. 1896–1912), they cancelled them with the town postmarks such as were in use when the stamps were in current use, and arranged the dates of the postmarks to correspond.

Sets of stamps with light postmarks were sold to collectors by the Australian Post Office at below face value from 1913 to 1966; some stamps are more common thus than postally used. The high value stamps were sold in unused condition with a 'SPECIMEN' overprint.

It is nearly always possible to tell a C.T.O. stamp from one postally used in the ordinary course as the pseudo-used stamp looks clean and fresh and its postmark is probably clear and neat; in many cases, too, the stamp will still have its gum! Many respected postal administrations today provide through their philatelic bureaux a C.T.O. service for their customers who require 'fine used' stamps. Often the cancellations used differ from those used in normal postal duties—for example the cancellations used by the Jersey Post Office. Such C.T.O. stamps are sold to collectors at full face value.

Cancelled to order stamp – light cancel in bottom left-hand corner

Remaindering of issues is not now so frequent as it used to be. It is a sign that a country puts money before its national honour since stamps are, in effect, government securities—promises to perform certain services on presentation of the stamp as proof that payment has been made. Invalidation is only carried out after due warning, so that the public can exchange their stamps for others still available for use, and this the man-in-the-street receives fair play. But what of the stamp collectors? Whether they will admit it or not, most governments (and certainly those which stoop to the practice of remaindering their issues) rely on stamp collectors to help them to balance their postal budgets. They charge the collector full value for stamps when they are issued and then, when they want to put out another set in order to draw more money from him, they have the effrontery to annul the value of what they have already sold him, by putting their surplus supplies on the market at a fraction of what he paid. Small wonder that such countries are not in high favour with collectors.

It must not, however, be assumed by the collector, when he buys a packet or set of stamps which contains cancelled-to-order stamps, that the vendor is trying to take advantage of him. Stamps of this kind are regarded as saleable and collectable, and it must be remembered that C.T.O. stamps (remainders or otherwise) are often cheaper than the same stamps either unused, or postmarked in the course of post.

Attention must also be drawn to stamps which, while apparently C.T.O. owe this appearance to a special feature of the postal service. The Netherlands had a system by which, when correspondence was posted in bulk, it was not necessary to put a stamp on each item, but the total postage due on the whole lot was reckoned, and the sender had only to hand in sheets of stamps to the total value, for cancellation. Naturally he handed in stamps of high face value, for he received them back after they had been postmarked, and he was then able to sell them to collectors. Here, there is no suggestion of double dealing. The stamps, even if they were not affixed to letters, were cancelled in the ordinary routine of the postal service, and were as much genuinely postmarked as if they had franked a letter from Amsterdam to Djakarta. The result of the system was that the collector got his high value modern Dutch stamps in used condition much more cheaply than he would otherwise have done, the man who posted the batch of correspondence got part of his money back, and everybody was happy.

Mention of this method of paying postage brings us to another system, also used for saving time, when correspondence is posted in bulk. Postmarking the stamps on a batch of thousands of circulars or letters occupies a great deal of time and therefore someone thought of the 'precancel'. This is, in effect, a cancellation of some kind *printed* on the stamp before it is sold to the public. As the stamps are already cancelled before they are stuck on the letters, the time of the postal clerks is saved and economy achieved. Certain safeguards are necessary, however, for obviously there is always a possibility that pre-cancelled stamps which have once been used, may be rescued and used again, in fact frauds of this kind on a large scale have been detected in the U.S.A.

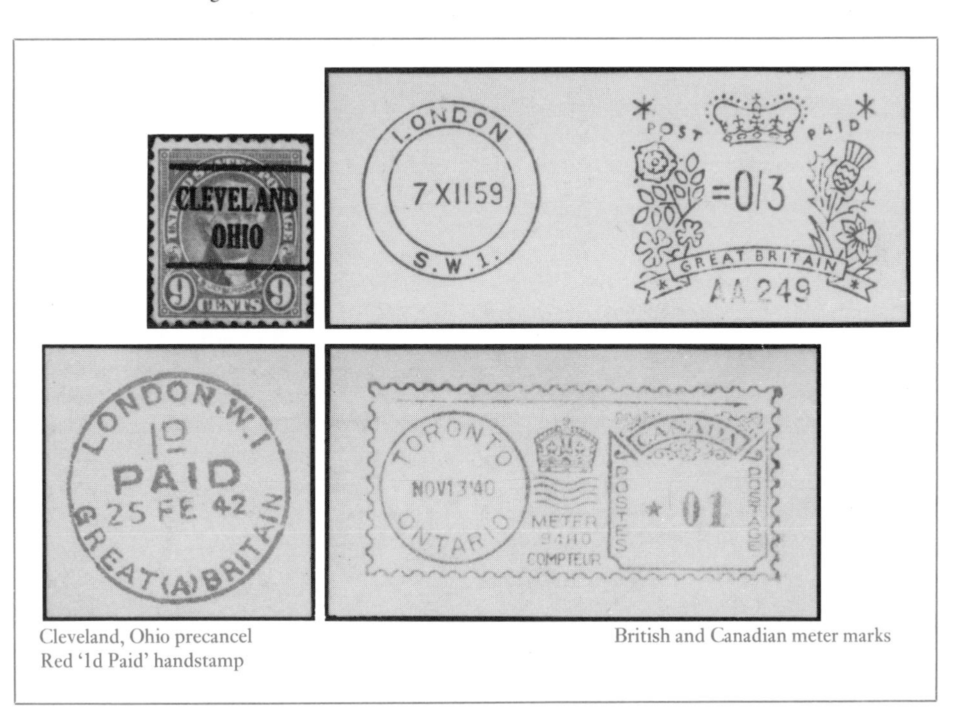

Cleveland, Ohio precancel
Red '1d Paid' handstamp

British and Canadian meter marks

Another method of dealing with big lots of circulars and correspondence, all of which have to be franked at the same rate, is by an automatic franking machine. No stamp is necessary. The sender simply hands in his batches of letters, etc., to the post office, agrees with them the number, and the amount of postage payable on each, and pays down a lump sum in settlement. The whole batch is then run through a machine which prints a frank on the envelope (usually in red) which will bear some such legend as 'Paid 3d' or 'Second Class Paid' and the date, time and place of posting. Similar handstamps are used on packets and parcels posted in large quantities. A rebate is sometimes given to senders of extremely large quantities of mail in one posting and postmarks inscribed 'R' are used on such mail.

Postmark and stamp also meet together in the machines which are now supplied to large commercial firms in many countries. These take the form of a kind of postage-meter, which is set by the local post office to provide a given value of franking, and is then locked, and handed over to the firm using it. By working a lever it is possible to impress on correspondence a device indicating that postage of a given amount has been paid, together with the date of posting, and some index letter or number which shows which machine made the device. Correspondence thus franked causes no further trouble to the post office, save that the weight has to be checked to see that the correct postage has been indicated. When the meter runs down, *i.e.* when it has franked letters to the value for which it was set, it is taken to the post office for re-setting, when a further sum is paid for the franking it will do on its next run. Collectors apply the term 'meter-mail' to such correspondence.

Sometimes these office franking machines are so arranged that they will print an advertisement of the firm which uses them on the envelope or wrapper, in addition to the frank and postmark. This is only a development of the practice of postal authorities using postmarking machines which incorporate in the cancelling die some announcement or advertisement, which is thus printed on correspondence at the time of postmarking.

These advertising or 'slogan' postmarks cover a very wide field. They are peculiarly appropriate for postal announcements, but they are also used for general government propaganda on such subjects as voting at elections, keeping Sunday, using the telephone, investing in loans, wise farming, careful driving, and a host of other matters. They are employed, too, for announcements regarding the charms of health resorts (since 1963 in Great Britain), the holding of exhibitions, fairs and fêtes, appeals for charitable funds and notices of important forthcoming events. In Great Britain the first such slogan postmark was used in 1917 and extolled the population to 'BUY NATIONAL WAR BONDS NOW'. Perhaps the most frequently encountered modern examples are 'REMEMBER TO USE THE POST CODE' and the annual 'A HAPPY CHRISTMAS FROM THE POST OFFICE'. Some of the designs for these slogans are attractive and there is a growing interest in them.

Slogan postmarks – including one extolling stamp collecting

Postmark advertisements of commercial firms have been tried and proved unpopular for the same reason as advertisements attached to stamps, the announcement of one firm too frequently went out on the correspondence of a rival.

Another type of postmark deserving of attention is that which indicates that no postage is payable, and which therefore takes the place of a stamp. Many governments use such franking postmarks in their various offices. These are similar to the bulk posting postmarks, being usually struck in red. Those used in Britain are inscribed 'OFFICIAL PAID'.

Some collectors make a point of securing an envelope franked with stamps postmarked on the day of issue—such envelopes are known as first day covers. Originally collectors had to make do with ordinary handstamps or machine postmarks. More recently (in Britain since 1963) postal authorities have provided specially worded 'FIRST DAY OF ISSUE' postmarks (machine or handstamp) at selected post offices.

Gibraltar red 'Official Paid' postmark

Wimbledon Lawn Tennis Tournament special handstamp

Perhaps the most popular type of postmark is the special handstamp. As long ago as 1862 the British Post Office provided special postal facilities at the South Kensington exhibition. The postmark was inscribed 'I E/W' (*International Exhibition/Western*). Until comparatively recently these handstamps were provided by the Post Office itself and normally applied only to mail posted at exhibitions (often stamp exhibitions), congresses and conferences. Amongst the most popular with collectors are those used at the Chelsea Flower Show

(1932–53) and at the Wimbledon Lawn Tennis championships (since 1948). Nowadays any individual or company may sponsor a special handstamp from the Post Office. The actual handstamp is used by P.O. staff only and remains the property of the P.O. A box is sited at the event or premises of the sponsor and all mail posted therein will receive the special handstamp. Collectors may also send covers to the Head Postmaster of the town where the handstamp is to be used, the covers will be cancelled and returned through the normal post. All covers must bear the appropriate postal rate and an additional fee for the special handstamping service (currently 3p). Many of these special handstamps are used on the day of issue of new stamps – some are provided by the P.O. itself (always at the Philatelic Bureau in Edinburgh and at least one other office)—others are sponsored, usually by stamp dealers. Sometimes quite large numbers of different handstamps are available—for example 12 and 20 different cancellations were used on 4 August 1980 and 22 July 1981 respectively on the stamps commemorating the 80th birthday of Queen Elizabeth the Queen Mother and the wedding of the Prince of Wales and Lady Diana Spencer. Often the numbers of covers cancelled are very large—nearly 200,000 covers were stamped with the two P.O. handstamps for the Queen Mother issue (Philatelic Bureau and Glamis Castle, Forfar).

British 'First Day of Issue' postmarks

The total number posted to receive the three P.O. cancellations for the Royal Wedding issue (Philatelic Bureau, London EC and Caernarfon) may have approached 1 million. At the other end of the scale, the numbers posted to receive handstamps for smaller events—local stamp exhibitions, football matches, etc. are usually in the range 2500 to 10,000, although occasionally it can be even lower—especially if little advance publicity is given. Any modern special handstamp with which under 1000 covers were cancelled can be regarded as scarce. However interest in these handstamps is not great and thus prices tend to be low. Even scarce cancellations are rarely worth more than a pound or two. Collectors can obtain advance information about these cancellations from the P.O.'s fortnightly *Postmark Bulletin* (see chapter 25) and details are sometimes given in the philatelic press. The number of different handstamps used each year is nowadays quite considerable—running into several hundreds.

Special handstamp commemorating the birth of Prince William

STAMPEX handstamp

Of particular interest to philatelists are those used at stamp exhibitions and congresses. A special Jubilee Exhibition was held at London's Guildhall in 1890 to commemorate the 50th anniversary of the 1d postage. The Post Office provided a special handstamp incorporating the royal cypher and the coat of arms of the city of London. A similar exhibition was held at South Kensington in July—several different postmarks were provided and a special charge of 1d was made for the handstamping service. The first Philatelic Congress of Great Britain (see Chapter 23) was held at Manchester in February 1909 and a special handstamp used on mail posted there. A special handstamp has been used at most Congresses since—pictorial cancellations have been used since 1939. The London stamp exhibitions of 1912 and 1923 were the first to be commemorated with special handstamps, such a postmark has been a regular feature of the National Stamp Exhibition (STAMPEX) since 1953 and of the British Philatelic Exhibition since 1966. The handstamps used at the London International Stamp Exhibitions in 1950 and 1960 featured the Maltese Cross and Tudor Rose respectively, in 1970 the Philympia Exhibition P.O. used a differently designed postmark on each day—as did the P.O. at the 1980 Exhibition at Earl's Court. The 1983 STAMPEX handstamp took the form of a hot air balloon—in commemoration of the bicentenary of manned flight. Mail posted at the Gibbons Catalogue Centenary Exhibition at the Royal Festival Hall in February 1965 was given a special handstamp which incorporated the famous S.G. 'Butterfly' logo.

As well as the sponsored handstamps used at exhibitions and other events for a day, week or relatively short period, the P.O. has in recent years introduced a number of handstamps which are in permanent use and intended for use on mail posted by philatelists. The first of these was introduced on 19 February 1969 when the Queen opened the National Postal Museum. The handstamp featured the Maltese Cross cancellation and was struck in black. This was replaced in 1972 by another datestamp—again featuring the Maltese Cross but this time struck in red—as the original Cross had been. The design was again changed in 1980. 'Tourist handstamps' were introduced at the London Chief Office and the Trafalgar Square Branch P.O. in August 1972, the former incorporated the Rowland Hill statue in the design, the latter Nelson's Column. These continued in use until September 1981 when new designs were introduced—along with other handstamps used at philatelic counters elsewhere (see Chapter 23). A special handstamp was introduced at Windsor in 1973, at Heathrow Airport in 1976 and at Britain's most northerly Post Office—Haroldswick on the island of Unst in the Shetlands in 1972. Other postal administrations use such tourist cancels—for example the Australian P.O.

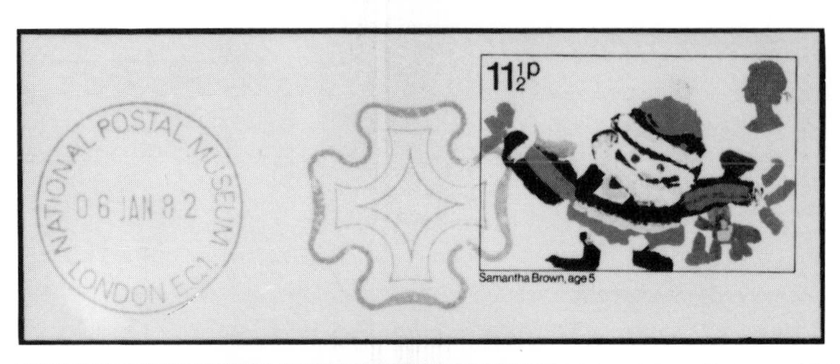

National Postal Museum Maltese Cross handstamp

Swedish Postal Museum postmark

The Guernsey P.O. applied a special handstamp to mail posted at its Postal Museum from June 1971 until February 1982; the Swedish Postal Museum has used a number of different handstamps over the years.

One group of postmarks of great interest to collectors are those connected with the Royal Family. A Court Post Office operates from Buckingham Palace and official mail despatched from this office goes to London's South West District P.O. where it receives the normal 'Official Paid' handstamp in red. However registered mail receives a 'Buckingham Palace' handstamp and covers bearing this postmark are keenly sought after. The Court Post Office is not open to the public and collectors are not permitted to send in covers for postmarking. A similar Court P.O. is situated at Windsor Castle and temporary offices are established at Sandringham, Balmoral and the Palace of Holyroodhouse (Edinburgh) when the Queen is in residence. Again these cancellations are eagerly sought by collectors and sometimes command quite high prices. More easy to obtain are those used at the House of Commons—most mail is machine cancelled but the machine die is inscribed 'HOUSE OF COMMONS/SW1'. A handstamp is used on registered mail and packets. A House of Lords handstamp is sometimes used but there is no P.O. in the Lords. A red 'Official Paid' cancel is used on mail sent out by the staff of both Houses (*e.g.* the Speaker's Dept., the Lord Chancellor's

Office, etc.). Members of Parliament are supplied with official paid envelopes for writing to their constituents—the normal House of Commons machine cancellation is applied to these.

Akin to postmarks are cachets and these are favoured by some collectors and included in their postmark collections. Cachets are usually applied by individuals or organisations not by the Post Office. Occasionally the British P.O. have used them—for example on mail posted on the last day of the Tutankamun Exhibition at the British Museum (31 December 1972) alongside the special handstamp, and the Jersey P.O. applies one to mail posted at the Jersey Postal Museum in St. Helier. For the most part they are applied to picture post-cards sold and/or posted at tourist sites. Possibly the earliest of these is that introduced at Land's End early in this century and used until the late 1940s (many different types were used). Similar cachets were introduced at John O'Groats in *c.* 1905, at Beachey Head (Eastbourne) in *c.* 1909 and at Snowdon in *c.* 1920. Several different cachets have been used at Llanfair P.G. on Anglesey—showing the full 58-letter name of the village. Although unofficial they are popular with some collectors and certain of the early ones or scarce types do fetch quite high prices.

House of Commons machine postmark

Summit of Snowdon tourist cachet

In Chapter 21 mention is made of the privilege of 'franking' mail enjoyed by members of both Houses of Parliament until 1840 whereby mail bearing their signature travelled free of postage. A similar system of franking using metal stamps inscribed with the name of a senior official was used by government departments from the 1850s. Later the name of the official was replaced by that of the department concerned. These indicated to the P.O. that no postage was payable and such mail was given the 'Official Paid' postmark. The use of these 'handstamped franks' or 'official cachets' continues today in a few government offices.

Altogether the study of postmarks is very interesting and there is today a small (but growing) number of philatelists who collect postmarks *per se*, the stamp being of secondary importance. However, for the majority of philatelists, postmarks are only of importance in providing additional information about their stamps—*i.e.* the date of the postmark provides additional confirmation that a stamp is from a scarce printing when it is known that the printing was in use for a short period of time.

Covers

A *cover* is any envelope, wrapper or other cover of correspondence. Many stamps are so common in used condition that it is not worth keeping them on the envelope and most collectors who are interested in stamps as such do not want to save them still affixed to covers. However, uncommon stamps and stamps having rare or unusual obliterations are best kept on cover and once removed are worth considerably less. Covers need not bear stamps—*e.g.* correspondence sent before 1840 (usually referred to as Postal History—see Chapter 21) and 'Official Paid' mail. In addition to ordinary covers—that is envelopes which conveyed normal private or business correspondence, the collector will frequently come across philatelic covers—*i.e.* those prepared with the collector in mind. Normally these will be specially designed envelopes posted on the day of issue of new stamps (first day covers) or else souvenir items posted to receive exhibition postmarks, etc. Some collectors go further and define as a philatelic cover any envelope (without special design) posted by or to a philatelist to receive a particular cancellation.

Falkland Islands first day cover

First Day Covers are not universally popular with collectors—indeed the purist collector regards them as unnecessary and unworthy of including in a collection. But this is now very much the viewpoint of the minority of collectors and there is a substantial (and growing) band of collectors who only collect such covers and do not concern themselves with mint or used stamps. In the early days of first day cover collecting, philatelists affixed the new stamp(s) to a plain cover which they addressed to themselves and posted in the normal way—the stamps being obliterated with either a machine cancellation or a handstamp depending on the usual method of postmarking at the local post office. By the mid-1930s several postal administrations provided special postmarks on first days of issue and gradually the plain cover was superseded by specially designed ones—produced either by the Post Office or by stamp dealers or philatelic societies.

The British P.O. was slow to recognise the great interest in such covers and not until 1963 did they provide first day of issue facilities. Special boxes were provided at 20 post offices on 21 March 1963 when the Freedom from Hunger stamps were released and covers posted therein were given normal cancellations but care was taken to ensure these were of a high standard—clear and easy to read. For the next issue—Paris Postal Conference stamp (7 May), the covers were given a special 'First Day of Issue' machine cancellation. First Day of Issue handstamps were introduced in April 1964.

Now special philatelic posting boxes are provided at most main post offices and mail handstamped at the nearest Head Post Office. The design and size of the 'First Day of Issue' handstamps has varied somewhat over the years—initially they were large (49 mm in diameter) later reduced to thimble-size (22 mm diameter) and now most are a standard 26 mm across. Those used at post offices in Wales are inscribed in both English (First Day of Issue) and Welsh (*Dydd Cyhoeddiad Cyntaf*). The Post Office first produced their own first day cover envelopes for the Shakespeare stamps and collectors could order these to be addressed and posted to them and cancelled with the Stratford-upon-Avon 'First Day of Issue' postmark. The P.O. charged 7s 2d for the complete service—6s for the stamps, 6d for the envelope and 8d for affixing the stamps and addressing the cover.

From the next issue (Geographical Congress) blank covers were sold (6d each) to collectors who could address them and post them locally. A complete service was also provided. The covers addressed and posted by the P.O. were given the Post Office Philatelic Bureau handstamp. Post Office covers have been provided for most special issues since 1964 and are usually of fairly simple design so as not to detract too much from the stamps which are, after all, the main feature of any cover. Similar specially designed covers are marketed by many stamp dealers and organisations—they are sold either blank for customers' own use or offered completely serviced—with stamps already affixed and cancelled. Some are extremely elaborate in design—a few perhaps too much so—but are extremely popular and for a particularly important event such as the Royal Wedding (July 1981) produced and sold in very large quantities. Normally these covers will be posted to receive a cancellation of a place associated with the subject of the stamp issue—for example many first day covers of the Darwin stamps (10 February 1982) were posted to receive the Down House, Downe, Orpington, Kent handstamp (Darwin lived at Down House).

Nowadays first day cover collecting is big business and the vast numbers involved means that not all covers are actually prepared, posted and cancelled on the actual day of issue. The P.O. allows most dealers 'pre-release facilities' whereby they obtain supplies of new stamps a week or so before the official issue date in order to stamp up their covers. These are then handed in *en bloc* at a post office, cancelled with the handstamp required and returned to the dealer. Thus the individual covers will not have travelled through the post and will not have been subject to the slight damage in transit which befalls most mail—*i.e.* minor damage to corners, etc. Hence the accusation by the purist collectors that such covers are not genuine postal items and unworthy of a place in a collection. This accusation cannot be denied—but it does not stop many thousands of collectors from acquiring these covers and gaining pleasure from so doing. However any collector who wants a genuine item should ensure that he (or his agent) posts the cover into a philatelic posting box and that it arrives in the normal postal delivery. Some will still want to post covers into the normal letter boxes so that the stamps are cancelled with a routine (officially termed 'operational') postmark. There is nothing wrong in this—but such covers will be worth little if ever offered for sale to a dealer as so few collectors now want covers with operational postmarks.

In recent times a 'craze' has developed for covers autographed by a person connected with the stamp issue. Collectors will of course buy whatever they want and can afford, but discretion should be exercised by purchasing from reputable dealers and high prices only paid where the signature is of direct relevance.

Akin to first day covers are souvenir covers produced for events where a special handstamp is to be used—for example STAMPEX, the B.P.E. and the Philatelic Congress of G.B. The majority of collectors wanting specimens of the postmarks will want them on the official souvenir cover and these are normally readily obtainable at the event for a small charge (nowadays about 10p–40p each). Collectors should however be wary of paying too highly for souvenir envelopes—it is the stamp and postmark that is the important feature and dealers/organisations asking £1 or more for a cover bearing a low value definitive stamp with modern special postmark are perhaps asking collectors to dig rather deeply into their pockets. In some cases some of the profits from the sale of such covers goes to a charitable purpose—here individual collectors will decide to what extent they wish to support such charities. The P.O. have produced souvenir covers from time to time—for STAMPEX (1972), for the Queen's Silver Jubilee Tour and for the 60th anniversary of the Post Office Railway (1977).

As well as covers produced and marketed through the Philatelic Bureau, several P.O. Regional Headquarters and some local Head Post Offices have produced commemorative covers which were on sale in the areas concerned. For example the Welsh Postal Board produced an attractive cover for use with special handstamps to mark the first visit to the Principality after their marriage of the Prince and Princess of Wales in October 1981. Some 50,000 covers were sold to collectors and souvenir-hunters. Normally these covers are produced in sufficient quantities that they are of fairly modest value. Occasionally, however, because of poor publicity very few are sold and then consequently a much higher price is realised when they change hands.

Gibraltar 'P.H.Q.' card showing Royal Wedding stamp

Since at least the 1940s picture postcards reproducing the design of a stamp or a view on which a stamp design was based have been popular with collectors in Europe. Normally collectors affixed the stamp to the picture side of the card and posted it to receive the appropriate local cancellations. Such cards are known as maximum cards—meaning the item has the maximum relationship between stamp, card design and postmark. Some of the early maximum cards are now in great demand and realise high prices.

In Britain collectors showed little interest until the mid-1960s and the craze for these did not really take-off until the P.O. launched the first of its own picture cards in 1973. The first issue reproduced the 1973 3p Cricket stamp (*SG 928*) and was sold at 5p each at main post offices. The card reproducing the $3\frac{1}{2}$p stamp commemorating Princess Anne's wedding (*SG 941*) proved highly popular and some 190,000 cards were sold. Starting with the Roses stamps (*SG 1006–1009*) of June 1976 the P.O. have issued cards for all values in each set of commemorative stamps. These cards are known as 'PHQ cards' since they are authorised by Postal Headquarters and each has a PHQ reference number on the reverse.

In 1971 the Head Postmaster at Dorchester produced a souvenir postcard featuring the wall paintings in his office. This was followed by other locally produced cards and interest was taken in this venture by regional headquarters. Since 1974 all regions (except Northern Ireland) have produced cards. Initially sales were small (2000–4000) but, with better publicity and attractively produced designs and printing, interest has grown and the print run

Swedish P.O. card depicting popular stamps of 1980

of some cards exceeds 50,000. Amongst the most popular subjects featured have been historic letter boxes and postbuses. Several catalogues of these interesting cards have been produced and some are listed in the *Stanley Gibbons Postcard Catalogue*. These cards are generally described as 'Regional Cards' to distinguish them from the PHQ cards produced for sale throughout the country. Regional cards are on sale only at post offices in the regions concerned and at the National Postal Museum in London and by post from the Philatelic Bureau in Edinburgh.

Since 1969 the National Postal Museum has issued various sets of cards featuring some of the most interesting stamps and documents in its collections. A special set of cards was put on sale in August 1979 to commemorate the centenary of the death of Sir Rowland Hill and individual *Special Series* cards have appeared since January 1981 as souvenirs of special exhibitions held at the Museum. These '*SS* cards' have proved very popular, demand exceeding the limited print runs of the first few issues.

As interest in postcards having a philatelic connexion has grown, so more countries are producing them. Jersey issued the first of its PHQ-type cards in 1978, Guernsey in 1980 and the Isle of Man in 1982. Nauru, Switzerland, the Bahamas, Portugal, Malta, Gibraltar and New Zealand are amongst the other countries to have started in recent years. The Swedish P.O. (and its Postal Museum) have produced many interesting cards but only in 1981 began to issue cards which exactly match stamp designs—the first of these reproduced the beautiful 2K.40 stamp featuring Kari Sylwan and Harriet Andersson in the film *Cries and Whispers*—one of five stamps commemorating Swedish Film History. This proved highly popular and was quickly sold out. This card and its successors were sold only with the stamp already affixed and cancelled with a commemorative postmark.

CHAPTER TWELVE
Cinderella Philately

Since the middle of this century there has been an appreciable revival of interest in local stamps, bogus issues, revenues, telegraph stamps and the like—the so-called 'Cinderellas of Philately'. These had been relatively popular in the late 19th century and early 20th century but thereafter their appeal had waned and only a small number of collectors sought them and even fewer studied them in any detail. Often collectors who came across such items mounted them at the back of their albums—away from the more respectable postage stamps—and thus they were often referred to as 'back of the book' stamps. One reason for the lack of interest and the almost hysterical reaction of some philatelists towards Cinderella material was the relative lack of information about them, there being few catalogues, handbooks or articles produced. In some cases the reaction to these stamps was based purely and simply on ignorance as to what they were and an unwillingness to find out.

There is no absolute definition of what comprises a cinderella stamp, but two 'working definitions' are used by members of the (British) Cinderella Stamp Club and are as good as any—(1) any item resembling a postage stamp that is not an official government postage stamp and (2) any stamp not listed in the standard catalogues; which in the case of British philatelists means the Gibbons catalogues. In a few cases a stamp which might be classified as cinderella has achieved catalogue recognition but for the most part the second of the two definitions given holds true. Essentially 'cinderellas' fall into two main groups—(1) those produced by official government agencies but not for use as postage stamps and (2) those produced by non-official organisations or by individuals. Amongst the official cinderellas are revenue stamps, savings stamps, telegraphs, and telephone stamps, unissued stamps, essays and proofs, testing stamps, some Christmas seals. Let us look briefly at each type.

Revenue or Fiscal stamps are issued to denote payment of different fees and taxes—either national or local. The earliest British revenue stamps were used in the 1690s to denote payment of various duties on legal documents. The stamps were not printed on gummed paper and affixed to the document (*i.e.* adhesive stamps) but were embossed directly on the document or on a piece of paper (known as 'base paper' and usually coloured) previously affixed to the parchment. Until *c.* 1875 these embossed impressions were uninked. The use of these embossed impressions has continued into the decimal era, stamps of various values between 5p and £2·50, embossed in blue or vermilion can still be found on legal documents. Some of the embossed stamps are inscribed with their value, others state the purpose for which they are applied—for example 'ATTESTED COPY' (1797–98), 'BANKRUPTCY' (1849–*c.* 1922). Amounts range from 1d to £50,000 (1961). Most include a pictorial motif—royal arms, floral emblems, etc. a few include royal portraits (*e.g.* Patent Office stamps of 1892–1903). As these stamps are not used for postal purposes and are non-adhesive, there is relatively little interest in them. However, those that do collect, tend to be studious types who research the subject in great detail. Surprisingly perhaps, there is a fairly extensive literature on the subject. From 1711 some revenue stamps were printed directly on to paper rather than embossed. Such stamps were applied to paper from which almanacs and newspapers were to be produced. Normally they are printed in red and bear national emblems. The first 'Newspaper stamp' of 1712 has a face value of one halfpenny and is inscribed with the royal motto of Queen Anne—*Semper Eadem* (Always the Same). For a short while from 1855 to 1870 the 'newspaper stamp' allowed the newspaper to be sent by post free of charge. As a result the newspaper stamps of this period are of some interest to postage stamp collectors as the 'newspaper stamps' served the same purpose as stamps on postal stationery.

Of greater interest—because of their more direct affinity to postage stamps—are revenue stamps printed like ordinary postal issues—often on adhesive paper, perforated or rouletted and watermarked. The earliest of these would appear to be the Post Horse duty stamps of 1779 although details of their use is unclear. In 1782 duties were applied to medicines—stamps showing that duty had been paid were affixed to jars and boxes. The use of these stamps continued until after the First World War. In 1786 similar duties were applied to toiletries—hair powders and perfumes—and jars and packets were sealed with a stamp which indicated payment of the duty. Most of these stamps were destroyed when the packages were opened and few have survived intact today. Occasionally an unused packet of pills or plasters is found—still with the stamp affixed. Similar duties were applied to hats and gloves in 1784—the stamps denoting payment of the duty being affixed—by pins—to the garments. However most of the stamps printed on adhesive paper were intended or used on legal documents: the following are known (dates of first stamps indicated): Admiralty Court (1855), Bankruptcy (1873), Board of Agriculture (1889), Chancery Court (1856), Civil Service (1872), Colonial Office (1900), Common Law Courts (1866), Companies Registration (1867), Companies Winding Up (1891), Consular Service (1886), Contract Note (1888), Copyhold & Commission (1872), Customs (1860), Diplomatic Service (1964), District Audit (1879), Draft (1853), Estate Duty (1895), Excise Revenue (1916), Foreign Bill (1854), Foreign Office (1923), Foreign Service (1951), House of Lords (1902), Income Tax (*c.* 1927), Inland Revenue (1860), Insolvency (1971), Judicature Fees (1875), Lancashire Chancery Court (1875), Land Commission (1886), Land Registry (1873), Law Courts (1873), Life Policy (1854), Magistrates Courts (1962), Matrimonial Causes (1858), Metropolotian Police (1907), Passport (*c.* 1910), Patent (1872), Paymaster General's Service (1890), Pedlar's Certificate (1873), Police Courts (1876), Probate (1858), Public Records (1873), Railway Rates Tribunal (1922), Rail & Road Traffic Act Appeals Tribunal (1947), Receipt (1853), Register House Scotland (1873), Transfer Duty (1888).

Many of these stamps were superbly printed in recess by postage stamp printers such as Perkins, Bacon & Co. and Thomas De La Rue, show the monarch's portrait, and are as attractive as postage stamps. There is a growing interest in them as some now command quite high prices. Fortunately for collectors interested in them, there are catalogues available. In addition to those used by central government departments, some local authorities used stamps to denote payment of fees in connexion with legal services for which they were responsible—these authorities being: City of London (Guildhall, Mansion House Justice Room and Lord Mayors Court, 1869–92), Gloucestershire (1870), Isle of Ely (1870), Northamptonshire (1870), Sheffield (Town Hall, Court House, 1891–2), Southampton (Town Court, County Court, 1878–80), and Winchester (Justice Court, 1888). Revenue stamps have also been issued by the governments of Guernsey, Jersey and the Isle of Man; these continue in use and are normally pictorial in design and popular with collectors of the stamps of these islands.

Excise Revenue stamp

New South Wales and Guernsey fiscal stamps

G.B. £1 Telephone savings stamp

Perhaps the revenue stamps most frequently seen by members of the public are those issued in connexion with the National Health and National Insurance schemes since 1912 and which used to be affixed to all National Insurance cards (now only to cards issued to the self-employed). The stamps were/are sold at post offices and it was a common sight to see a young clerk sent to the local post office each week to buy the stamps needed to affix to insurance cards. Collectors can still purchase unused stamps at post offices but stamps once affixed to cards became the property of the Secretary of State for Social Services and it is an offence to retain them. The stamps on cards surrendered to the Department of Health and Social Security are normally cancelled by being perforated with holes. Any cards bearing such stamps which come into collectors' hands have somehow 'escaped' from the Department and collectors are advised to return them.

In 1960 'Prescription Charge' stamps were introduced and sold in vending machines at certain hospitals. These stamps are believed to be still in use. Since 1972 stamps have been affixed—at post offices—to television licences to denote payment of the relevant fee. The design incorporates a TV screen motif and the legend 'TV LICENCE FEE PAID'. Separate stamps are issued for monochrome and colour licences and the colours of the stamps change when the licence fees are increased. The initial issues had the actual fee printed on them—£7 black and white and £12 (colour). These stamps should only be issued affixed to licence forms and cancelled with the counter datestamp; mint copies should not exist and where they have been sold, P.O. regulations have been broken. Collectors are advised to keep the stamps on the complete licence form. Since 1979 stamps have been issued at post offices which can be affixed to savings cards for the payment of telephone bills. The stamps cost £1 and £5 each and depict a telephone handset. As there is no obligation to affix these stamps to the card, collectors may legitimately obtain mint specimens of these stamps.

A few British revenue stamps could also be used for postal purposes and are hence known as 'Postal Fiscals' and are listed in the *Gibbons Catalogue*. These comprise surface-printed adhesives inscribed 'Receipt', 'Draft', 'Draft Payable on Receipt' and 'Inland Revenue (issued 1853–81) and embossed stamps from dies not appropriated to any special purpose (from 1883 onwards). Collectors are referred to the *Part 1 Catalogue* for a listing of these postal fiscal issues; used on cover they are scarce and command quite high prices. Similar postal-fiscal stamps are listed for the Australian states of Queensland, South Australia and Tasmania as well as many other places. All British definitive stamps are both postage and revenue stamps and from 1883 until 1967 all definitives were inscribed 'Postage & Revenue'—the only exception being the Edward VIII stamps and high values. Even some commemoratives were so inscribed. These stamps used for revenue purposes—usually with manuscript cancellations—are from the point of view of most collectors worth considerably less than the same stamp postally used with a postmark. However, some values will have seen little use as revenues and consequently will not be easy to find in that condition. Most commonly used for revenue purposes was the 2d stamp which covered the duty on receipts until this was abolished in 1969. Old receipts are frequently found with these stamps affixed and 'cancelled' with a signature, a rubber-stamped signature or some machine-printed wording showing that the receipt had been authenticated. Occasionally the 2d stamp will have been overprinted to denote the organisation which used it; such stamps were normally only used for receipt purposes. The only use nowadays of postage stamps for revenue purposes is on Post Office post bus services. The driver issues the passenger with a ticket comprising a small printed card on which is affixed postage stamps covering the fare for the journey and the stamp(s) cancelled with a rubber 'Postbus' handstamp. These handstamps are not usually used for postal purposes—*i.e.* for cancelling stamps on letters or cards. Such postbus tickets have been in use since 1973 and some of the early ones are now quite difficult to obtain.

The main types of British revenues have been outlined above. Similar issues exist from most countries, Argentina, Italy and the U.S.A. having particularly large numbers of different issues—made by both central and local government agencies. It has been estimated that to date about $\frac{1}{4}$ million different postage stamps have been issued and probably twice this number of different revenue stamps. Some issues have been carefully studied and catalogued but many are little known and the collector wishing to include these in his collection will often find it difficult to obtain much information about them. Most dealers do not stock revenue stamps as such but will usually have some to offer—perhaps as part of a collection of postage stamps they have purchased—and will be pleased to sell them at modest prices. Revenue stamps are popular in the U.S.A. where the American Revenue Association publishes a magazine *The American Revenuer* devoted to this type of material.

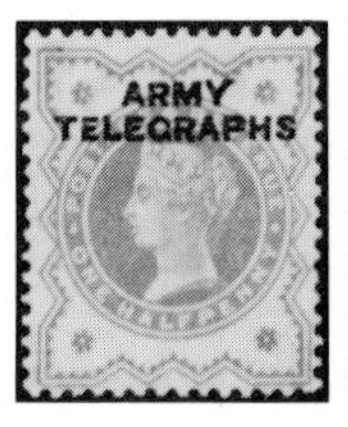

Telegraph stamps

1923 'Mercury' air mail essay

Another official Cinderella issue is the telegraph stamp. In Britain postage stamps were affixed to telegram forms to show that the fee had been paid. In the 1870s the Treasury were concerned that the P.O. should keep accurate accounts of the revenue derived from the telegram service and to facilitate this special telegram stamps were introduced in 1876 and remained in use for five years. Values ranged from ½d to £5. Although telegram forms bearing used stamps were supposed to be destroyed, many escaped and came on to the philatelic market. Prior to the 'nationalisation' of the telegram service by acts of 1868 and 1869 there were several private telegraph companies which issued their own stamps. Most prominent of these was the Electric Telegraph Company. Some railway companies—such as the South Eastern Railway and the London, Chatham & Dover Railway also operated telegraph services and issued stamps. Some of these are now rarely seen. Until 1940 Gibbons listed British telegraph stamps in their catalogues but these were dropped as a wartime expediency and not reintroduced. P.O. telegraph stamps are, however, listed in the *G.B. Specialised Catalogue Volume 1*. Telegraph stamps have been issued by several Post Offices apart from Britain and by many private telegram companies—such as the Canadian Pacific Railway. P.O. telegraph stamps which were also valid for postal use are listed in the *Gibbons Catalogue* (for example Argentina), stamps issued solely for telegraph use are outside the scope of the catalogue.

One group of cinderella items eagerly collected by many philatelists are unissued stamps, essays and proofs. Unissued stamps are stamps officially authorised and prepared but which—for some reason—were not put on sale at post office counters. These are usually noted in the catalogue as 'Prepared for use but not issued'. For example the famous 2d Tyrian Plum of Great Britain—prepared for issue in May 1910 but cancelled when King Edward VII died. A few copies 'escaped' and are offered from time to time on the philatelic market; they were never put on general sale. In January 1954 the Sudan issued a set of three stamps commemorating Self-Government. A few sheets were released in error having the inscription 'SELF GOVERNMENT 1953' instead of '1954'. These were not valid for postage and are footnoted in the catalogue below the proper stamps (*S.G. 140–142*). The term 'unissued' is really illogical, as the stamps exist and were issued—even though they were not intended to be. The term 'Erroneously Issued Stamps' would perhaps be more accurate. However, relatively few have appeared and most collectors can build up a collection of the stamps of their chosen country or theme without ever coming across an 'unissued stamp'.

Essays, proofs and colour trials have been mentioned in Chapter 5 (Anatomy of the Stamp) and we need not repeat the details here. In addition to essays made by printers on behalf of official Post Offices, essays are sometimes also produced on behalf of private individuals, companies and stamp societies. These are more frequently encountered by collectors than essays for official postage stamps—which are normally kept only in P.O. archives. Such private essays are sometimes produced in the form of souvenir labels or sheets for stamp exhibitions, for example the 'Ideal Stamp' and the 'Mercury' Air Mail essay sold at London exhibitions in 1912 and 1923 respectively. The 'Ideal Stamp' comprised a suggested design for a George V definitive stamp—it was printed by Waterlow Brothers & Layton and 24,000 were sold at the exhibition. It can be found in several colours, both perforated and imperf. The Mercury Air Mail essay—also found in several colours—was prepared as a design for a British official air mail stamp but the P.O. decided against any such issue. This stamp was printed by De La Rue & Co. and copies can normally be obtained for a few pence. Replicas of this stamp—printed in purple and imperforate—were produced in connexion with a stamp exhibition in 1974. Several exhibition souvenir sheets have reproduced rejected designs for official stamps—printed with the permission of the Post Office. The 1963 Stampex Sheet showed the six stages in the printing of the Hong Kong $20 Annigoni portrait stamp—in effect miniature colour proofs of the stamp. The sheet was printed by Harrison & Sons Ltd who printed the actual stamps.

One of the most interesting essays of recent times was prepared in early 1965 by Stanley Gibbons Ltd as part of their campaign for pictorial definitive stamps. This comprised a sheet containing 12 designs for low value stamps: $\frac{1}{2}$d Hovercraft, 1d Sailing, 1$\frac{1}{2}$d White Horse, Berkshire, 2d Tower of London, 1$\frac{1}{2}$d Jodrell Bank Radio Telescope, 3d Canterbury Cathedral, 4d Exports, 5d Sheep, 6d Houses of Parliament, 9d Winscale Atomic Reactor, 1s H.M. The Queen at Trooping the Colour and 1s 3d The Queen at the State Opening of Parliament. The sheet was printed—in blue—by Harrison & Sons Ltd in photogravure; the designs were by Jock Kinneir, FSIA. Other exhibition souvenir sheets have taken the form of posthumous proofs or colour trials of issued stamps—the reproductions being printed by the printer of the original stamp using the same printing die. The British Philatelic Exhibition sheets from 1971 onwards are good examples of this. Of a similar nature are 'black prints'. True black prints are similar to proofs, being printed by the same printing process and printer as the actual stamps but in black rather than the issued or trial colour.

Stanley Gibbons's designs for new British definitives (*1965*)

The first black print of British stamps reproduced were the four 1953 Coronation stamps. A black print of the 1977 Silver Jubilee stamps was produced for the 1977 Festival of Stamps sponsored by the Stamp Collecting Promotion Council. Black prints of the 1978 Horses and Cycling stamps were produced for *Stamp Collecting* magazine and given away free to readers and prints of the 1978 Buildings and 1979 Rowland Hill miniature sheets were included in the catalogue of the London 1980 stamp exhibition. The Austrian Post Office has produced black prints of many of its stamps—these are given out to the press and copies are keenly sought-after by philatelists and black prints have been produced for several European stamp exhibitions reproducing Swiss, West German and Italian stamps. Needless to say these black prints are not valid for postage even though they have been produced with the consent of the relevant Post Office. Allied to these are the so-called 'Philatelic Documents' issued by the French P.O. since 1973. These comprise a large sheet of high-quality paper (210 × 297 mm) on which is printed the official announcement of the stamp issue, connected illustrations, a single-coloured proof specimen and the actual stamp with first day cancellation. Bearing a proof, these documents are obviously of interest to collectors of cinderella material as well as to collectors of French stamps. The documents are listed in the *Stanley Gibbons Catalogue: Part 6 France.* In addition the French P.O. also make available imperforate copies of most of their stamps; these are not valid for postage and hence can be regarded as Cinderella items rather than postage stamps. They are not listed although a note about them is included.

British Philatelic Exhibition souvenir sheet

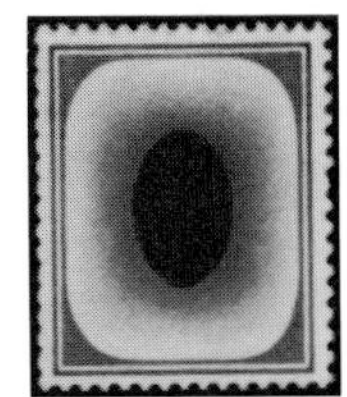

G.B. 'Poached Egg' stamp coil testing label

Several Post Offices have used 'Test Stamps' in connexion with coil machines. These are dummy stamps—printed ordinary postage stamp size and used by postal engineers to test that stamp vending machines are working correctly. The first British ones were used in the 1930s—they comprise a stamp printed in green, the design of which resembles a 'poached egg'—hence this sobriquet has been frequently applied to this stamp. Later issues were printed in grey and double-sized labels in pink were produced in the mid-1950s to test machines dispensing commemorative stamps. These stamps should not be available to collectors but they have reached the philatelic market and can normally be obtained quite cheaply. The Danish, Swedish and French Post Offices have produced similar stamps.

The British P.O.—along with many others—runs special centres for training staff in counter work, including the sale of stamps. Ordinary postage stamps are used at these centres, the front of the stamps being overprinted with thick black bars. Such stamps are not intended for philatelic sale although supplies have reached the market. The P.O. point out that such material is technically stolen property and collectors are advised to leave well alone.

Several Post Offices sell Christmas seals to be used on Christmas cards and mail. These are not to be confused with charity stamps as they have no postal validity whatsoever. The first of these seals was issued by Denmark in 1904, funds raised from the sale of these seals (or labels)—going to sick and poor children. In the U.S.A. the seals are sold in aid of tuberculosis victims. Some of the U.S. issues have featured childrens' paintings, the Norwegian P.O. has issued seals showing a map of Norway and the Danish P.O. country churches. The British P.O. has not adopted this idea, although Christmas seals have been produced by numerous charities.

Other 'official cinderellas' include registration labels and air mail stickers and the like. Most British post offices have their own registration label—these are of common design and include the name of the office. Some of the smaller and temporary offices do not have specially prepared labels but add the name by datestamp or in manuscript. Similar labels are used by nearly all countries. There are relatively few collectors of these labels as the extent of the collection is potentially vast—there are over 20,000 post offices in the United Kingdom alone. More popular are the labels used at temporary offices especially if a special handstamp is also used. Such labels are normally collected on cover. Air mail stickers or etiquettes also have a small following—most of the labels are of strictly utilitarian design but some of the earlier ones depict aeroplanes and make more attractive items. Until *c.* 1975 the British label was bicoloured, worded 'BY AIR/Par Avion' and included an airmail motif. The current label comprises the wording in white against a blue background. Similar labels are available for other P.O. services—Recorded Delivery (introduced 1962), Express Delivery and Special Delivery (until 1980), Royal Mail Special Delivery and Swiftair (since 1980), Receipted Parcel service and 'Nightrider' parcel delivery services. Not all are easy to obtain and when mounted up with appropriate notes as to their use, they can make an interesting display.

Perfins—stamps perforated with initials might be classified as 'official cinderellas' in that the stamps are proper postage stamps even if the perforating is carried out privately. These stamps can be found from most countries. In Britain the practice started in the 1860s and over the years thousands of government departments, local authorities and private firms have obtained such stamps. The perforation is intended as a security device to prevent staff from pilfering stamps. Normally collectors can only obtain these in used condition as mint examples will have 'escaped' from post rooms. Most collectors regard perfins as damaged stamps and hence they are of little monetary value. However some are very difficult to obtain and to perfin specialists are great rarities. Books and articles have been written—in particular the perfins of the British railway companies seem popular.

When one turns to cinderella stamps produced by non-P.O. organisations, the scope is almost endless. Such items range from local stamps produced in connexion with non- or semi-official postal services, to forgeries of official postage stamps, fakes and bogus issues. Local stamps are popular with cinderella collectors-a local stamp is described in *Philatelic Terms Illustrated* as a stamp '. . . whose validity and use are limited in area to a prescribed district, town or country, or on certain postal routes where there is no official service, issued by civic municipalities, private firms and landowners, etc., sometimes in conjunction with official postal administrations'. In 1899 Stanley Gibbons produced a *Priced Catalogue of the Local Postage Stamps of the World* as Part 3 of their four-volume *Catalogue*. Previously local stamps had been listed in the main body of the catalogue, but interest then did not justify continued publication and this was the only edition of the 'Locals Catalogue'. It contained 122 pages of closely-set listings: evidence of the considerable number of local stamps issued. For Great Britain the catalogue included listings of the railway letter stamps and notes (but not listings) referring to the stamps of the circular delivery companies and Oxford and Cambridge college stamps. There was a sizeable listing of Scandinavian local posts and of the Russian Government Locals or Zemstvos—stamps issued by local municipal or district authorities for the purpose of supplementing the Imperial postal service. It is estimated that over 10,000 different Zemstvos exist—some extremely rare. A very rare local is the 1 boo stamp issued by Sutherland & Co. in *c*. 1870. Only two copies are known and seven copies of a similar $\frac{1}{4}$ boo stamp. James Wilson Sutherland ran a livery stable in Tokyo (then called Yedo), from which he operated 'The Yedo Mail' using four-horse coaches. A postboy on horseback is depicted on the two stamps. Readers interested in knowing more about rare and unusual locals are referred in particular to the chapter relating to them in *Rare Stamps* by L. N. and M. Williams, published in 1957 and reprinted in serial form in *Gibbons Stamp Monthly*, 1972.

College Stamp – St. John's, Oxford

Lundy local

For many collectors, their first encounter with local stamps will be modern British locals. At the present time there are nearly 100 private postal services which issue their own stamps. These private services can be grouped into five main types: island stamps, airway and railway letter stamps, bus parcel stamps, railway parcel stamps and ship parcel stamps. The island issues are probably the best known and the most collected. The first of these appeared in 1929—issued by the owner of Lundy—a small island in the Bristol Channel. Until 1926 the British P.O. had operated a sub-office on the island but closed it as the population was so small it was uneconomic. The owner—Martin Coles Harman—then decided to operate his own postal service and the stamps covered the cost of taking the mail to the mainland for posting. The Lundy stamps had to be affixed to the back of envelopes or to the top left hand corner of postcards, normal British stamps had to be affixed to prepay the postage once the letters/cards were posted on the mainland. This service still operates and is the oldest island post in the world. The normal term for these island stamps is *local carriage labels* devised some years ago by a committee of the British Philatelic Association and the Philatelic Traders Society.

Twenty years went by after the issue of the Lundy locals before a second island—Herm near Guernsey—followed suit. Since then a considerable number of stamps have appeared for various offshore islands. Some of these stamps have been issued for a *bona fide* local post, others are basically tourist souvenirs and others bogus. A list of the islands concerned—with notes as to their status appears after the listing of Postal Fiscal stamps in *Stanley Gibbons Part 1 Catalogue*.

Airway and railway letter stamps can be regarded as semi-official, in that the companies which issue them do so under authority of the Post Office. The Railway Letter Service began in 1891 to provide an express service, principally for sending urgent mail after the last regular post had gone. Each 'railway letter' had to bear the normal postage stamp (to comply with P.O. monopoly of letter carrying) and a special railway letter stamp issued by the railway company. When the service started about 70 companies issued stamps—nearly all in a common design, the stamps costing 2d and being printed in various shades of green. Later the fee was increased to 3d and 4d and most companies issued stamps in these denominations. The stamps continued in use until the 1920s and 1930s when the number of letters carried began to decline and it was not worth while having special stamps printed; parcel stamps (see below) were then used instead. In 1948 the railways were nationalised and British Railways inherited the service from its predecessors. B.R. continued using parcel stamps on railway letters until *c*. 1955, since when such letters are given an unvalued parcel label (with the fee paid entered in manuscript) or simply the rubber datestamp of the station of despatch. Of greater interest to collectors—and in particular to thematic collectors—are the stamps issued since the mid-1950s by several private railways. These stamps are produced mainly for collectors; proceeds from their sale going to help preserve the railways' locomotives and permanent way. The first such stamps were issued by the narrow-gauge Talyllyn Railway in mid-Wales in 1957, since then the following companies have also started a railway letter service and issue stamps: Festiniog, Ravenglass & Eskdale (1969), Bluebell, Welshpool & Llanfair (1975), Llanberis Lake (1976), Romney, Hythe & Dymchurch (1978), Mid-Hants, Keighley & Worth Valley, Kent & East Sussex (1979), Railway Preservation Society of Ireland (1981), North York Moors (1981) and Great Central (1982).

Modern railway letter stamp – Festiniog Railway (*Wales*)
Bus parcel stamp – Crosville Motor Services (*Chester*)
1981 Christmas charity post stamp (*Beacon Hill Scouts, Essex*)

The Airway Letter Service is similar to the railway service, letters being carried between airports and either posted on arrival or held for collection. The first such service was operated by Great Western Railways who operated an air service between Cardiff and Plymouth in 1933. Special 3d stamps showing an aeroplane were used. The only company now carrying airway letters is British Airways who have issued colourful and attractive stamps since 1951.

The Post Office has never had a monopoly for the carriage of parcels and over the years a vast number of companies have competed with the P.O. for such trade. Railway companies carried parcels from their early days and issued stamps from 1855 onwards. Later tram and bus companies did likewise and today nearly 60 bus companies still operate parcels services and issue stamps (many others carry parcels but no stamps are issued). For the most part these stamps are of rather unattractive design, simply letterpress printed and bear the name of the company and value. In the 1930s Brighton Corporation Transport had attractive perforated stamps depicting buses and Crosville Motor Services of Chester still issue stamps showing some of their vehicles. The stamps are normally two-part—a receipt section given to the sender of the parcel and the 'stamp' itself which is affixed to the parcel.

The early parcel stamps of the railway companies are more popular and at the beginning of this century there was sufficient interest in them to justify publication of a catalogue. Interest has revived in recent years—mainly through the efforts of the Railway Philatelic Group. Some of these parcel stamps are of attractive designs—featuring the coats of arms of the railway companies or similar motifs. Today British Rail still use parcel stamps on bundles of newspapers carried by train but the stamps are of purely utilitarian design. Across the Irish Sea, parcel stamps are still used by the nationalised Coras Iompair Eireann (Irish Transport Company); the design of these stamps has remained unchanged since 1916. Only one shipping company now issues parcel stamps—the Isle of Sark Shipping Company in the Channel Islands. Pictorial stamps featuring maps, ships and island scenes were issued in 1980.

In addition to these five main groups, stamp-like labels are used by other carriers such as Securicor, Courier Express, etc. These labels are not inscribed with a denomination and hence have relatively little appeal to collectors. Only one company—TNT Parcels Express of Warwickshire—have denominated stamps depicting the company's delivery vans and lorries. A local parcel delivery service operates in Alderney and stamps have been used since 1975.

In 1981 Parliament changed the law affecting the P.O.'s monopoly of letter carriage. Private operators may carry urgent letters provided that they charge a minimum of £1 per letter. At the time of publication only one operator of such a service has produced stamps. Charities are allowed to carry Christmas cards—but no other mail—in the weeks preceding the Christmas festival. About a dozen such posts were operated during the Christmas period in 1981, more in 1982. Some issued stamps, others stamped mail with a cachet. In all cases the delivery area was limited but several thousands of cards were accepted and delivered.

Most of the cinderellas detailed above are/were issued in connexion with a postal (delivery) service. Others are of a purely souvenir or propaganda nature. Mention has already been made of some exhibition items which reproduce essays or postage stamps. There are many other souvenir sheets and labels, some most attractively designed and printed. The first philatelic exhibition labels were produced for the Vienna Philatelic Exhibition of 1881, the first British example was for the London 1890 Exhibition at the Portman Rooms, Baker Street and comprised the undenominated 'Britannia' type stamps of Mauritius overprinted 'L.P.E./1890' in red (L.P.E. =London Philatelic Exhibition). For the 1897 Exhibition, labels depicting the Mulready envelope design were produced and there were several labels (depicting Viking ships) prepared for the Manchester International Exhibition of 1899. The 1923 London Exhibition gave rise to labels featuring a biplane and for the International Air Post exhibition of 1934 labels were produced showing a plane over Tower Bridge. The Bridge also featured on labels—produced in miniature sheet format—for the Stamp Centenary Exhibition in London in 1940. Twelve labels depicting the first Postmaster-General—Henry Bishop—and early postmarks were produced for the 1960 London International Stamp Exhibition at the Festival Hall. Most of these labels can be obtained from stamp dealers and a selection of them on an album page makes an interesting display.

Stanley Gibbons have produced a number of labels worthy of a place in a cinderella collection. In 1905 Gibbons took over the firm of G. Hamilton-Smith of Gracechurch Street in the City of London. Hamilton-Smith had produced a number of advertising labels depicting London Buildings—Parliament, Somerset House and the General Post Office. At least one of these labels (Parliament) was reprinted after the takeover, the company name Hamilton Smith being replaced by Stanley Gibbons. These labels are not often seen. In 1957 Harrison & Sons Ltd demonstrated perforating on the Gibbons stand at the Boys and Girls Exhibition at Earl's Court. Sheets of labels were perforated and given to visitors; they were printed in mauve and depict the Cape of Good Hope triangular and the *Simplified Catalogue*.

Propaganda labels issued for a variety of reasons are of interest to some cinderella collectors. In recent years the Scottish Philatelic Secretariat (now part of the Alba Stamp Group) has issued a vast number of labels commemorating Scottish persons and events which have not been found sufficiently important to warrant an issue of postage stamps. Similar labels have appeared in Wales and in Cornwall. Many propaganda labels were used in Ireland from 1865 to 1922 featuring the Irish harp and patriots.

We come now to the real 'nasties' of the philatelic world—forgeries, fakes and bogus issues. Forgeries are of interest to three types of collector. Firstly, the specialist one-country collector often requires copies for his collection—to mount alongside the genuine stamp. Secondly, the general collector will want to know about them so as to ensure the stamps he buys are genuine. Thirdly, there is the cinderella collector who will want a forged stamp simply because it *is* a forgery. Whereas the specialist will want the forgery to mount alongside the genuine, the cinderella collector of forgeries will want the genuine to compare to the forgery.

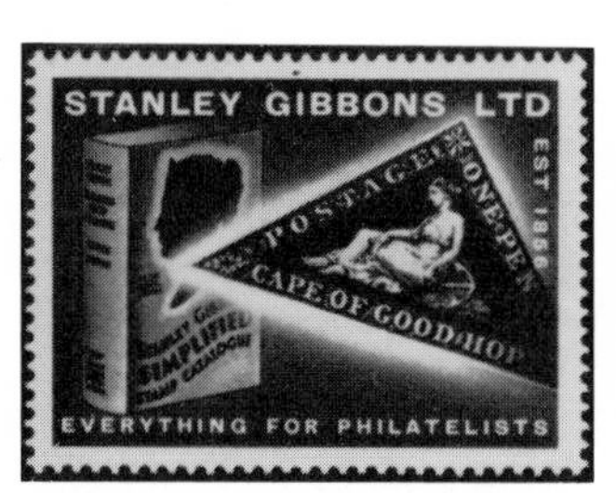

Stanley Gibbons advertising labels

Forgeries of Western Australia and British Guiana stamps

In case anyone should be deterred from taking up stamp collecting by reason of the existence of forgeries, it should be said that the inexperienced collector can collect on normal lines, and build up a collection of thousands of stamps, without ever seeing a forgery.

A forgery is an imitation of a stamp, surcharge, or overprint, made to deceive either the postal authorities (a 'postal forgery') or the collector (a 'philatelic forgery'). Forgery on a scale sufficient to make profits by deceiving a Post Office is now only rarely practised, but in the early days of postage stamps it was quite frequent. Unused copies of some of these forgeries are quite common but used copies, which have actually passed through the post, are in many cases very much more valuable (particularly on cover) than the genuine stamps they imitated.

Postal forgeries are usually of stamps of low denomination—stamps in common use. Particularly susceptible to postal forgeries were the stamps of France and Spain, where stamps were sold not only at post offices but at tobacconists, newsagents, etc. The forger was, therefore, able to find a ready market for his 'stamps', offering the less reputable shopkeeper a tempting discount on the forgeries. Other countries that have suffered postal forgeries include Argentina, Australia, Austria, China, Germany, Greece, Japan, Netherlands and the U.S.A. Great Britain has not suffered greatly from forgeries. The most notorious is the so-called 'Stock Exchange forgery' of the 1871 one shilling stamp. Forgeries were used on telegram forms sent from the Stock Exchange P.O. Being on these forms meant the forgery was less likely to be detected and the one shilling stamp enabled the forger to make a handsome profit on his activities. The stamps were not discovered until 1898 by a leading stamp dealer.

Philatelic forgeries are usually of rare stamps—designed to fool the collector. Over the years there have been a number of notorious forgers—Georges Fouré, Francois Fournier, the Spiro Brothers and perhaps the most famous of all, Jean de Sperati. Fouré's main work comprised forgeries of early issues of German postal stationery although he also undertook the production of fakes by skilfully changing the colour of a stamp. Francois Fournier (*1864–1917*) marketed forgeries in a big way, in his 1914 price list he offered some 3671 different forgeries for sale—some produced for him by other forgers—and claimed he had 20,000 regular customers. However, he was not a total rogue, advising his clients that the stamps he offered them were reproductions—he disliked the term forgery.

The Spiro Brothers were lithographic printers in Hamburg and in the 1860s and 1870s produced over 500 forgeries of stamps. These were produced in sheets of 25 on ungummed paper and sold unused or with forged cancellations—often as many as five different cancellations being applied to each sheet of stamps.

Jean de Sperati (*1884–1957*) forged no fewer than 566 different stamps (of nearly 100 different countries) between 1909 and 1953. A detailed work on the forgeries was published by the British Philatelic Association in 1955 so that collectors can now readily identify his work. Sperati forged only one British stamp—the 2s brown of 1867 but numerous Commonwealth stamps (including Australia and Mauritius) and foreign issues (France, Germany, Spain and Switzerland).

A reprint is on rather a different footing from the forgery for it is often printed from the original plate, block or stone from which the 'originals' were printed, but after the issue of them had ceased. In early times, it was not thought to be wrong to make fresh printings from the plates, after the stamps had gone out of use. Postal authorities adopted the attitude that if those mad collectors wanted them, and there were no originals available, they could make some more. And they did! Not many collectors appreciated the difference in those days—as can be seen from the collections which were formed at the time.

Sometimes the plates were sold to a dealer with the remaining stocks of a withdrawn issue ('remainders'), and then he went on making reprint after reprint as needed. The reprints made by Nicholas F. Seebeck of South American stamps in the 1890s are notorious. Seebeck was a New York stamp dealer and also a bank official, in which position he was able to have stamps printed. He supplied stamps free to the postal administrations of Ecuador, Honduras, Nicaragua and Salvador. In return he kept the original plates and all unsold stamps at the end of their period of use. Seebeck made many reprints of the stamps—these are still common in unused condition, but postally used copies are rare. The practice of reprinting has now virtually ceased as most countries ensure that printing plates are securely held.

Some reprints have been made by governments for official purposes. It sometimes happened that a postal authority was asked for complete sets of their old stamps, for presentation to a museum or some visiting dignitary. If no stocks were found, but the plates were available, they were put to press again, and sets of official reprints resulted. Reprints are sometimes easier to obtain than the original stamps, and where they are printed from the original plates or stones, they provide valuable material for purposes of study, whether they are from official or unofficial printings. Most specialised collections worthy of the name, therefore, include all known reprints for comparison with the original stamps.

Fakes, like forgeries, result from an attempt to deceive but differ from forgeries in that they comprise at least a part of a genuine stamp. The most usual types of fakes are cleaned and repaired stamps and genuine stamps re-gummed or with a forged overprint. Cleaning is mainly directed to taking out pen or fiscal cancellations with chemicals, either leaving the stamp in 'unused' condition, or else going a stage further and providing it with a forged postmark.

Repairing is carried out with the object of improving the condition of a stamp. The desire for wide margins on imperf. stamps has made it profitable to take a stamp with little or no margin, and to graft lovely wide margins on to it. The work is most delicately done, and is quite imperceptible in most cases until an expert sense is acquired. The early octagonal-shaped stamps of Ceylon have frequently been provided with new corners in this way (the stamps were so often cut to shape in the past in order to fit the spaces in stamp albums).

To a defective perforated stamp margins can be added and perforated, though it is not easy to imitate a particular gauge and style of a perforation satisfactorily. If there is a thin spot on the paper of the stamp, or even a hole, the repairer will fill the deficiency, even to the extent of painting in the missing portion of the design on the paper with which he patches the hole.

There are numerous variations of the faker's art, which in some cases amount to partial forgery. Thus, in the standard key-type stamps of the British Colonies, one value may be very rare. A stamp of similar colour, in the same type, but perhaps of a different denomination, or from another colony, has the inscriptions removed, and the result is a genuine design, with blank spaces into which the faker paints the inscriptions of the rare stamp. He has overcome the difficulty of imitating the genuine paper by using an actual stamp as his basis. In some cases, the faker will bleach out the whole of the design of a stamp and will print a new one on the resulting piece of blank paper, which will itself be genuine, and have a genuine watermark, and genuine perforations.

Faking of rare colours is not difficult if one has the necessary knowledge. A rare shade may be produced from a common one, or colours can be changed entirely, for example from violet to grey or red to brown. Therefore, beware of uncatalogued 'errors of colour' or of rare shades offered to you from a doubtful source, or at a very low price.

Watermarks can be faked—a common stamp printed on unwatermarked paper is given a 'watermark' to transform it into the more valuable version of the stamp printed on watermarked paper. Faked watermarks are normally produced by pressure, in which case they show clearly when the back of the stamp is looked at, but when it is looked through, the watermark is not transparent. A faker who wants to make a really good job of it, will thin the paper down very carefully by scraping, thus producing the characteristics of a true watermark. The results of his work should be easily visible under magnification, however, for the fibres of the paper will be broken.

Rare postmarks are keenly sought, and the faker can have a profitable time imitating these while overprints and surcharges have always been fair game to him.

The most notorious of all producers of philatelic fakes was Raoul Charles de Thuin (*1890–1975*) of Mexico who from the 1930s to the 1960s produced thousands of fake overprints, surcharges and cancellations on stamps and covers—either using a cliché impression or hand drawing and tracing. Many of these fakes were of rare overprints and district numbers on Latin American stamps and with forged postmarks were clever enough to fool even some experienced postal historians.

The forger or the faker has never had any great difficulty in producing his wares. In fact it is probably easier, with modern methods, to produce fairly good forgeries and fakes than it ever was in the past. On the other hand, expert collectors and dealers are now better equipped to detect them. After years of reliance on experience and intuition, experts now turn to science for help, using instruments which have made the work of the forger and faker very much more difficult to market. Apart from this, collectors are supplied with more information about forgeries through the philatelic press and the societies. A good information service is vital as the collector who wanders in the dark without any information about forgeries and fakes is the one who is going to get scared. If from magazines or books, he can learn to identify forgeries, he will be much better able to protect himself, and will feel safer to that extent. In addition to modern technical aids and published works on how to identify forgeries, the collector has at his disposal organisations which carry out expertisation work and issue certificates of authenticity.

To detect a forgery of an entire stamp should not be difficult, provided that a genuine stamp is available for comparison. It is not hard to imitate the design of a stamp with fair accuracy, but apart from this, the paper, colour and (in the case of unused stamps) gum, also have to be accurately reproduced, and this is not so easy. In forging used stamps, a postmark has to be applied, and we have already seen how the forger can go wrong in this direction in applying a type of postmark not used concurrently with the stamp. Forged overprints and surcharges are not always easy to detect, for the basic stamp is usually genuine, and only the ink and the shape and spacing of the lettering are available for comparison. Measurement of the various parts of the overprint with a graduated rule, or screw-adjustment compass, will sometimes serve to identify a forgery, but one must, of course, first be certain that there is no variation in the genuine overprint. Examination of the colour and appearance of the ink is often helpful. The depth may vary, and the ink may be shiny instead of dull, or rough instead of smooth. Such differences will provide grounds for suspicion.

An instrument much used by experts is the ultraviolet or quartz lamp, which uses U.V. rays to analyse the materials placed under it. Thus if two pieces of paper, similar in appearance but differing in actual composition, are placed side by side under the lamp, they will appear of different colours. Similarly if two stamps which appear to be printed in ink of exactly the same colour are placed under the lamp, and one of them is a forgery, it will show, under the rays, that its ink is made up of different ingredients from that in which the genuine stamp was printed.

The value of such an instrument in detecting forgeries is obvious, but unfortunately it does not readily indicate differences between black substances, so that for overprints it is not of much use except where they are in coloured inks. Reprints, like forgeries, are distinguished by their colour, paper and gum.

In detecting cleaned stamps the ultra-violet lamp is a very effective aid, for penmarks which have been 'removed' by the use of chemicals, and are invisible to the naked eye, still show clearly under the lamp. However, cleaning nearly always leaves some results on the paper or colour of the stamp, and the expert can often detect these changes without the use of the lamp. Even the inexperienced collector will gradually be able to notice differences that will put him on his guard. A word of warning is necessary regarding the use of the ultra-violet lamp. It has been found that marks caused quite innocently, will show up in the lamp, and give rise to suspicion. For example, a drop of water which has fallen on an unused stamp may appear as a blot when viewed under the rays.

Repairing can often be detected by the trained eye, or by the feel of a stamp, though it is frequently marvellously done, margins being grafted on with no visible sign of what has happened. There are two tests that the collector can apply. Firstly, if a repaired stamp is dipped in benzine, the added portions will frequently stand out clearly with a different appearance. Secondly, by using the U.V. lamp, the added paper is nearly always seen at once. However, if a stamp has been 'backed', *i.e.* if the whole of the back of the stamp has been reinforced by added paper, neither test will work.

The inexperienced reader may ask, 'How can I best protect myself against acquiring forgeries and fakes?'. The best advice is to buy only from reputable dealers who guarantee every stamp they sell. Mistakes may occur but the best firms make very few, and the customer can, therefore, deal with them and be confident that he is getting what he pays for. Bargain-hunters run a vastly increased risk of getting a forgery or fake. If you buy a scarce stamp cheaply, it could pay you to have the stamp examined by one of the recognised expert committees. In Britain expertisation is undertaken by the Royal Philatelic Society and by B.P.A. Expertising Ltd. A fee is charged, and if the stamp is genuine, a certificate, with photograph, is provided. The certificate will be a valuable asset if you ever wish to sell the stamp. These committees do not, however, value or identify stamps.

Some dealers may allow you to have a stamp expertised before you definitely decide to take it. If this is not possible, and the stamp turns out to be bad, you are advised to return the stamp to the dealer requesting a refund. It he does not agree to this you will probably decide not to do business with him again, but if he takes back the stamp, and refunds your money, you may assume that he is honest. However, it might be as well to have the next few stamps you buy from him examined. By using the services of recognised expert committees even the inexperienced collector can safeguard himself. Yet too many collectors prefer to assume that every stamp they obtain at bargain price is genuine, thus postponing disillusionment till they—or their heirs—come to sell the collection. Then it is too late to learn wisdom, or to recover the money.

Often associated with forgeries and fakes are bogus stamps. These are in a different category entirely as they do not imitate actual postage stamps, they are 'stamps' for non-existent countries or for real countries which did/do not have any postal service and, therefore, have no requirement for stamps. In the early days of the hobby, when communications were not so well organised, fairly frequent attempts were made to market stamps of a mythical kingdom, or of a place which was very unlikely to need postage stamps.

Fred Melville in his book *Phantom Philately* (published in 1924) gave details of many of these bogus stamps. The stories of some of them make interesting reading. For example, a series of Brunei was produced in the 1890s by a European on the spot, who was quite willing to sell these stamps to dealers, without mentioning the fact that there was at the time no postal service for which they could be used. Bogus issues were made for Clipperton Island, Sedang and Trinidad (an island in the South Atlantic), the last two by persons claiming to be the kings of the respective territories. They had no more right to the title than their labels had to be called postage stamps.

Bogus stamps – Clipperton Island and Sedang

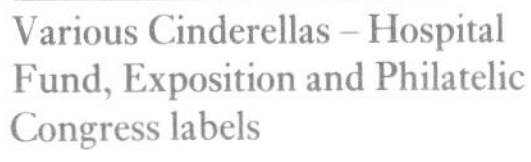

Various Cinderellas – Hospital Fund, Exposition and Philatelic Congress labels

Perhaps the most famous 19th century 'bogies' were the 'stamps' of Moresnet, for they never existed. J. B. Moëns, a leading European dealer and publisher of *Timbre-Poste*, was extremely annoyed by the fact that other journals frequently lifted information about the latest stamps from his magazine. He decided to play a trick on his rivals. One month in his magazine he listed, described and illustrated a new issue for the state of Moresnet—a small Belgian town near the German border—and the next issues of a dozen or so Continental stamp magazines all listed the new issue. The stamps only existed in M. Moën's imagination!

Included in the category of 'bogus' or 'phantom' issues are the so-called 'Sun Gate' stamps of Bolivia. An archaeologist interested in the Inca ruins of Tiahuanaco planned a series of stamps which would, when fitted together, represent the famous 'Sun Gate' there. He came to Europe and had the stamps printed, flaming in bronze and gold, and very impressive they looked. Foolishly he did not obtain authority from the Bolivian Government and disclosed his scheme to some people in the stamp trade. The philatelic press at once denounced the stamps as an unauthorised issue, and the Bolivian Government disowned them.

Bogus stamps are still manufactured although not on the same scale as in the past. The only recent British examples are stamps produced in the 1960s for the Isle of Soay, off the coast of Skye. Ostensibly these were 'local carriage labels' to carry mail from the island to Skye but they were not authorised by the owner and never used. They were declared bogus by the Stamp Trade Committee of the Philatelic Traders Society and the British Philatelic Association. Elsewhere the record is not so clean; for example, from Japan have emanated bogus stamps commemorating the establishment of government in the Marshall Islands (in the Central Pacific Ocean). These appeared in 1979 but had no postal validity as the islands were under U.S. trusteeship and ordinary U.S. stamps were in use. Included in the set was a 75c value claimed as the 'largest stamp in the world' having a surface area of 17,600 sq. mm. The largest official stamp is that issued by China in 1913–14 (10c Express Letter stamp, *SG E266/267*) which has a surface area of 17,360 sq. mm.

The range of cinderella material is so vast that the examples described in this chapter are but the tip of the iceberg. Hopefully the general collector will look upon cinderella items as interesting—and perhaps amusing—realising that many collectors find fascination and pleasure in them, even if he decides not to include them in his collection. In recent years more has appeared in print about such stamps and this has encouraged interest—particularly in the U.S.A. and Scandinavia—and there are several societies which collectors of cinderella stamps can join. The most prestigious society is based in Britain—the Cinderella Stamp Club (founded in 1959).

PART TWO
The Stamp Collection

CHAPTER THIRTEEN
Basic Equipment

I am not going to advocate the purchase of a very elaborate outfit by the beginner, but I do suggest that stamps, at any stage of their career, deserve the best possible album their owner can afford to give them, for properly housed they give him more pleasure to look at, and are also a source of greater interest to his friends. I also advise the purchase and use of suitable accessories according to the progress made by the collector in technical knowledge.

In the past the most elementary form of album used to be a cheap exercise book; stamps were mounted by stamp-edging or *selvedge*. While an exercise book was certainly better than no album at all, the use of stamp edging, sticky tape or similar gummed paper ruined many good stamps. Today some new collectors still use such materials but their use should be banished at once from the mind of any reader of this book. Proper stamp hinges are specially made so that, once thoroughly dry, they may be peeled away from both the stamp and the album page, and leave scarcely a mark on either.

It is worth mentioning here that even the best hinges do leave a mark on the gum of mint stamps. Nowadays many collectors insist that the mint stamps in their collection are *unmounted*, *i.e.* they do not even show a trace of a hinge mark. The whole question of unmounted mint condition and how it affects both the storage of stamps and the market prices of stamps is discussed in Chapter 15.

Stamp albums themselves are of two main types: *printed albums* (fastbound or loose-leaf) or *blank albums* (which are always loose-leaf and contain pages ruled with tiny squares to assist the neat arrangement of stamps).

Modern printed stamp album

For the general collector making his first steps in the hobby, an album with printed pages is advisable. If the number of stamps he is likely to posses in the near future is under a thousand or so, the first collection should be formed in one of those albums which have squared pages headed by the name of the country or countries whose stamps they are to contain, possibly supplemented by illustrations of stamps and by brief geographical and historical details of the countries concerned. In such an album, a small number of stamps shows to the best advantage, while they would be lost in the pages of a bigger album. Then, too, the collector using these simple albums, learns to identify stamps as belonging to a particular country, without concerning himself too specifically about the order in which the stamps were issued.

It cannot be too strongly emphasised that from the earliest stages of the hobby it should be the ambition of every collector to possess a stamp catalogue, perhaps at first a simplified one, but as soon as possible a general catalogue, even if the latter seems complicated at first sight. Once he uses a catalogue, the collector will really begin to know his stamps. The elementary catalogues will show him what is available looking at stamps in the most unscientific way, but the more advanced catalogues will show him that many of his stamps may be divided and sub-divided into groups and that stamps he thought were duplicates can, by the more advanced system of classification, be considered as different stamps.

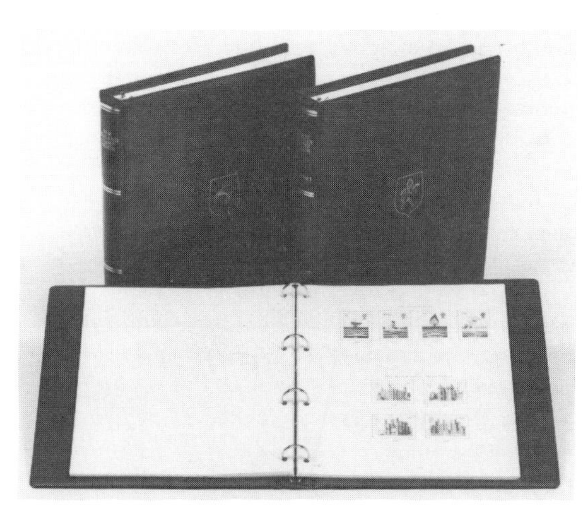

Gibbons One-Country albums

The next type of printed album is one in which there are definite spaces for each stamp. These are sometimes numbered and cross-referenced to a catalogue listing on alternate pages of the album, as in the case of the Gibbons *Windsor* album for British stamps. Alternatively, the squares provided for the stamps bear illustrations of the items to be mounted in each one; this is the style used in the Gibbons *One-Country* albums. Once a collector has bought the basic album he purchases a *supplement* each year which gives him new pages for the previous year's new issues, so that his album is kept up-to-date. The demand—in recent years—for unmounted mint stamps has brought about the publication of albums in which transparent mounts are already affixed—normally referred to as 'Hingeless albums'. Gibbons produce such albums for British, Channel Islands, Isle of Man, Australian, Canadian and New Zealand stamps. This type of album is very popular indeed on the Continent, and the European publishers produce a range which covers almost every country in the world. British collectors are usually less inclined to collect in printed albums, preferring the flexibility afforded by blank, loose-leaf albums, but printed albums are available for Great Britain and the more popular Commonwealth countries.

The provision of a definite space for each stamp makes collecting much more fascinating, and the collector begins to learn something of the order in which stamps were issued and of the relations between those of different countries. Quite large collections can be formed in this type of album, and many collectors are content to use them throughout their philatelic career. It is advisable, however, that they should be supplemented by the use of blank, loose-leaf albums or stock books to include anything interesting which comes along, and for which there is no space in the main album, for example, air covers, special postmarks, distinct shades, etc. It is in such a supplementary album that the collector will be able to express his growing knowledge and give rein to his individuality, for the printed album gives him little scope for growth.

To most collectors there comes a time when, either the collection outgrows the printed album, or knowledge and enthusiasm are irked by the restraints which its hard and fast limitations impose. Then the collection may be transferred entirely to blank albums, whose loose leaves can be arranged in any order as the owner may wish. There is absolute freedom when collecting in blank albums, but placed on the collector is the task of arranging his stamps, for he has nothing to guide him. Here the catalogue is more essential than ever, but its lists should only be taken as a basis, and the collector should feel himself absolutely free to arrange his stamps in the way he considers best, for slavery to a catalogue is unnecessary and regarded by more serious philatelists as the sign of an immature collector.

When selecting a stamp album of any kind, and particularly when choosing loose-leaf albums, whose efficiency depends on the proper functioning of some kind of retaining mechanism (a springback in the simplest kind, or pegs, rings, or projections engaging in holes or slots, in the more elaborate albums), it is a mistake to be too economical. Go to a good British maker, and select the best you can afford of the particular type of album you are buying, and you will be sure of getting quality.

We shall learn more about blank albums when considering the arrangement of a stamp collection, and the only advice that is necessary at this stage is to avoid cheapness and eschew complicated mechanical devices (such as are used for some types of loose-leaf ledgers), for holding the leaves, as these are quite unsuitable for stamp albums.

An album, a catalogue, a pair of stamp tweezers and some stamp hinges or transparent mounts and a subscription to at least one stamp magazine are the essentials of the outfit. The philatelic journals supplement the catalogue by listing all the newest stamps, by giving additional information regarding stamps already in the catalogue and by publishing helpful hints about collecting and articles telling what other people have found out in studying particular issues.

Stamp tweezers are an essential tool; they can be bought quite cheaply. With a little practice it is possible to handle, hinge, and mount stamps in the album without touching them with the fingers at all. Tweezers are also very useful for removing stamps from the water, when 'floating' them, and for this reason they should be made of non-rusting metal. They can be had with points ridged (or 'milled') so that they grip the stamps better, or with plain points. The gripping portion is also in varying shapes, more or less pointed, or with a kind of 'spade' end. The important thing is that your tweezers should be non-rusting, and that there are no really sharp edges where the points meet, as these might damage your stamps. You can test any tweezers offered you, by picking up a piece of plain paper with them, and seeing whether they leave any serious mark.

To turn to less essential parts of the outfit, I would put first a good magnifying glass. Some of the cheap ones are quite powerful, but the glass in them is rarely true, and thus the small details which you want to examine may be distorted, and the value of the magnifier lessened. A good glass of fairly small field of the type which folds so that it can be carried in the pocket, is recommended. A really good magnifying glass will cost several pounds, but a quite serviceable one can be obtained for about £1, and even these cheaper ones are much better than no glass at all. There are also several kinds of illuminated magnifiers which are powered by torch batteries and brightly illuminate the stamp under inspection.

Next in usefulness comes the duplicate book, in which you will keep your stamps until they can be transferred to the album pages, or where you will store duplicates awaiting exchange. These books are made in all sizes—from small pocket-sized to the large 'stock book' type. The pages are not of the kind used in albums but are provided with strips of transparent material stuck to each page, which form pockets into which the stamps can be slipped and from which they can easily be removed. A supply of transparent envelopes of various sizes will also be found useful for sorting and storing cheaper stamps.

When the early stages have been passed, there are several accessories which will help you to examine stamps from the more technical point of view. A device for detecting watermarks is invaluable. The simplest form of this is a black tray on which the stamp to be examined is placed face downwards. On many stamps the watermark can be seen straight away, but it may be necessary to pour a few drops of *benzine* on to the stamp. This wets it and it clings to the tray. The watermark can now usually be seen quite clearly. The benzine will quickly evaporate and will normally have caused no damage to the stamps. Benzine can cause the ink to run on certain photogravure-printed stamps.

Perforation Gauge

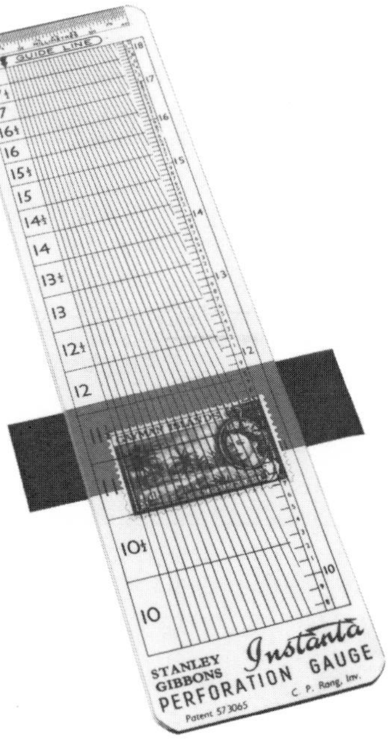

A more recent invention, the Morley-Bright detector, relies on the fact that in a watermarked stamp the design of the watermark coincides with a thinning of the paper (for notes on how watermarked paper is produced see Chapter 5). The stamp is placed on a piece of glass under a plastic sheet on which ink is scraped thinly, thus revealing the watermark. This system can also produce 'prints' of the watermark which form a permanent record and can be cut out and mounted beside the stamp in the album.

A perforation gauge comes next on this list of accessories, but again this is a relatively inexpensive item. The most accurate gauge is the Gibbons *Instanta*, which measures all perforations from 9.8 to 18.2 on a decimal scale. (See Chapter 5 for a description of the standard system for expressing gauges of perforation.) When using the *Instanta* it is important to place the gauge on top of the stamp (rather than placing the stamp on top of the gauge) in order to minimise inaccuracies due to light being refracted by the clear plastic out of which the gauge is made.

There are times when direct measurement, either of the stamp itself, or of an overprint or surcharge, is necessary to prove genuineness or otherwise, or to make a distinction between two issues. Two kinds of instruments are used by philatelists for this work—a millimetre scale (engraved on ivory or other material) and a pair of small dividers, with screw adjustment, which can be set to the distance it is required to measure and then applied to the part of the stamp that is being examined.

For heading the pages in a blank album, books of gummed labels can be bought. These bear the names of the various stamp-issuing countries and places, and are cut out and stuck in place. If you collect only one country, and want to head a large number of standard-sized leaves with the same information, say just the country name, dry transfer lettering may be the answer. Alternatively it could be worth approaching a small printer for a quote.

Do try to avoid the temptation of making any wording too ornate or of using red or other coloured inks; this detracts from the clarity of the heading and takes the eye away from the stamps on the page which are, after all, the most important feature.

There are quite a number of luxuries which can be added to the collector's outfit. Nearly every year sees the production of some new philatelic gadget, but as long as the collector has the basic philatelic equipment outlined in this chapter, he will not go too far wrong.

CHAPTER FOURTEEN
How to Obtain Stamps

There are three principal ways of getting together stamps for a collection, by gift, by exchange and by purchase. Most junior collections are started by a present from a relative, either of an old collection no longer wanted by its owner, or of a stamp packet. As other gifts of stamps are received, duplicates are acquired and these are used as 'swaps' for exchanging, and so the collection is built up, until one day, when there is a little spare pocket-money in hand, a dealer's shop is visited, or he is asked to send an 'approval book', and then the serious stage is reached.

The adult collector is rather at a disadvantage in the matter of presents, but if there is anyone who remembers his birthday or Christmas in the appropriate way, there is nothing to prevent him dropping a hint that he prefers stamps or philatelic accessories to ties of the wrong colour or cigars of the wrong kind. The hint should, however, be accompanied by a written description of the stamps he wants, for there is nothing more helpless than the non-collector who is attempting to buy stamps for a collector. He may be a general collector, or he may collect the stamps of one country only, as the dealer kindly points out, and eventually the poor bemused non-collector may leave the stamp shop and buy the usual brand of pseudo-Havanas.

The business man has, of course, the opportunity of begging stamps from his friends who have correspondence with countries abroad, and even if he is not interested in these current stamps he should take them, either for the benefit of some younger collector or with a view to possible exchange for something he does want. Many collectors have built up quite good general collections by the happy chance of being in a position to secure the stamps from a big world-wide business correspondence. One specimen of each stamp goes into their albums, and the rest are kept and either exchanged, or sold to a dealer in quantity, so that there is a continual flow of stamps, and of cash which can be turned into more stamps.

'Never miss anything' is the motto of the keen collector, and this is why even the man who collects the stamps of only one country should have some knowledge of those of the rest of the world. In any case he should never miss the chance of picking up stamps, especially when they are offered to him gratis. To sniff and say: 'Oh, thanks, but I don't collect that', is to miss the opportunity of securing specimens which can possibly be exchanged or sold. Unless funds are plentiful the stamps one does not want can help pay for the stamps one needs.

When the occasional gift and the results of 'swapping' fail to satisfy the desire for a quickly expanding collection, the aid of the dealer must be enlisted. In the early days of one's collection, quantity appeals rather more strongly than quality, and this is where the stamp 'packet' comes in. The dealer who receives an order for 100 different stamps, each of which has to be looked out separately, is forced to charge for his labour, and those stamps are therefore much dearer when bought separately than they are when purchased in a packet. In a packet, of course, you do not have any choice, beyond what is afforded by the grouping in the dealer's list, that is to say he may have, in addition to his whole world packets, packets containing British Commonwealth stamps only, or packets of pictorial stamps.

Stamp Packets

The best start for a collection is the biggest whole world mixed packet you can afford to buy, for you want to avoid duplicates and if you start with a small packet, the larger packets will almost certainly contain the same stamps over again. The cost per stamp naturally increases in the larger packets, which contain stamps which are harder to get, but it is still far less than the cost of the same stamps if bought separately one by one. When the contents of the packet have been absorbed in the album, other packets may be bought, until it is clear that this method of purchase is bringing in too many duplicates. The latter are always useful for exchanging purposes, but it is better to get stamps one really wants if possible.

When mixed packets have helped as much as they can, it is time to turn to one-country packets. These, as the name implies, include the stamps of one country only. There may be several size packets of a particular country in the dealer's list, 20 different, 50 different and 100 different, and it is as well to realise that, as in the case of the mixed packets, the larger one-country packets will often include the stamps that are in the smaller ones of the same country, plus others. Therefore buy the largest, if you can, straightaway. The advantage of these one-country packets is that they give the collector the chance of buying to fill his weaker countries, for example Iran. Looking at the dealer's list he sees that he can get, for a modest sum, 25 different Iranian stamps. Even if the three stamps he already possesses are included (and it is quite likely that they are not), he is sure of adding 22 stamps to his Iran page, none of which will be duplicates. In this way, many countries can be built up to a reasonable degree of strength, and only a very few duplicates will be acquired. Similar packets are now available for particular themes rather than countries, *i.e.* animals, sport, transport, etc. These contain stamps of more than one country. Their appeal is growing rapidly as thematic collecting becomes even more popular.

The third stage brings us to the set of stamps which only includes the stamps of a single issue. Some dealers' lists will give the date and a fairly detailed description of the contents of the set. Others will quote the Stanley Gibbons catalogue numbers or similar recognised identification. Thus one knows exactly what is on offer. Comparing the description or catalogue number with one's collection, it is an easy matter to select sets which will contain very few duplicates. Do not refuse to buy sets of which you already possess the commonest stamps. For these low values you are paying very little, and even if their cost is not taken into account, the better stamps in the set will still be far cheaper than if bought separately. As new sets are continually appearing, set buying may continue until the collection is in quite an advanced stage.

There may still be gaps, however, and these will have to be filled by buying stamps singly. This can be done in two ways. The first method is for the collector to send the dealer a wants list, a description of the stamps he wants, quoting the reference numbers of a recognised catalogue. Always give the name of the country as well as the catalogue number, and state whether unused (mounted or unmounted) or used stamps are required. The dealer will then send you what he can supply of these stamps and usually these are sent on approval, so that if they are not exactly as required they can be returned. If the stamps are of sufficient value, the dealer may only supply a quotation rather than the actual stamps. Alternatively, he may supply the stamps straightaway if adequate references are sent with the wants list.

The second method of buying stamps singly is to ask the dealer for an approval section. These selections are arranged on sheets or in books, each stamp being priced separately. The simplest form of selection will include the cheaper stamps of several countries, and some of the larger and longer-established dealers have quite a good range of these approval sheets. For collectors who need a more advanced type of selection, books are available containing the stamps of only a single country, or perhaps of one issue only. If you are to take full advantage of such a service as this, it is essential that you should give the dealer full details of the stamps you are collecting. It is no good merely saying you want a selection of the stamps, of say, France, if you take nothing but French stamps issued before 1920 or only used copies with Colonial postmarks. The dealer will send you a general selection of France, in which there may be nothing of interest. Tell him exactly what issues you are collecting, whether you want unused or used, if you collect pairs or blocks, and so on, and then he will be able to send you the sort of selection you really want to see. Give him some idea, also, of the prices of stamps you wish to see; it is no good him sending you stamps priced up to £5 each, if you want stamps priced in the 10p–25p range. For the same reason, he will not continue to send you stamps on approval, unless you buy a reasonable amount. Some dealers are more lenient in this respect than others, hoping that if you do not buy today, you may be tempted later, but it is obvious that no business man can afford to waste time, energy and postage on someone who is obviously not a buyer. If, however, you are prepared to spend a few pounds when a cheap approval sheet is sent to you, or more when better books arrive, you will probably be very satisfied with the service the dealer will give you, and will be able to spend many happy hours comparing his stamps with yours and filling the gaps in your album. Do be fair, however, and return his stamps within the stipulated time limit, for the dealer has other customers waiting to see them. The quicker he can get his stamps back, as a general rule, the less he has to allow on his expense account for stock lying idle, and the cheaper he can sell. When returning approval sheets or books make sure they are adequately packed to avoid damage in the post. If the dealer has sent them to you by recorded delivery or registered post, they should be returned to him by the same service.

The keen collector is always hoping for a 'find'. The young collector will be quite satisfied if he finds a stamp catalogued at £1 in a 50p packet. The acquisition of bargains is just as interesting to the adult collector, and his superior knowledge often enables him to take advantage of the carelessness of dealers, or their lack of detailed knowledge. The man who specialises in the stamps of one or two countries nearly always knows more than the dealer who has to handle the stamps of the whole world, and there is nothing unsporting in using that knowledge to pick up minor varieties that the dealer has overlooked.

In fact, dealers, and in particular those who have to employ a large staff, often give the collector the chance to make very interesting finds. Apart from mistakes, the trader simply does not have time to sort all his stock on the most advanced specialist lines. If he buys common stamps at so much a hundred, he is not going to waste expensive staff time in getting them to search for a few minor varieties which will add a pound or two to the value of his stamps. He will be satisfied if he gets his normal rate of profit by selling them all as standard stamps, and if the collector gets a bargain here and there, the dealer knows that that may be an inducement for him to return in the hope of finding others. Cheap approval sheets are, in many cases, prolific sources of 'finds', for the stock used for these has to be handled very quickly, and is often not sorted for varieties of perforations, watermark or shade.

Though the stamp dealer does not mind his customers making finds, he does very strongly object to the customer who will buy from him nothing but bargains—those who come into dealers' shops and sit for hours looking through books of stamps in the hope of 'spotting' something. They often waste the time of the dealer's staff and give him practically no return. Stamp dealers will always try to help a genuine collector who does a reasonable amount of business with them, but the man who looks for bargains and nothing else is unlikely to be given much of welcome.

The search for philatelic treasure, like the search for sunken gold, is beset with perils. Wherever he goes hunting, the collector must first be sure of his own knowledge. The man who thinks he is getting bargains in old stamps because he is getting them at cheap prices may have disappointment in store, for very few people nowadays are sufficiently foolish or ignorant to sell the scarce stamps of the older issues at bargain prices. The first thing that should enter a collector's mind, when presented with what he thinks is a bargain, is caution—whether the treasure be in an apparently old collection, in a dusty shop, or in a club exchange book. Club exchange books are particularly dangerous to the inexperienced, for the overworked secretary cannot possibly guard his members against the ignorance of the majority of their friends. One seldom sees a collection, formed on 'bargain-hunting' lines, which is worth more than a small fraction of what the owner has paid for it. Those who show a profit are those whose owners pay good prices for their best stamps, realising that then they are getting what they are paying for, both as regards genuineness and condition.

Most collectors dream of coming across a hoard of old and (hopefully) valuable stamps. Many collectors still come across something—a small batch of old family letters perhaps—which will yield some stamps but very rarely will these be of much value. Stories about the discovery of rare stamps in old cupboards, desks, trunks, attics, etc. are part of philatelic folk-lore. A whole book could be written on them but, charming though they may be, they are of little practical help to the new collector and may even be discouraging to those who feel 'I will never have such luck'. Most philatelists will not 'strike lucky' in a big way however long they collect stamps, but this need not detract from the pleasure the hobby can give them.

To the inexperienced reader who finds old stamps, the following is sound advice: If the stamps are on their original envelopes, do not try and soak them off until you have taken expert advice. Many of the old stamps have greater value on their original envelopes. If the stamps are in sheets or blocks, do not take one of them off to send as a sample to anybody, or for your own collection. In the case of many old stamps, the value of a block or sheet is far more than that of the number of single stamps it contains. If the stamps or envelopes are creased or folded, do not try to straighten them out unless you are sure you can do so without further damage, or separating the stamps along the lines of perforation. Above all, if the sheets or envelopes have not been folded, do not fold them in any way, as so many people do, in order to get them into an envelope for transmission by post. The fresher the stamps or envelopes, the greater will be their value, so keep them packed flat until an expert has seen them. Do not rely on the advice of some friend who claims to know all about stamps. The more a collector claims to know, the less he usually does know. The real experts very rarely vaunt their knowledge. In any case of doubt, the best advice you can get is from a dealer of really high reputation. He has to maintain that reputation, which has been built up by years of straight dealing, and though he will make a profit on the sale of your stamps, he will not rob you.

CHAPTER FIFTEEN

The Question of Condition

To the collectors of early days, even damaged stamps appeared worthy of a place in their albums, but nowadays the philatelist should exercise a certain discretion in the stamps which he admits to his collection, and here he will meet for the first time the magic word 'condition'.

The 'condition' of a stamp applies the relation which its completeness, freshness and general appearance bear to what may be imagined to be the ideal specimen of that particular stamp. An unused stamp in perfect condition would be as fresh as on the day it came from the printing-press, with colour bright, on clean and uncreased paper, and with its gum untouched. If it is an imperforate issue, it must have margins on all four sides as wide as can possibly be obtained, and certainly the scissors which separated it from its neighbours should not have touched even the outermost line of its design. As far as perforated stamps are concerned, perfect condition excludes any shortness of tooth in the perforation, and good centering is essential. This means that the printed design must be at an even distance from the rows of perforations which bound it, at top and bottom and on right and left.

Poorly centred modern stamps like these 'Machins' are commonplace. Extremely poorly centred copies (like the Bulgarian stamp) are of little value

This search for stamps in perfect condition has become a craze with many collectors. The search for the perfect item can be carried to an extent that, in any other connexion, would be regarded as eccentric. Collectors have been known to spurn and regard as of no account rare and interesting stamps simply because they do not reach their extreme standards of condition. What should we think of the collector who would rather have a gap in an otherwise complete collection than take the finest known specimen of a stamp because it does not measure up to his imaginary standard? It is, of course, for each individual to decide what he will collect—but it would be foolish for the ordinary collector to follow these 'super conditionists' for not only would he exclude many quite sound stamps from his albums, but he would make the hobby much more expensive for himself and his fellows. If the dealer who buys 100 copies of a particular stamp, has to discard half of them, not because they are damaged, but because they do not quite come up to the standard of the fastidious, then whoever buys the remaining stamps must pay double the price for them.

The collector who thinks solely of investment should certainly cultivate sound judgment as to condition when buying the rarer stamps. If he buys inferior copies he should ensure that he does not pay more than their value—which will often be only a fraction of the top price of the fine specimens. The average collector will be well advised not to worry unduly about condition, but fill his spaces with any stamps that are not defective or heavily postmarked for damaged and unsightly stamps are an eyesore on the album page.

The stamp at left is a fine used and worthy of a place in a collection, the stamp at right should be discarded

Postmarks should be cut out neatly – not to an odd shape

The removal—hopefully the replacement—of these damaged and ugly stamps is, therefore, the first step to be taken by the collector who is preparing to mount his stamps. The next is to remove all superfluous paper from the remainder. If you know that stamps are printed in fast colours, any which are on pieces of envelope may be placed in warm water until the paper can be peeled off. Stamps printed in many of the modern inks and all stamps printed on 'chalky' paper, or in inks of a deliberately fugitive character, must be treated more carefully. They may either be floated face upwards on the surface of a tray of water, until the damp has penetrated the adherent paper sufficiently to enable it to be detached, but not enough to affect the colour of the stamp. A sponge or a wad of damp blotting paper in a shallow trough or tray can be used instead of water. It is preferable that the water should not touch the surface of the stamp. Sufficient time should be allowed for the water to penetrate the paper and dissolve the gum before trying to remove the stamp from the paper. Always allow five minutes and then try slowly to remove the stamp. If it comes away easily fine; if not leave it for a few more minutes. Some of the more stubborn specimens may require as much as half an hour. Always be patient if you do not want to damage the stamps.

It is not always desirable to remove stamps either from whole envelopes or from pieces. Many early stamps, whether 'on cover' (the whole envelope) or 'on piece', are worth much more in this state and the advice of experienced collectors should be sought. Often part of the envelope should be retained to show an interesting postmark in which case the paper should be cut to a neat rectangle, and not trimmed round the postmark.

Cleaning stamps in the ways employed by fakers (see Chapter 12) should not be undertaken by the collector, but there are one or two things which the ethics of the hobby permit to be done by way of improving defective specimens. Stamps whose colours have been 'oxydised', may be restored to their natural tones by a bath in peroxide of hydrogen. (This affects the gum of unused stamps so the peroxide should be applied very carefully to the surface of the stamp only using a camel hair brush.) Used stamps printed in fast colours, which look as if they are dirty, may often be improved by a good hot bath. Creases may be removed or rendered less prominent, by the use of a hot iron and damp blotting paper, but only when the colours are fast. If there are grease spots on a stamp, they can be taken out by ironing the stamp with a hot iron through clean blotting paper, or by immersion in benzine.

Mention has been made earlier of the current wish of most collectors of unused stamps for unmounted mint specimens. Any collector obtaining unmounted mint stamps is strongly advised to keep the stamps in that condition—*i.e.* he should not mount them using stamp hinges. He should, therefore, keep the stamps in a stock-book or mount them using transparent mounts. Two kinds of mounts are sold by Stanley Gibbons—'Gibbons Gard' and 'Gibbons Hawid' mounts. 'Hingeless albums' with mounts already affixed are also produced. Used stamps can, of course, be mounted using stamp hinges—as there is no gum to disturb. Nevertheless a good quality hinge should be used to avoid any damage to the paper when it is removed.

Collectors today pay far greater attention to the question of condition than the philatelists of yesteryear. Always handle your stamps carefully—always with stamp tweezers and ensure they are kept in proper albums or stockbooks and that the cupboard in which they are stored is neither too hot, nor cold and particularly not damp.

The value of your collection will depend both on the type of stamps you collect and the condition in which they are preserved. Even if your stamps are not valuable, you should aim to keep them in good condition. Guidance on mounting is given in Chapter 17.

CHAPTER SIXTEEN
How to Identify Stamps

It is when he tries to identify his stamps and allot them to their particular countries that the collector finds the need for a catalogue, for although few countries do not put their names on their stamps at all, many others do not call themselves by the name we are accustomed to use in English, and a third group use alphabets with which we are not familiar. It is, therefore, very helpful, for the collector, before starting to identify his stamps, to make a thorough study of his catalogue, paying particular attention to the illustrations and trying to memorise the characteristics of the various countries and groups of colonies.

When undertaking the identification of a mixed lot of stamps, the beginner should put on one side at once all those which bear the name of the country in English, or which he can identify without difficulty. He will, of course, have no difficulty with names which differ very little from the English equivalents, such as Brazil, Chile, or the French Colonies which end in a final 'e' where the English name ends in 'a' such as 'Indo-Chine', 'Mauritanie', etc.

In attempting to identify stamps with quite unfamiliar names, it is sometimes helpful to remember the equivalent for the word 'post' (or 'posts') in various languages. Thus the French word is *postes*, the Spanish *correos*, the Portuguese *correio* or *correios*, and so on. This does not take us far, however, as many countries have their stamp inscriptions in French, and most countries of South and Central America use Spanish or Portuguese on their stamps.

Perhaps the widest indications are given by the standard designs used by the former colonies of various European states. If the catalogue illustrations of the former French, German, Portuguese, Dutch and Spanish colonies are studied, it will soon be easy to recognize the standard types in each group, and after this, allotment to countries is easy.

The first word in a stamp inscription is not always the name of the country. It may mean 'Republic', 'Kingdom', 'Postage Stamp', 'Post' or many other things, but a little practice will enable you to pick out the name. In some cases the name of the country is in the overprint, stamps of another country having been converted for use by this method.

Inscriptions on stamps cover such matters as the postal value of the stamp, its purpose, the country from which it comes, and sometimes the subject of its design, or the event in connexion with which it was issued. Overprints cover much the same field. The average collector is too often content to study the inscriptions only so far as they enable him to identify a particular stamp but they are in many cases worthy of more than this superficial scrutiny. Stamps of Palestine (1927–45), had lettering in English, Hebrew and Arabic—

typifying British rule endeavouring to hold the scales of justice evenly between Jew and Arab. On stamps of Russia an inscription in Esperanto may be found, evidently intended to convey a message to those unfamiliar with Russian characters. Other stamps of Russia, with inscriptions in three or four languages, indicate the wide area under Soviet rule.

French and Spanish and Portuguese stamps inscribed 'Postes', 'Correos' and 'Correio'

Palestine stamp inscribed in Hebrew, Arabic and English

Early Ceylon stamp simply inscribed 'CEYLON' and modern issue with name in English (*Sri Lanka*), Singhalese and Tamil

Changes in stamp inscriptions are equally revealing. East India, of the Honourable East India Company, gives place to 'India' under the rule of the Queen-Empress. The Orange Free State changes its name after the Boer War to Orange River Colony. In Ceylon (now Sri Lanka) the adoption of Singhalese as the official language of that country in the face of violent Tamil opposition was reflected in her stamp inscriptions. Where 'Ceylon' in English was formerly given greater prominence, the Singhalese version later became the more prominent, with the English and Tamil inscriptions in much smaller type. A later innovation was the printing of stamps inscribed in Singhalese and Tamil alternately in the same sheet. The emotive word 'republic' appears on the issues of one country after another. So the story of the world is told.

Other changes are brought about by the granting of independence to British Commonwealth territories and the formation or dissolution of Federal alliances. Hence Gold Coast has become Ghana and the member countries of the former Rhodesia and Nyasaland Federation, Southern Rhodesia, Northern Rhodesia and Nyasaland, are now Zimbabwe, Zambia and Malawi. Tanganyika and Zanzibar have a political alliance as Tanzania, and North Borneo, a member of the Malaysia Federation, has become Sabah.

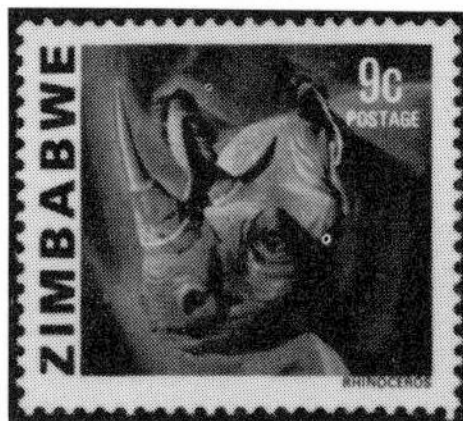

Changes in country name – Southern Rhodesia now Zimbabwe, Northern Rhodesia now Zambia and Nyasaland now Malawai

In the following list the collector will find explanations of the inscriptions most likely to cause him trouble. The name given in capitals is the country under which the stamps will be found in the Gibbons catalogue (Parts 1–22).

A

A & T. Overprint on French stamps for ANNAM AND TONGKING.

Açores. AZORES.

Admiralty Official. Overprint on British stamps 1903.

A.E.F. FRENCH EQUATORIAL AFRICA. The issue of 1938 was inscribed with this abbreviation of *Afrique Equatoriale Française*.

Afghanes. AFGHANISTAN. Mostly inscribed in French with **Postes Afghanes**, but occasionally in English **Postage Afghan(istan)** or mixtures of both languages.

Africa. A general issue in 1898 for PORTUGUESE COLONIES.

Africa Occidental Espanola or **Territorios del Africa Occidental Espanola.** SPANISH WEST AFRICA.

Africa Orientale Italiana. ITALIAN EAST AFRICA.

Afrique Equatoriale Française. FRENCH EQUATORIAL AFRICA.

Afrique Occidentale Française. FRENCH WEST AFRICA.

Albania, with surcharge in para currency on Italian stamps, for ITALIAN P.O.S IN THE LEVANT—Offices in Turkish Empire.

Alexandrie. ALEXANDRIA, the French Post Office in this Egyptian port.

Algérie. ALGERIA.

Allemagne Duitschland. Stamp of Belgium over-printed during BELGIAN OCCUPATION OF GERMANY 1919–21 for use in the Rhineland.

A.M. Post Deutschland. GERMANY Allied Occupation, the 1945 issue by the Military Government in the Anglo-American Zone.

A.M.G. F.T.T. TRIESTE. Overprints on Italian stamps 1947–54 for Allied Military Government—Free Territory of Trieste.

A.M.G. V.G. Stamps of Italy overprinted for Allied Military Government in VENEZIA GIULIA AND ISTRIA.

Amtlicher Verkehr K. Württ. Post. WURTTEMBERG Official Stamps.

Andorre. ANDORRA (French Post Offices).

Anna(s). (1) British stamps surcharged in this Indian currency were for BRITISH POSTAL AGENCIES IN EASTERN ARABIA. (2) Surcharges on French stamps were for FRENCH P.O.S IN ZANZIBAR.

A.O. (*Afrique Orientale*) Belgian Congo stamps overprinted for Belgian Occupation of RUANDA-URUNDI.

A Payer Te Betalen. Postage Due stamps of BELGIUM.

A Percevoir. (*To Collect*) Postage due stamps of BELGIUM, FRANCE, GUADELOUPE, CANADA, EGYPT and MONACO.

A Percevoir Timbre Taxe. Postage due stamps of FRENCH COLONIES.

Archipel des Comores. COMORO ISLANDS.

Army Official. (1) Overprint on British stamps 1896–1902. (2) Overprint on Sudan stamp 1905.

Assistência D.L. no. 72. Portuguese Colonies fiscal stamps overprinted as Educational Tax for TIMOR 1936–37.

Autopaketti. Stamps of FINLAND for use on parcels carried by road.

Avion Nessre Tafari. Airmail stamps of ETHIOPIA 1931.

Avisporto Maerke. Newspaper stamps of DENMARK.

B

B. Overprinted on Straits Settlements stamps for use in British Post Office in BANGKOK, Siam.

B in an oval. Overprinted on stamps of BELGIUM to signify Railway Official usage.

Baden. (1) Issues 1851–68 before Baden's postal administration was incorporated with that of the German Empire. (2) GERMANY Allied Occupation, French Zone issues of 1947–49.

Bánát Bacska. Stamps of Hungary overprinted for RUMANIAN OCCUPATION OF HUNGARY.

Baranya. Hungarian stamps overprinted or surcharged for SERBIAN OCCUPATION OF HUNGARY.

Bayern. BAVARIA.

B.C.A. Stamps of Rhodesia overprinted for British Central Africa Protectorate.

B.C.O.F. Japan 1946. British Commonwealth Occupation Force. Stamps of Australia overprinted for BRITISH OCCUPATION OF JAPAN.

België. BELGIUM.

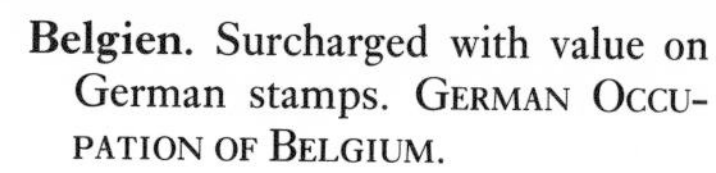

Belgien. Surcharged with value on German stamps. GERMAN OCCUPATION OF BELGIUM.

Belgique. BELGIUM.

Belgisch Congo. BELGIAN CONGO.

Benadir. SOMALIA.

Bengasi. Overprint on Italian stamps, for ITALIAN P.O.S IN THE LEVANT.

Berlin. Overprints 1948–49 for GERMANY—West Berlin.

BMA Malaya. (*British Military Administration.*) Overprint on Straits Settlements stamps.

B.N.F. Castellorizo. (*Base Navale Française*) Overprint on French Levant stamps for Occupation of CASTELROSSO.

Board of Education. Overprint on British stamps 1902.

Böhmen und Mähren. BOHEMIA AND MORAVIA.

Bollo Postale. SAN MARINO.

Bosnien Hercegovina or **Bosnien herzegowina.** BOSNIA AND HERZEGOVINA.

Brasil. BRAZIL.

Braunschweig. BRUNSWICK.

British Occupation. Overprint on Russian stamps for BATUM.

British Somaliland. Indian stamps overprinted for SOMALILAND PROTECTORATE.

Buchanan. Registration stamp of LIBERIA 1893.

Bureau International d'Education. International Education Office, of the UNITED NATIONS.

Bureau International du Travail. International Labour Office, of the UNITED NATIONS.

C

Cabo Jubi or **Cabo Juby.** Overprint on Rio de Oro, Spain or Spanish Morocco stamps for CAPE JUBY.

Cabo Verde. CAPE VERDE ISLANDS.

Calchi or **Carchi.** Italian stamps overprinted for Khalki, AEGEAN ISLANDS.

Calimno or **Calino.** Italian stamps overprinted for Kalimnos, AEGEAN ISLANDS.

Camb. Aust. Sigillum Nov. NEW SOUTH WALES 1850.

Cambodge. CAMBODIA.

Cameroons U.K.T.T. (*United Kingdom Trust Territory*). Nigerian stamps overprinted for SOUTHERN CAMEROONS.

Caso. Italian stamps overprinted for Kasos, AEGEAN ISLANDS.

Castellorizo or **Castelloriso.** CASTELROSSO.

Cavalle. CAVALLA, also spelled Kavalla.

Čechya Morava. BOHEMIA AND MORAVIA.

C.E.F. (1) *Cameroons Expeditionary Force*; Overprint on German Colonial stamps for the British Occupation of the Cameroons. CAMEROUN. (2) (*China Expeditionary Force*) Overprint on Indian stamps for use by CHINA EXPEDITIONARY FORCE.

Cefalonia e Itaca. Stamps of Greece overprinted for Italian Occupation of CEPHALONIA AND ITHACA.

Cent Surcharge on German stamps (also **F.** for franc). GERMAN COMMANDS in World War I covering Belgium and Northern France.

Centesimi and **lire** Surcharges on stamps inscribed **K.u.K. Feldpost** were produced in 1918 for the AUSTRO-HUNGARIAN MILITARY POST.

Centesimo (or **centesimi**) **di corona.** Stamps of Italy were surcharged in this currency for use in ITALIAN AUSTRIA 1919.

Centimes. German and Austrian stamps surcharged in this currency were issues for GERMAN P.O.S IN TURKEY, 1908 and for AUSTRIAN P.O.S IN CRETE.

Centimos. Surcharged on French stamps for use in FRENCH P.O.S IN MOROCCO.

Centrafricaine, République. CENTRAL AFRICAN REPUBLIC.

Československo. CZECHOSLOVAKIA.

CFA. (*Communité Financielle Africaine*) Overprint on stamps of France for REUNION.

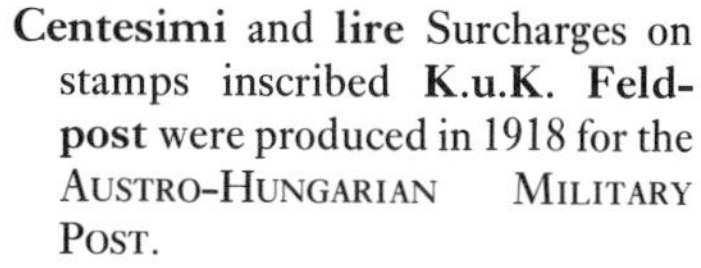

C.G.H.S. (*Commission de Gouvernement Haute Silésie*) Overprint on German stamps for UPPER SILESIA.

Chemins de Fer Spoorwegen. BELGIUM Railway Parcels stamps.

China. Overprint on Hong Kong stamps for issues of CHINA: BRITISH POST OFFICES, also on stamps of Germany for GERMAN P.O.S IN CHINA.

Chine. Surcharged on French and Indo-Chinese stamps for FRENCH P.O.S IN CHINA; also used as inscription.

Cilicie. CILICIA.

Cinquantenaire 24 Septembre 1853 1903 and eagle. Overprint on French Group 'Tablet' type for NEW CALEDONIA.

Cirenaica. CYRENAICA.

Co. Ci. (*Commissariato Civile*). Yugoslav stamps overprinted for Italian Occupation of SLOVENIA.

Colombia. Most issues are from the Republic of that name. Those showing a map of Panama and inscribed Colombia, however, are from PANAMA.

Coloniali Italiane. General issues for ITALIAN COLONIES used in Cyrenaica, Eritrea, Italian Somaliland and Tripolitania.

Colonie Italiane. Overprint on Italian stamps for use in ITALIAN COLONIES.

Colonies de l'Empire Français. FRENCH COLONIES.

Colonies Postes. Though also inscribed **République Française** the 1881 'Commerce' type was a general issue for FRENCH COLONIES.

Comité Français de la Liberation Nationale. With R.F. or République Française. FRENCH COLONIES.

Comores, Archipel des. COMORO ISLANDS.

Confed. Granadina. COLOMBIA.

Confoederatio Helvetica. SWITZERLAND.

Congo. (1) Overprints on Belgian Congo stamps for newly independent CONGO (Kinshasa), 1960. (2) As inscription or overprint on key-types of Portuguese Group for PORTUGUESE CONGO.

Congo Belge. BELGIAN CONGO.

Congo Français. FRENCH CONGO.

Congo Français Gabon. GABON.

Congo, République de. Inscription used both by CONGO (Kinshasa) 1961–64—the former Belgian Congo—and by CONGO REPUBLIC (Brazzaville) 1959–70, the former French possession.

Congo, République Populaire du. Inscription on stamps of CONGO (Brazzaville) since 1970.

Congreso de los Diputados. SPAIN Official Stamps.

Constantinopol Posta Romana. Overprint on Rumanian stamps for RUMANIAN P.O.S ABROAD—Constantinople.

Constantinopoli. Overprint on Italian stamps for ITALIAN P.O.S IN THE LEVANT.

Corée, Postes de. KOREA.

Corfu. (1) Overprint on Italian stamps for Italian Occupation of CORFU. (2) Overprint on Greek stamps for Italian Occupation of CORFU AND PAXOS.

Corona. Surcharge on Italian stamps for use in ITALIAN AUSTRIA.

Cos or **Coo.** Overprinted on Italian stamps for KOS, AEGEAN ISLANDS.

Côte d'Ivoire. IVORY COAST.

Côte Français des Somalis. FRENCH SOMALI COAST.

Cour Permanente de Justice Internationale or **Cour Internationale de Justice.** Overprint or inscription for Court of International Justice. The Hague, Netherlands.

Crete. Surcharge or inscription on French Group designs for FRENCH P.O.S IN CRETE.

D

D de A. (*Departamento de Antioquia.*) COLOMBIA—Antioquia.

Danmark. DENMARK.

Dansk Vestindiske øer or **Dansk Vestindien.** DANISH WEST INDIES.

Datia. DUTTIA.

DDR. (*Deutsche Demokratische Republik*) German Democratic Republic. EAST GERMANY.

Dédéagh. DEDEAGATZ.

Deficit. Postage Dues of PERU.

Demokratska Federativina Jugoslavija. Croatian stamps surcharged in 1945 for Regional Issues of YUGOSLAVIA Democratic Federal Republic.

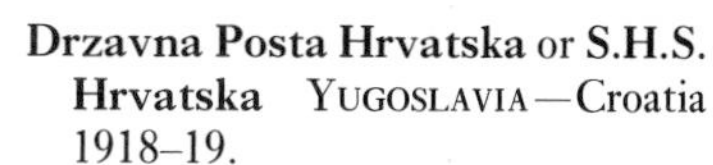

Deutsch-Neu-Guinea. German stamps overprinted or as inscription for NEW GUINEA when a German Colony.

Deutsch-Ostafrika. German East Africa, the former name for TANGANYIKA.

Deutsch-Sudwestafrika. SOUTH WEST AFRICA when a German Colony.

Deutsche Bundespost. WEST GERMANY (inscription used since 1950).

Deutsche Bundespost Berlin. West Berlin issues, (inscription used since 1955).

Deutsche Demokratische Republik. *see* **DDR.**

Deutsche Feldpost. GERMANY. Military Fieldpost stamps.

Deutsche Flugpost or **Deutsche Luftpost.** GERMANY. Airmail issues 1919–38.

Deutsche Nationalversammlung. GERMANY. Issue of 1919 for National Assembly.

Deutsche Post. GERMANY of the immediate postwar period, including Allied Occupation issues, stamps for West Berlin until 1954, West Germany 1949, and East Germany 1949.

Deutsche Post Berlin. GERMANY, 1952–55 issues of West Berlin.

Deutsche Post Osten. Surcharges on German stamps for POLAND under Nazi Occupation.

Deutsche Reichspost. GERMANY. Issues of 1872–87.

Deutsches Reich. GERMANY. Issues of 1902–43. Stamps additionally inscribed **General Gouvernement** are from POLAND under Nazi Occupation.

Deutschösterreich. AUSTRIA.

Dienstmarke. GERMANY. Official stamps.

Diligencia. URUGUAY (1856–57).

Dios Patria Libertad. Early issues of DOMINICAN REPUBLIC.

DJ. Overprint on Obock stamps for DJIBOUTI.

Dominicana, República. DOMINICAN REPUBLIC.

Drzavna Posta Hrvatska or **S.H.S. Hrvatska** YUGOSLAVIA—Croatia 1918–19.

Drzava S.H.S. YUGOSLAVIA—Slovenia.

Drzava S.H.S. Bosna i Hercegovina. Overprint on Bosnian stamps for YUGOSLAVIA— Bosnia and Herzgovina.

Duc. di parma Piac. Ecc. PARMA.

Durazzo. Surcharges on Italian stamps for ITALIAN P.O.S IN THE LEVANT.

E

E.A.F. (*East African Forces*) Overprint on British stamps for use during British Occupation of SOMALIA.

East India Postage. Victorian stamps of INDIA. If surcharged with a crown and value in cents they are first-issue STRAITS SETTLEMENTS.

EE. UU. DE C., E.S. DEL T (*Estados Unidos de Colombia, Estado Soberano del Tolima*) First issue of TOLIMA.

E.E.F. (*Egyptian Expeditionary Force*) PALESTINE stamps issued under British Military Occupation and Civil Administration.

Eesti. ESTONIA.

Egeo. Overprint on Italian stamps for AEGEAN ISLANDS.

Egypte, Royaume d'Egypte or **Postes Egyptiennes.** EGYPT.

Eire. IRELAND (REPUBLIC).

Elsass. Overprint on German stamps for GERMAN OCCUPATION OF ALSACE.

Emp. Ottoman. TURKEY (1876).

Empire Franc. Abbreviation of *Empire Français*. On some early issues of FRANCE and FRENCH COLONIES.

En. Denomination for yen on stamps of JAPAN.

Equateur. ECUADOR (1887).

E.R.I. 6d. Surcharge on 6d. ORANGE FREE STATE stamp in 1902 during British Occupation.

Escuelas. VENEZUELA. Originally fiscal stamps, also valid postally.

Espana. SPAIN. Similar inscriptions have been **Estado Español, República Española** and **La Cruz Roja Española**. The word **España** often appeared on stamps of Spain's Overseas Provinces, such as IFNI or RIO MUNI, in addition to the Province name itself.

Est Africain Allemand Occupation Belge/Duitsch Oost Africa Belgische Bezetting. Overprint on stamps of Belgian Congo for Belgian Occupation of RUANDA-URUNDI.

Estado da India. PORTUGUESE INDIA.

Estados Unidos de Nueva Granada. COLOMBIA (1861).

Estensi, Poste. MODENA.

Estero. Overprint on slightly modified Italian stamps for use in ITALIAN P.O.S IN THE LEVANT.

Estland Eesti. GERMAN OCCUPATION OF ESTONIA.

Etablissements Français dans l'Inde. INDIAN SETTLEMENTS, former French territories now part of India.

Etablissements (or **Ets.**) **Français de l'Océanie.** OCEANIC SETTLEMENTS.

Etat Indépendant du Congo. Congo Free State. Renamed BELGIAN CONGO in 1908.

Ethiopie, Etiopia Empire d'Ethiopie or **Postes Ethiopiennes.** ETHIOPIA, sometimes called Abyssinia.

Eupen & Malmédy. Overprint on Belgium stamps for use in these districts during the BELGIAN OCCUPATION OF GERMANY.

Exposicion General (or **Gral.**) **Española.** SPAIN (1929).

Exposicion Gral. Sevilla Barcelona. SPAIN (1929).

F

Feudatory State Raj Nandgam. NANDGAON.

Filipinas (or **Filias.** PHILIPPINE ISLANDS while a Spanish Colony.

Fiume Rijeka. Overprint with date 3-V-1945 on Italian stamps for VENEZIA GIULIA AND ISTRIA—Yugoslav Occupation.

Florida. With picture of heron. URUGUAY air stamp.

Forces Francaises Libres Levant. Surcharge on Syrian and Lebanese stamps for FREE FRENCH FORCES IN THE LEVANT.

Føroyar. FAROE ISLANDS.

Franc. Surcharges in this currency on Austrian stamps were for AUSTRIAN P.O.S IN CRETE.

Franco. Design showing a woman seated (Helvetia) on the 1854 issue of SWITZERLAND.

Franco Bollo. (*Postage Stamp*). The first stamps of ITALY were thus inscribed without country name. They were perforated: similar imperforate stamps are from SARDINIA.

Franco Bollo Postale. With designs showing crossed keys and denominations in bajocchi, scudo or centesimi, are stamps of the PAPAL STATES.

Franco Marke. BREMEN (1856).

Franco Scrisorei. RUMANIA (1862).

Francobollo di Stato. Official stamps of ITALY.

Freimarke. (*Postage Stamp*) Stamps with no country name and portrait are from PRUSSIA; stamps with large numerals from THURN AND TAXIS.

Frimaerke Kgl. Post. The second word is short for **Kongeligt**, or Royal. Stamps inscribed in (rigsbank) skilling are early issues of DENMARK; similar designs, but in cents, are from the DANISH WEST INDIES.

G

G. Overprint on Stamps of Cape of Good Hope for GRIQUALAND WEST.

G et D (or **G & D**) *Guadeloupe and Dependencies.*

GAB. Overprint on French Colonial Stamps for the first issue of GABON.

G.E.A. *German East Africa.* Overprint on Kenya and Uganda stamps for use during British Occupation of TANGANYIKA.

Gen.-Gouv. Warschau. (*General Government Warsaw*). Overprint on stamps of Germany for GERMAN OCCUPATION OF POLAND.

General Gouvernement. POLAND under Nazi Occupation.

Georgie (La) or **Republique Georgienne.** GEORGIA. (1919–21) The country is now part of the U.S.S.R.

Gerusalemme. Overprint on Italian stamps for ITALIAN P.O.S IN THE LEVANT—Jerusalem.

G.F.B. (*Gaue Faka Buleaga*). On Government Service. Official stamps of TONGA

Giornali Franco Bollo Stampe. Stamps for printed matter from ITALY (1862) and SARDINIA (1861).

G.K.C.A. Surcharge on newspaper stamps of YUGOSLAVIA for the Carinthian Plebiscite (1920).

Golfo de Guinea. Overprint on stamps of Spain for SPANISH GUINEA.

Govt. Parcels. Overprint on British stamps for official use (1883–1902).

G.P.E. Overprint on French Colonies stamps for GAUDELOUPE.

Granadina, Confed. Early issues of COLOMBIA when the country was the Granadine Confederation.

Grand Liban. LEBANON 1924–26 when known as Greater Lebanon.

Grande Comore. GREAT COMORO.

Grenville. Registration stamp of LIBERIA 1893.

G.R.I. Overprint on Stamps of German New Guinea and Marshall Islands during Australian occupation of NEW GUINEA and on German Colonial issue for SAMOA under New Zealand administration 1914.

Grønland. GREENLAND.

Grossdeutsches Reich. GERMANY. Inscription adopted by Nazi State 1943–45. Stamps additionally inscribed **General Gouvernement** are from POLAND under Nazi Occupation; or additionally **Böhmen und Mähren** from BOHEMIA AND MORAVIA.

Guine. PORTUGUESE GUINEA. The words **Portuguesa** or **Portugueza** often appeared in conjunction.

Guinea (or **Guinea Contial) Española.** SPANISH GUINEA.

Guinea Ecuatorial, República de. EQUATORIAL GUINEA.

Guinée. Found on the stamps of FRENCH GUINEA. When the country became independent in 1958 the inscription became RÉPUBLIQUE DE GUINÉE and the stamps are listed under GUINEA.

Guinée Française. FRENCH GUINEA.

Gultig 9. Armee. Overprint on German stamps. Ninth Army Post during GERMAN OCCUPATION OF RUMANIA.

Guy. Franç. *Guyane Française.* Overprint on French Colonies stamps for FRENCH GUIANA.

Guyane Française. FRENCH GUIANA.

G.W. Overprint on stamps of Cape of Good Hope for GRIQUALAND-WEST.

H

Hadhramaut. One of the ADEN PROTECTORATE STATES.

Harper. Registration stamp of LIBERIA (1893).

Haut (or **Ht.**) **Sénégal-Niger.** UPPER SENEGAL AND NIGER.

Haute Silésie. UPPER SILESIA.

Haute-Volta. UPPER VOLTA.

H.E.H. The Nizam's Government. HYDERABAD.

Hejaz & Nejd (or **Hedjaz & Nedjde**). SAUDI ARABIA.

Helvetia. SWITZERLAND. If with additional inscriptions as Bureau International du Travail, Union Postale Universelle, etc., these are stamps of the UNITED NATIONS—GENEVA HEADQUARTERS.

Herzogth. (or **Herzogthum**) **Holstein.** SCHLESWIG-HOLSTEIN. Herzogthum means Duchy.

Herzogth. Schleswig. SCHLESWIG-HOLSTEIN.

H.H. Nawab Shah Jahan Begam. Early stamps of BHOPAL.

H.I. Postage. HAWAII. Abbreviation for Hawaiian Islands.

Holkar State. INDORE.

Hrvatska. CROATIA.

Hrvatska SHS. Overprint on Hungarian stamps for YUGOSLAVIA—Issues for Croatia. (1918).

I

I.E.F. Overprint on stamps of India for INDIAN EXPEDITIONARY FORCES. (1914).

I.E.F. 'D'. Overprint on Turkish fiscal stamps for MOSUL.

Ile de la Réunion. REUNION.

Ile Rouad. Overprint on French Group keytypes for ROUAD ISLAND.

Iles Wallis et Futuna. WALLIS AND FUTUNA ISLANDS.

Imperial British East Africa Company. BRITISH EAST AFRICA.

Imperio Colonial Portugues. PORTUGUESE COLONIES Postage Dues.

Impuesto (or **Impto.**) **de Guerra.** War Tax stamps of SPAIN.

India Inscription on Portuguese Group keytype stamps used in PORTUGUESE INDIA.

India Portuguesa (or **Port.** or **Portugueza**). PORTUGUESE INDIA.

Indo-Chine. INDO-CHINA.

Instrução D.L. no. 7 de 3-2-1934. Overprint on Portuguese Colonies fiscal stamps for Educational Tax issues for TIMOR (1934–35).

Instruccion. VENEZUELA. Fiscal stamps, intended to collect a tax for schools; also valid postally.

I.R. Official. (*Inland Revenue.*) Overprint on British stamps (1882–1902).

Irian Barat. WEST IRIAN. Name given to West New Guinea after its transfer to Indonesian rule in 1963.

Island. ICELAND.

Islas Galapagos. GALAPAGOS ISLANDS.

Isole Italiani dell' Egeo. Overprint on Italian stamps for the AEGEAN ISLANDS.

Isole Jonie. Overprint on Italian stamps during occupation of IONIAN ISLANDS.

Istra. Surcharges on Italian stamps. VENEZIA GIULIA AND ISTRIA—Yugolsav Occupation. The same word was included in later definitive stamps when the area was under Yugoslav Military Government.

Itä-Karjala Sot.hallinto. Overprint on Finnish stamps for use in FINNISH OCCUPATION OF EASTERN KARELIA.

Italia or **Poste Italiane.** ITALY.

J

Jam. Dim. Soomaaliya (or **Jum. Dim. Somaliya**). Stamps of SOMALIA since 1970 when the country was renamed Somali Democratic Republic.

Janina. Surcharge on Italian stamps for ITALIAN P.O.S IN THE LEVANT. They were for Janina, the present-day Ioannina in Greece.

Jeend (or **Jind** or **Jhind**) **State.** Overprint on Indian stamps for JIND.

Jubilé de l'Union Postale Universelle. SWITZERLAND commemoratives of 1900.

Jugoslavija. YUGOSLAVIA.

K

Kalayaan nang Pilipinas. JAPANESE OCCUPATION OF PHILIPPINE ISLANDS.

Kamerun. Overprint on stamps of Germany for use in the German Protectorate, listed under CAMEROUN.

Karki. Overprint on Italian stamps for Khalki, AEGEAN ISLANDS.

Karnten Abstimmung. Overprint on Stamps of AUSTRIA for the Corinthian Plebiscite.

Karolinen. CAROLINE ISLANDS.

Keneta. Stamps of HAWAII including such inscriptions as Elua Keneta or Akahi Keneta.

Kenttäpostia Fältpost. Military Field Post of FINLAND.

Kenya Uganda Tanzania or **Kenya Uganda Tanganyika Zanzibar.** The Postal Administration of EAST AFRICA issues stamps inscribed with these combined country names.

Kgl. Post. Frm. (*Kongeligt Post Frimaerke* = Royal Post, Postage Stamp). Found on 1864 issue of DENMARK.

Kibris Türk Yönetimi or **Kibris Turk Federe Devleti Postalari.** Turkish Cypriot Posts, listed under CYPRUS.

K.K. Post-Stempel. (*Kaiserlich und Königlich* = Imperial and Royal.) (1) With denominations in kreuzer, the first issue of AUSTRIA. (2) The same design but in centes was from LOMBARDY AND VENETIA, formerly known as Austrian Italy.

Klaipeda. Inscription or surcharges for MEMEL—Lithuanian Occupation.

Korea or **Republic of Korea**. SOUTH KOREA.

Kraljevstvo Srba, Hrvata i Slovenaca. (1) Overprint or surcharge on Bosnian stamps 1919 for YUGOSLAVIA—Issues for Bosnia and Herzegovina. (2) The inscription (or first word changed to **Kraljevina**) was used also for Kingdom of the Serbs, Croats and Slovenes, the early issues of YUGOSLAVIA proper.

K.S.A. Kingdom of Saudi Arabia.

K.u.K. Feldpost. AUSTRO-HUNGARIAN MILITARY POST.

K.u.K. Milit. Verwaltung Montenegro. Overprint on stamps inscribed **K.u.K. Feldpost** were produced in 1917 for the AUSTRO-HUNGARIAN MILITARY POST—Issues for Montenegro.

K.u.K. Militärpost. Austro-Hungarian Military Post in BOSNIA AND HERZEGOVINA.

L

L. Marques. Overprint on Mozambique stamps for LOURENCO MARQUES.

La Canea. Overprint on Italian stamps for ITALIAN P.O.S IN CRETE.

Land-Post Porto-Marke. BADEN Postage Due stamps.

Lansa Sobreporte. COLOMBIA—Private Air Companies.

L.A.R. Stamps of LIBYA from 1969 after the country became the Libyan Arab Republic.

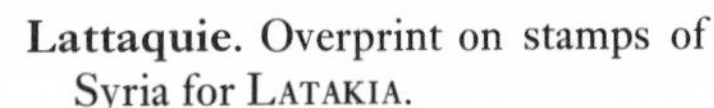

Lattaquie. Overprint on stamps of Syria for LATAKIA.

Latvija or **Latwija**. LATVIA. Some inscribed **Latwijas Pasts.**

Latvija 1941. 1. VII. Overprint on Russian stamps for GERMAN OCCUPATION OF LATVIA.

Latvijas PSR. Stamps of LATVIA were thus inscribed after absorption into the U.S.S.R. in 1940.

Lero or **Leros**. Overprint on Italian stamps for Leros, AEGEAN ISLANDS.

Levant. (1) Overprint on British stamps for post offices in the Middle East (2) Overprint on Polish stamps for the POLISH P.O. IN TURKEY.

Levante. Surcharge with para and piastra on Italian Express Letter stamps for ITALIAN P.O.S IN THE LEVANT.

Liban or **République Libanaise.** LEBANON.

Lietuva or **Lietuvos pastas.** LITHUANIA.

Lignes Aeriennes F.A.F.L. Surcharge on Syrian stamps for Free France Forces in FRENCH LEVANT.

Lima. Some early issues of PERU.

Lipso or **Lisso**. Overprint on Italian stamps for Lipsoi, AEGEAN ISLANDS.

Litwa Srodkowa. CENTRAL LITHUANIA.

Lösen. Postage Due stamps of SWEDEN.

Lothringen. Overprint on stamps of Germany for GERMAN OCCUPATION OF LORRAINE.

Lubiana, R. Commissariato Civile Territori Sloveni Occupati. Overprint on Yugoslav stamps in 1941 for Italian Occupation of SLOVENIA.

M

Macau or **Macav**. MACAO.

Mafia, G.R. Post. Overprint on Indian Expeditionary Forces stamps for British Occupation of TANGANYIKA.

Magyar Posta or **Magyar Kir. Posta**. HUNGARY.

Magyarorszag. HUNGARY.

Mahra State. One of the ADEN PROTECTORATE STATES.

Malagache, République. MALAGASY REPUBLIC, the former Madagascar.

Malagasy, Repoblika. MALAGASY REPUBLIC.

Malmédy. Overprint on stamps of Belgium for BELGIAN OCCUPATION OF GERMANY.

Marianen. Overprint on German stamps for MARIANA ISLANDS.

Maroc. (1) FRENCH MOROCCO. (2) For a few years after independence the same inscription was used for MOROCCO (SOUTHERN ZONE) before the change to **Royaume du Maroc**, Kindom of Morocco.

Marocco or **Marokko**. Overprint on stamps of Germany for GERMAN P.O.S IN MOROCCO.

Marruecos. (1) SPANISH MOROCCO, both for Spanish P.O.s there and when a Spanish Protectorate. Longer inscriptions were sometimes used. (2) During 1956–57 **Marruecos** signified MOROCCO—NORTHERN ZONE. (3) Spanish stamps overprinted **Correo Español Marruecos** were for Spanish P.O.s and Tangier P.O.s of SPANISH MOROCCO.

Marschall (or **Marshall**) **Inseln**. MARSHALL ISLANDS.

Mauritanie. MAURITANIA.

Mecklenb. Schwerin. MECKLENBURG-SCHWERIN.

Mecklenb. Strelitz. MECKLENBURG-STRELITZ.

Medellin. The 1888 issue of the Colombian Department of ANTIOQUIA was thus inscribed, after the chief town.

M.E.F. MIDDLE EAST FORCES. Overprint on British stamps for use in former Italian Colonies occupied by British Forces.

Mejico, Correos. MEXICO.

Melaka Malaysia. MALACCA.

Memelgebiet. Overprint on stamps of Germany for MEMEL.

Memento Avdere Semper. Overprint on Yugoslav stamps for FIUME AND KUPA ZONE.

Militärpost Eilmarke. BOSNIA AND HERZEGOVINA Newspaper Stamps.

Militärpost Portomarke. BOSNIA AND HERZEGOVINA Postage Due stamps.

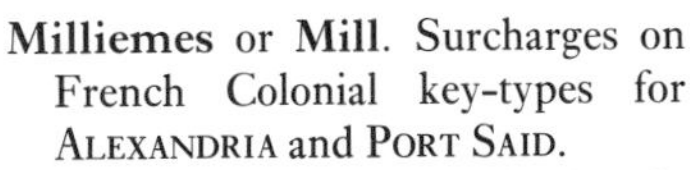

Milliemes or **Mill**. Surcharges on French Colonial key-types for ALEXANDRIA and PORT SAID.

Moçambique and **Provincia de Moçambique**. MOZAMBIQUE.

Monrovia. Registration stamp of LIBERIA 1893.

Montevideo. URUGUAY 1858–59. Also used on an air stamp of 1925.

Moyen Congo. MIDDLE CONGO.

MQE Surcharge on French Colonial stamps for MARTINIQUE.

M.V.i.R., (*Militärverwaltung in Rumänien* = Military Administration in Rumania.) Surcharge on stamps of Germany for GERMAN OCCUPATION OF RUMANIA.

N

Napoletana, Bollo della Posta. NAPLES.

Nationaler Verwaltungsausschuss 10.XI.1943. Overprint on Italian Occupation stamps for MONTENEGRO—GERMAN OCCUPATION.

Nations Unies Office Européen or **Nations Unies Helvetia.** UNITED NATIONS—GENEVA HEADQUARTERS.

N.C.E. Surcharge on French Group stamps for NEW CALEDONIA.

Nederland. NETHERLANDS.

Nederlands (or **Ned.**) **Nieuw-Guinea.** NETHERLANDS NEW GUINEA.

Nederlandsch (or **Ned.** or **Nederl.**) **Indië.** NETHERLANDS INDIES.

Nederlandse (or **Ned.**) **Antillen.** NETHERLANDS ANTILLES.

Nepriklausoma Lietuva 1941-VI-23. Overprint on Russian stamps for GERMAN OCCUPATION OF LITHUANIA.

Nezavisna Drzava (or **N.D.**) **Hrvatska.** CROATIA. Inscription of overprint on Yugoslav stamps.

N.F. Overprint on Nyasaland stamps for Nyasa-Rhodesian Force during British Occupation of TANGANYIKA.

Nieuwe Republiek. NEW REPUBLIC.

Nippon. JAPAN.

Nisiro or **Nisiros.** Overprint on Italian stamps for Nisiros, AEGEAN ISLANDS.

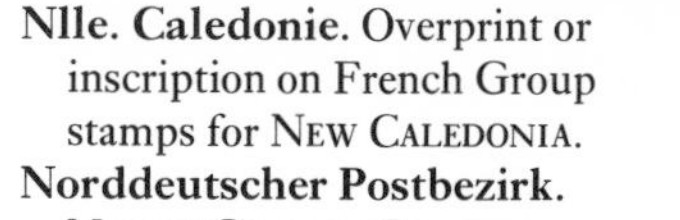

Nlle. Caledonie. Overprint or inscription on French Group stamps for NEW CALEDONIA.

Norddeutscher Postbezirk. NORTH GERMAN CONFEDERATION.

Noreg. NORWAY.

Norge. NORWAY.

Nouvelles Hebrides. NEW HEBRIDES.

NP. (*Naye paise*) Surcharge on British stamps for BRITISH POSTAL AGENCIES IN EASTERN ARABIA.

N. Sembilan. NEGRI SEMBILAN. From 1965 the inscription has read **Negeri Sembilan.**

NSB. Surcharge on French Colonies stamps for NOSSI-BÉ.

N.S.W. NEW SOUTH WALES.

Nueva Granada, Estados Unidos de. Inscription on 1861 issue of COLOMBIA when the country was the United States of New Granada.

N.W. Pacific Islands. Overprint on Australian stamps for NEW GUINEA.

N.Z. Inscription on NEW ZEALAND Postage Dues of 1899.

N.Z. Government Life Insurance Department (or **Office**). Official stamps for NEW ZEALAND government department.

O

Océanie. OCEANIC SETTLEMENTS.

Occupation Française. Overprint on stamps of Hungary for FRENCH OCCUPATION OF HUNGARY.

Occupation Militaire Française Cilicie. Surcharge on Turkish fiscal stamp or **O.M.F. Cilicie** on French stamps for the French Occupation of CILICIA.

Oesterreich. An alternative spelling for Österreich, AUSTRIA.

Oeuvres de Solidarité Française RF. FRENCH COLONIES 1943.

O.F. Castelloriso. (*Occupation Française*). Overprint on French stamps for Occupation of CASTELROSSO.

Offentlig Sak. Official stamps of NORWAY.

Oil Rivers. Overprint on British stamps for Oil Rivers Protectorate, known from 1893 as NIGER COAST PROTECTORATE.

Oltre Giuba. Overprint on Italian stamps or as inscription for JUBALAND.

O.M.F. Syrie. (*Occupation Militore Française*). With surcharge in milliemes, centimes or piastres on French stamps for French Military Occupation of SYRIA.

O.N.F. Castellorizo. (*Occupation Navale Française*). Overprint on stamps of France and French Levant for Occupation of CASTELROSSO.

Orange River Colony. Overprint on Cape of Good Hope stamps, or as an inscription for the former ORANGE FREE STATE. (1900–10).

Oranje Vrij Staat. ORANGE FREE STATE.

Organisation Internationale pour les Réfugiés. International Refugees Organization, listed under UNITED NATIONS.

Organisation Météorologique Mondiale. World Meteorological Organization, listed under UNITED NATIONS.

Organisation Mondiale de la Santé. World Health Organization, listed under UNITED NATIONS.

Orts-Post. SWITZERLAND 1850.

O.S. or **Off. Sak.** or **Offentlig Sak.** Official stamps of NORWAY.

Österreich. AUSTRIA. Some earlier stamps used a longer version: **Kaiserliche Königliche Österreichische Post.**

Ostland. Overprint on German stamps for GERMAN OCCUPATION OF RUSSIA. Ostland comprised the former Baltic States and White Russia.

Ottomanes, Postes. TURKEY 1914.

Oubangui-Chari or **Oubangui-Chari-Tchad.** UBANGI-SHARI.

O.W. Official. (*Office of Works*). Overprint on British stamps (1896–1902).

P

P (in an oval, with crescent and star). Overprint on Straits Settlements for PERAK 1878.

Pacchi Postali. (1) Parcel Post stamps of ITALY. (2) The design of these stamps is in two halves. The words **R. S. Marino** printed vertically between the halves signify Parcel Post stamps from SAN MARINO. (3) The presence of Arabic inscriptions on the halves signifies Parcel Post stamps for SOMALIA.

Packhoi. Surcharge on Indo-Chinese stamps for PAKHOI.

Pakke-Porto. GREENLAND Parcel Post stamps.

Palestine. (1) Overprint on E.E.F. stamps in three lines (with Arabic and Hebrew) for PALESTINE during period of Civil Administration under the British High Commissioner (1920–22). (2) Overprint in English and Arabic on Egypt and U.A.R. stamps for EGYPTIAN OCCUPATION OF PALESTINE (GAZA).

Para(s). British stamps surcharged in this currency were for BRITISH LEVANT. Similar surcharges on Austrian stamps were for AUSTRIAN P.O.S IN TURKEY; on French stamps for FRENCH LEVANT; on German stamps for GERMAN P.O.S IN TURKEY; on Italian stamps for ITALIAN P.O.S IN THE LEVANT; on Rumanian stamps for RUMANIAN P.O.S ABROAD; and on Russian stamps for RUSSIAN P.O.S IN TURKEY.

Parlamento a Cervantes, El. Official stamps of SPAIN.

Patmo or **Patmos.** Overprint on Italian stamps for Patmos, AEGEAN ISLANDS.

Pechino. Overprint on Italian stamps for Peking, ITALIAN P.O.S IN CHINA.

Pentru Cultura. Postal Tax stamps of RUMANIA 1932–34.

Persanes, Postes. IRAN. Before 1935 the country was called Persia.

Persekutuan Tanah Melayu. MALAYAN FEDERATION.

Pesa. Surcharge on German stamps for German East Africa, listed under TANGANYIKA.

Peseta(s). Surcharge on French 'Peace and Commerce' types stamps for use in FRENCH P.O.S IN MOROCCO.

P.G.S. (*Perak Government Service*). Overprint on Straits Settlements stamps for PERAK.

Piaster. (1) Austrian stamps surcharged in this currency were for AUSTRIAN P.O.S IN TURKEY. (2) German stamps similarly surcharged were for GERMAN P.O.S IN TURKEY.

Piastra. An 1893 25c of Italy surcharged 1 Piastra 1 was for ITALIAN P.O.S IN CRETE.

Piastre(s). (1) British stamps surcharged in this currency were for BRITISH LEVANT. (2) Similarly, French stamps for FRENCH LEVANT. (3) ITALIAN P.O.S IN THE LEVANT had surcharges Piastra (singular) or Piastre (plural). (4)

Surcharges on Russian stamps were for Russian P.O.s in Turkey.

Pilgrim Tercentenary. United States commemorative set of 1920.

Pilipinas. Philippine Islands. A similar inscription, **Republika ng Pilipinas**, was used during Japanese Occupation of Philippine Islands.

Piscopi. Overprint on Italian stamps for Tilos (Piskopi), Aegean Islands.

Plébiscite Olsztyn Allenstein. Overprint on German stamps during plebiscite in Allenstein.

Poczta Polska. Poland.

Pohjois Inkeri. North Ingermanland.

Polska. Poland.

Port Gdansk. Stamps of Poland overprint on for Polish Post in Danzig.

Porte Franco. Peru early issues.

Porteado Correio. Postage Due stamps of Portugal.

Porto Gazetei or **Porto Scrisorei.** Early issues of Rumania.

Porto Rico. Overprint on U.S. stamps for Puerto Rico during Military Occupation.

Portzegel. Surcharge for Netherlands Postage Due.

Post & Receipt. On stamps denominated in annas from Hyderabad.

Post Stamp. On stamps denominated in annas from Hyderabad.

Posta 15 or **Posta 35.** Surcharge on fiscal stamps from Tuva.

Postage Due. Stamps denominated in £.s.d. from Great Britain and from Australia.

Postal 1 Avo. Surcharged on fiscal stamp of Macao (1911).

Postat e Qeverriës së Përkohëshme të Shqipeniës. Albania 1913.

Poste Khedivie Egiziane. Some issues of Egypt in the last century when the country was ruled by a Khedive.

Poste-Locale. Switzerland 1850.

Postgebiet Ob. Ost. (*Oberbefehlshaber Ost.* = Commander-in-Chief East.) Overprint on stamps of Germany for the German Command covering the Russian Baltic Provinces in World War I.

Postzegel. On stamps without country name from Netherlands.

Preussen. Prussia.

Pro Juventute. Annual Children's Fund stamps of Switzerland.

Pro Plebiscito Tacna y Arica. Obligatory tax stamps of Peru. (1925–28).

Protectorado Español en Marruecos. Spanish Morocco.

Protectorat Français. Overprint on French key-type stamps for French Morocco.

Provincie Modonesi. Modena.

Provinz Laibach/Ljubljanska Pokrajina. Inscription or overprint on Italian stamps for German Occupation of SLOVENIA.

Pto. Rico. Abbreviation for PUERTO RICO when a Spanish Colony.

Pulau Pinang Malaysia. PENANG.

Puolustusvoimat Kenttäpostia. Military Field Post of FINLAND.

Puttialla State. Overprint on Indian stamps for PATIALA.

R

R(and value in figures) Surcharge on French Colonial stamps for REUNION.

Rarotonga. Surcharge on New Zealand stamps for COOK ISLANDS.

Rayon. Early stamps of SWITZERLAND.

Recargo or **Recargo Transitorio de Guerra.** War Tax stamps of SPAIN.

Regatul Romaniei (and values in bani, leu or lei.) Overprint on Hungarian stamps in 1919 for RUMANIA–Transylvania.

Regno d'Italia Trentinio 3 nov 1918. Overprint on Austrian stamps for ITALIAN AUSTRIA.

Regno d'Italia Venezia Giulia 3.XI.18. Overprint on Austrian stamps for ITALIAN AUSTRIA.

Reichspost. GERMANY. Issues under the Empire. (1889–1901)

Repub. Franc. (*Republique Française*) Early issues of FRANCE and FRENCH COLONIES.

República Oriental. URUGUAY.

Republique Française. FRANCE.

Retymno. RUSSIAN P.O.S IN CRETE – Rethymno Province.

R.F. (*Republique Française*).

R.H. (*Republique d' Haiti*). HAITI Postage Due stamps.

R.H. Official (*Royal Household*) Overprint on British stamps (1902).

Rheinland-Pfalz. GERMANY Allied Occupation, French Zone issues for the Rhineland-Palatinate. (1947–49).

Rialtar Sealadac na Héireann 1922. (=*Provisional Government of Ireland*) Overprint on British stamps for IRELAND (REPUBLIC).

Robertsport. Registration stamp of LIBERIA (1893).

Rodi. Inscription or overprint on Italian stamps for Rhodes, AEGEAN ISLANDS.

Romagne, Franco Bollo Postale. ROMAGNA.

Romana or **Romina.** RUMANIA.

Roumelie Orientale or **R.O.** Inscription or overprint on stamps of Turkey for EASTERN ROUMELIA.

Royaume de l'Arabie Soudite (or Saoudite). SAUDI ARABIA.

RSA. Abbreviation used since 1967 for Republic of SOUTH AFRICA.

R.S.M. Abbreviation for Repubblica di SAN MARINO.

Rumänien (and value in 'bani') on German stamps. GERMAN OCCUPATION OF RUMANIA.

Rupee(s). British stamps surcharged in this Indian currency were for BRITISH POSTAL AGENCIES IN EASTERN ARABIA.

Russisch-Polen. Overprint on stamps of Germany for GERMAN OCCUPATION OF POLAND.

S

S. Overprint on Straits Settlements Stamp for SELANGOR. (1882).

S. Marino, Repubblica (or **Rep.**) **di.** SAN MARINO.

S. Thomé e Principe. ST. THOMAS AND PRINCE ISLANDS. **Thomé** was spelled **Tomé** from 1913.

S. Ujong. SUNGEI UJONG.

Saargebeit. SAAR.

Sachsen. SAXONY.

Sahara Español. SPANISH SAHARA.

Sahara Occidental, Posesiones Españolas del. SPANISH SAHARA.

Salonicco. Surcharge on Italian stamps for ITALIAN P.O.S IN THE LEVANT. These were for Salonica, the present-day Thessaloniki in Greece.

Salvador. Inscriptions first read **Correos del Salvador** and then **Correos de el Salvador**. El Salvador.

Samoa i Sisifo. Samoa.

Sandjak d'Alexandrette. Overprint or surcharge on Syrian stamps for territory later renamed the Republic of Hatay.

Saorstát Eireann 1922. (=*Irish Free State*). Overprinted on British stamps for Ireland (Republic).

Sarkari, Overprint on official stamps of Soruth.

Sarre. Overprint on stamps of Germany and Bavaria for Saar while administered by the League of Nations. (1920).

Saurashtra. Soruth.

Scarpanto. Overprint on Italian stamps for Karpathos, Aegean Islands.

Scutari di Albania. Surcharge on Italian stamps for Italian P.O.s in the Levant. Scutari is presentday Shkodër.

Segnatasse. Postage Due stamps of Italy.

Seiyun. The Kathiri State of Seiyun was one of the Aden Protectorate States.

Serbien. (1) Overprint on Yugoslav stamps during German Occupation of Serbia. (2) Overprint on Bosnian stamps for Austro-Hungarian Military Post—Isssues for Serbia.

Shanghai China. Surcharge on U.S. stamps for United States Postal Agency in Shanghai.

Shihr and Mukalla. The Qu'aiti State of Shihr and Mukalla was one of the Aden Protectorate States. From 1955 inscriptions changed to Qu'aiti State in Hadhramaut.

Shqiperia. Modern stamps of Albania. Alternatives are **Shqipenia, Shqiptare, Shqipenië, Shqyptare, Shqipni, Shqipnija, R(epublika) P(opullore) e Shqiperise**.

S.H.S. (*Srba, Hrvata, Slovena,* = Serbs, Croats, Slovenes). Early issues of Yugoslavia.

Siam. Thailand bore this name before 1939 and during 1945–49.

Sicilia, Bollo della Posta. Sicily.

Simi. Overprint on Italian stamps for this Aegean Island.

Slesvig. The Plebiscite issues of Schleswig.

Slovenija Jugoslavija. Overprint on German, Hungarian and 'Provinz Laibach' stamps for Slovenian Regional Issues of Yugoslavia Democratic Federal Republic. (1945).

Slovensko (or **Slovenska Posta**). Slovakia.

Smirne. Surcharge on Italian stamps for Italian P.O.s in the Levant. There were for Smyrna, the present-day Izmir in Turkey.

S.O. 1920. Overprint on Czech and Polish stamps for East Silesia (Silésie Orientale).

Sobreporte. Special fee stamp of Colombia (1865).

Sociéte des Nations. Overprint on Swiss stamps for the League of Nations and listed under United Nations.

Solidarité Française Entr'aide de l'Aviation. French Colonies 1944.

Soomaaliya (or **Somaliya**). Modern stamps of Somalia.

Soudan (and Arabic characters). Overprint on Egyptian stamps for first issue of Sudan.

Soudan Français. French Sudan.

Sowjetische Besatzungs Zone. Overprint for Germany Allied Occupation, Russian Zone.

SPM or **St-Pierre M-on.** Surcharge on French Colonies stamps for St. Pierre et Miquelon.

Srodkowa Litwa. CENTRAL LITHUANIA.

Stampalia. Overprint on Italian stamps for Astipalaia, AEGEAN ISLANDS.

Stati Parmensi (or **Stati Parm.**). PARMA.

S.T. Trsta Vuja. TRIESTE Yugoslav Military Government.

STT Vuja (or **Vujna**). TRIESTE. Overprint on Yugoslav stamps for Zone B—Yugoslav Military Government. (1949–54).

SU (in an oval with crescent and star). Overprint on Straits Settlements stamps for SUNGEI UJONG. (1878).

Sud Kasai, Etat Autonome du. SOUTH KASAI.

Suidafrika (and **Republiek van Suid-Afrika**). SOUTH AFRICA.

Suidwes-Afrika. SOUTH WEST AFRICA.

Sverige. SWEDEN.

S.W.A. Overprint on South African stamps for SOUTH WEST AFRICA. Also as abbreviated inscription on stamps of that territory since 1968.

Syrian Arab Republic. SYRIA since 1961.

Syrie or **République Syrienne.** SYRIA.

Syrie Grand Liban (and surcharges in centiemes or piastres) on French stamps for SYRIA (1923). The stamps were valid in both Syria and Lebanon.

T

Tanger. (1) Overprint on stamps of France and French Morocco for FRENCH P.O.S IN TANGIER. (2) Similarly on stamps of Spain (including **Correo Español Tanger, Via Aérea Tanger, Correo Aéreo Tánger)** and as inscription for SPANISH MOROCCO—TANGIER.

Tangier. Overprint on British stamps for MOROCCO AGENCIES—Tangier International Zone.

Tassa Gazzette. Newspaper Tax stamp of MODENA (1959).

Taxa de Guerra. War tax surcharge found on fiscal stamps. From MACAO if denominated in 'avos'; from PORTUGUESE GUINEA in 'reis'; from PORTUGUESE INDIA in 'Rps.'; from PORTUGUESE COLONIES in '$'.

Taxa Porto Pentru Cultura. Postal Tax Postage Due stamp of RUMANIA 1932.

Tchad. CHAD.

Te Betalen Port. Postage Due stamps of NETHERLANDS, CURACAO, SURINAM.

T.E.O. (*Territoires Ennemis Occupés.*) (1) With surcharges in milliemes or piastres on French stamps for French Military Occupation of SYRIA. (2) In paras on French Levant stamps for CILICIA.

T.E.O. Cilicie. Overprint on Turkish stamps for French Occupation of CILICIA.

Terres Australes et Antarctiques Françaises. FRENCH SOUTHERN AND ANTARCTIC TERRITORIES.

Territoire Français des Afars et des Issas. French Territory of the Afars and the Issas, the former French Somali Coast renamed in 1967 after the principal tribes living there.

Territorios Españoles del Golfo de Guinea. Inscription or overprint on stamps of Spain for Spanish Guinea.

Tetuan. Handstamps on Spanish stamps for Spanish Morocco—Spanish P.O.s in Morocco.

Thirty Two Cents (and picture of a sailing ship). Liberia (1886).

Tientsin. Overprint on Italian stamps for that city. Listed under Italian P.O.s in China.

Tjeneste Frimærke. Official stamps of Denmark.

Tjenestefrimerke. Official stamps of Norway.

To Pay. Postage due stamps in decimal currency from Great Britain.

Toga. Tonga.

Togolaise, République. Inscription on stamps of Togo since 1962.

Toscano, Francobollo Postale. Tuscany.

Touva. Tuva.

Traité de Versailles etc. (in an oval). Overprint on German stamps for a plebiscite in Allenstein.

Transjordan. Name of the Hashemite Kingdom of the Jordan before 1949, stamps are listed under that name.

Trieste Trst (with date I.V.1945). Surcharge on Italian stamps. Venezia Giulia and Istria—Yugoslav Occupation.

Tripoli di Barberia. Overprinted on Italian stamps for Italian P.O.s in the Levant—Offices in Africa. This Tripoli is in Libya, distinguished by 'di Barberia' from Tripoli in the Lebanon.

Tripoli, Fiera Campionaria. (1) Tripolitania. Issues for Trade Fairs 1927–35. (2) Stamps for 1937–39 are listed under Libya.

TTTT (in four corners of stamps with large numeral). Postage due stamps of Dominican Republic.

Tunisie or **République Tunisienne.** Tunisia.

Türkiye (or **Turk**) **Postalari.** Turkey.

Türkiye Cumhuriyeti (or **T.C.**) **Postalari.** Turkey.

Two Pence (as denomination). Stamp showing Queen Victoria on throne. Victoria (1852).

U

U.A.E. United Arab Emirates.

U.A.R. (*United Arab Republic*). The U.A.R. was formed when Egypt and Syria united in 1958. Stamps of EGYPT were inscribed thus between 1958 and 1971 even though Syria had withdrawn in 1961. Stamps of SYRIA were inscribed **U.A.R.** or **République Arabe Unie** between 1958 and 1961.

UG. The famous typewritten stamps prepared by a Missionary for UGANDA (1895).

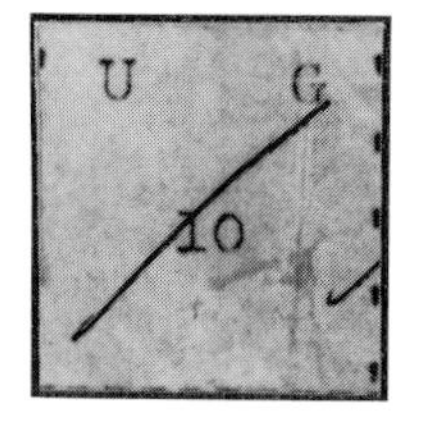

Ukraine. Overprint on German stamps for GERMAN OCCUPATION OF RUSSIA. Ukraine was one administrative area, Ostland the other.

Ultramar (on stamps with year dates). CUBA, also PUERTO RICO. The word means 'Beyond the seas' and appears also on fiscal stamps of MACAO and PORTUGUESE GUINEA.

U.N. Force (India) Congo. Overprint on stamps of India for INDIAN U.N. FORCE IN CONGO (1962).

UNEF. Overprint on Indian stamp for INDIAN U.N. FORCE IN GAZA (PALESTINE) (1965).

Union Internationale des Télécommunications. International Telecommunications Union, listed under UNITED NATIONS.

Union Postale Universelle. Universal Postal Union, listed under UNITED NATIONS.

UNTEA. (*United Nations Temporary Executive Authority*). Overprint on stamps of Netherlands New Guinea for WEST NEW GUINEA during U.N. Administration (1962–63).

U.S. UNITED STATES OF AMERICA.

V

Vallées d'Andorre. ANDORRA – French Post Offices.

Valona. Surcharge on Italian stamps for ITALIAN P.O.s IN THE LEVANT. Valona is present-day Vlonë in Albania.

Van Dieman's Land. TASMANIA first issues.

Vancouver Island. BRITISH COLUMBIA AND VANCOUVER ISLAND.

Vaticane, Poste. VATICAN CITY.

Venezia Giulia. Overprint on Italian stamps for ITALIAN AUSTRIA.

Venezia Tridentina. Overprint on Italian stamps for ITALIAN AUSTRIA.

Vilnius. Overprint on Russian stamps for GERMAN OCCUPATION OF LITHUANIA.

Vojna Uprava Jugoslavenske Armije. Surcharge on Yugoslav stamps for VENEZIA GIULIA AND ISTRIA – Yugoslav Military Government.

Vom Empfänger Einzuziehen. Inscribed on designs incorporating a crown above two crosses: DANZIG Postage Dues.

Vom Empfänger Zahlbar. Inscribed on design with large numeral. BAVARIA Postage Dues.

V.R.I. (and values in British currency). Overprinted for British Occupation of ORANGE FREE STATE.

W

Wendenschen Kreises. WENDEN.

Western Samoa. SAMOA.

Württemberg. (1) Issues when an independent kingdom are listed under WURTTEMBERG. (2) Issues 1947–49 from Allied Occupation, French Zone, appear under GERMANY.

Y

Y.A.R. YEMEN Arab Republic.

Yunnansen or **Yunnanfou.** YUNNANFU. Stamps used at the Indo-Chinese P.O. at Yunnansen. It was renamed Yunnanfu in 1906.

Z

Zanzibar. Surcharges on French stamps for FRENCH P.O.S IN ZANZIBAR.
Zona de Ocupatie Romana (in oval). Overprint on Hungarian stamps for RUMANIAN OCCUPATION OF HUNGARY – Debrecen.
Zona Occupata Fiumano Kupa. Overprint on Yugoslav stamps for FIUME AND KUPA ZONE.
Zona Protectorado Español or **Zona de Protectorado Español en Marruecos.** SPANISH MOROCCO.
Zone Française. GERMANY Allied Occupation, General Issue in the French Zone (1945–46).
Zuid Afrikaansche (or **Z. Afr.**) **Republiek.** TRANSVAAL.
Zuidwest Africa. SOUTH WEST AFRICA.

CHAPTER SEVENTEEN
Arranging the Collection

It is the easiest thing in the world to collect stamps, but judging by what one sees, it must be the hardest of tasks to keep a collection properly mounted and arranged. Many collections, quite important so far as their extent and the value of the stamps they contain are concerned, are kept in dilapidated albums, cardboard boxes, old exercise books, etc.

There are three main reasons why a stamp collection should be properly arranged. First, you get a lot of pleasure out of the hobby and it is only fair to treat your stamps decently in return. In the second place you can give people a lot of pleasure by showing them a collection which is arranged with care and method, and can thus add to your own pleasure and possibly make new recruits for the hobby. Thirdly, stamps properly kept are less likely to get damaged or soiled and lose their value, while a neatly classified collection is of more value if you ever wish to sell, not because a dealer will pay anything for pretty writing-up, but because it is easier for him to see what you have got.

The collector who is using the elementary type of printed album, described in Chapter 13, will have no difficulty as regards the placing of his stamps, for there is no specific position for each, and he has only to find the correct page. I have seen young collectors try to arrange their stamps in catalogue order in such an album, changing their places every time a fresh specimen came their way, but this, I think, is not advisable. The continual removals damage the album, and as there are not enough spaces for all the stamps of each country, and the collector does not know which ones he is going to get, any attempt to leave blanks for stamps still to come is doomed to failure.

In all types of printed album, the essentials are to exclude stamps still on paper, to admit no damaged or heavily postmarked specimens, and to see that you get the stamps in level. Lack of attention to the last factor frequently spoils the appearance of a collection, and as printed albums usually have ruled squares or lines, there is no excuse for putting stamps in crooked.

There are three main types of blank album; spring-back, peg-fitting and ring-fitting. In some albums the leaves lie quite flat when the album is open and this is a great advantage when inserting odd stamps or annotations, although when working for any length of time on the collection it is advisable to take the leaves out of the cover and work on a single leaf at a time.

Another point to be noted is the paper of which the leaves are made. A shiny paper looks attractive, but it is not easy to write on, and even the most peelable hinges are apt to mark its surface. The best leaf to select is one with a good writing surface, free from spots and lumps, and of as high a quality as you can afford.

The *quadrille* rulling, which forms the background of your page, and which is to serve as a guide to you in placing your stamps, should not stand out too boldly to the eye, but should be sufficiently visible for you to be able to distinguish each individual line without eyestrain by natural or artificial light.

In any type of album, it is advisable to protect the stamps as far as possible. In the fastbound printed album, there are usually spaces for stamps on every page, and stamps on opposing pages are liable to catch and cause damage, while in albums where the stamps are on one side of the page only, deterioration is caused by the rubbing of the stamps on the paper, which, particularly in the case of those printed on 'chalky' paper, causes the colour to offset on to the opposite page. There are some types of ink used for postmarks which also rub off in this way, with very unsightly results.

The solution to this problem is to interleave the album with thin, unprinted paper.

In spring-back albums the interleaving is best done by inserting sheets of smooth transparent paper, which any stamp dealer can supply. Albums with ring or peg fittings usually have leaves of a more elaborate type, with a sheet of transparent paper already attached to the inner (hinged) edge of the leaf.

Whatever album you decide on, make up your mind to treat it properly. Do not overfill a spring-back album, or the springs will eventually break. Do not use leaves of one type in a binder for which they were not intended. Keep the album in its box, if one is provided by the makers, and do not put a lot of heavy volumes one on top of the other; in fact it is advisable to keep albums standing upright on shelves, if possible.

The importance of using properly gummed hinges for affixing stamps in the album has already been mentioned. A peelable hinge is the cheapest item in the collector's expense account, so there is no excuse for false economy. The use of the hinges in the proper way is also important. It should be noted that hinges are only peelable when the gum is quite dry. If a stamp is mounted, and then found to be in its wrong place on the page, it should be left for an hour or so, before any attempt is made to remove it to its proper position. Detaching a hinge which is still damp is almost sure to damage the album page.

To hinge a stamp properly is a relatively simple task. Hold the hinge with the gummed side downward, and fold back about a third of it with your tweezers, pressing the crease down with your thumb (ready folded hinges are also available). The stamp is then placed face downward on the table with the top edge uppermost, and the turned back (smaller) portion of the hinge is lightly moistened with the tongue, and attached to the stamp within a fraction of an inch of the top edge and midway between the sides. The hinge must be clear of the top perforations or it will show when the stamp is mounted on the page.

You now have your stamp with one-third of the gummed side of your hinge attached to it, and with two-thirds lying free. Pull the free end away from the stamp, so that your tongue will not touch the stamp, and then lightly lick *the lower part* of the free end (*do not lick the free two-thirds all over*). The stamp can then be carefully placed in position on the page, by means of the hinge, and when it is in place it will be found that this method of hinging allows the stamp to be turned right back, for examination of the watermark, etc. without any damage being done to the perforations. This would be impossible if the hinge had not been placed right at the top of the stamp, or if the free part of the hinge had been licked all over. When mounting mint stamps, always lift the stamp after placing to ensure no excess moisture has 'stuck' it to the page.

When mounting pairs or blocks of four it is open to question whether the procedure adopted by some collectors of attaching the hinge to one stamp only, or, in the case of blocks, in the centre and close to the upper edge of the upper pair of stamps, is wise. The object of attaching the hinge to one stamp only is to avoid possible damage to the gum of two stamps. Placing the hinge at the top of a block of four certainly enables the back of the stamps to be examined easily, but in the case of both blocks and pairs the methods described leave the stamps insecurely attached to the page, and when the leaves are turned it too often happens that the stamps turn up or over themselves and can get badly creased, and ruined. Pairs should be mounted with a hinge on one of the two stamps, not with a hinge applied across the dividing perforation. On blocks the smaller portion of the hinge should be attached to the lower portion of the upper stamps, so that the stamps are firmly held.

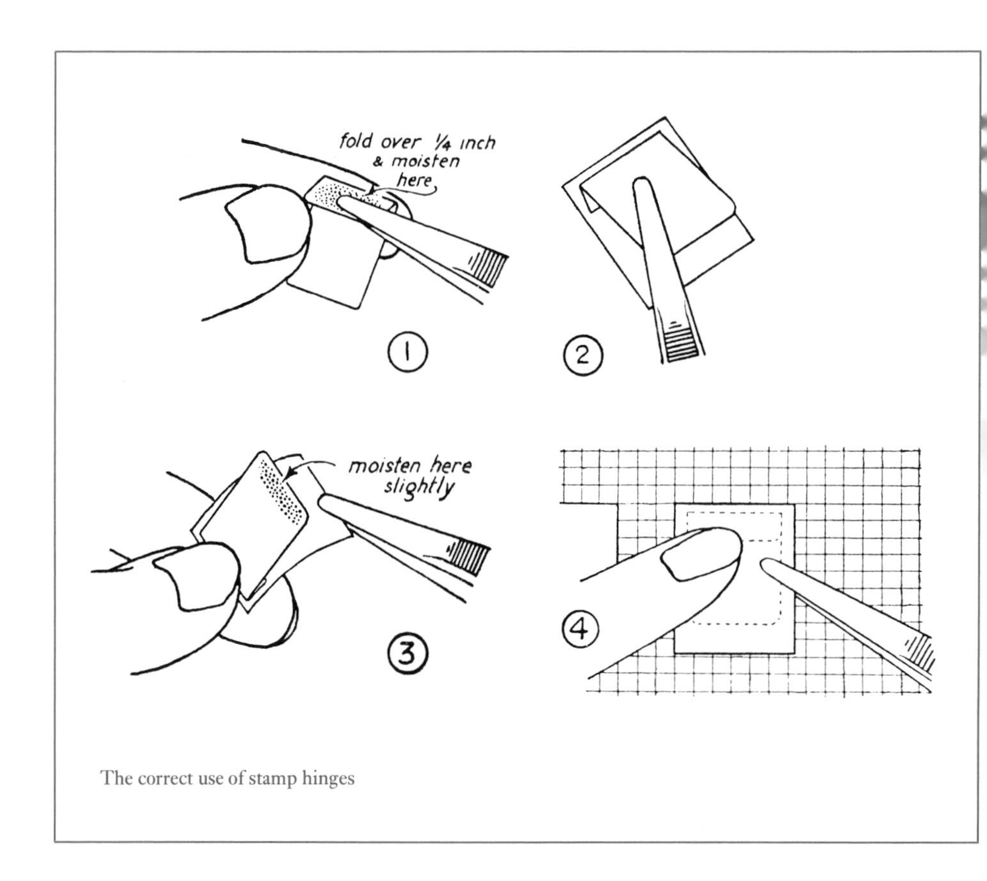

The correct use of stamp hinges

If hinges are not acceptable, *Gibbons Gard* and *Gibbons Hawid* mounts offer a large degree of protection to one's stamps. They are double-sided plastic protective mounts, with a transparent front and a black backing. *Gibbons Hawid* mounts are sealed on one side only, and *Gibbons Gard* mounts are sealed on two opposite sides. The *Gard* mounts therefore hold the stamps more firmly but can be used only if the stamps fit them exactly, whereas the *Hawid* mounts can be trimmed to fit any stamp.

Both *Hawid* and *Gard* mounts have adhesive on the back which is moistened with the tongue to affix the mounts to the album page. With *Gard* mounts, only the top half should be moistened and fixed to the leaf. The bottom half remains free. This half should be lifted and the stamp pushed gently into it as far as it will gö. If the mount is then allowed to flap back into place the stamp will be held securely.

Items which are taller than the deepest strip protective mount available may be mounted using two strips. For example, an item 100 mm deep may be mounted with two 55 mm *Hawid* strips, one at the top and one at the bottom. The two strips are joined at the back with a small offcut of the gummed backing or a piece of gummed paper. The protective mount can then be affixed to the page in the usual way, by moistening the gum along the welded edges. On the front, the two strips will overlap slightly, preventing the item inside from slipping out.

Stamp booklets provide a problem for the collector. They may be displayed 'exploded' on the page, that is, separated into their individual panes and then mounted up separately along with the front and back covers and any advertisement or information pages. But this diminishes their value and if it is wished to retain the booklet intact then photograph corners or a separate booklet album should be used. Modern folded booklets can be flattened out and displayed intact like a large block, using a *Hawid* or *Gard* mount if the booklet cover is not too thick.

Covers or postcards may be added to a collection and mounted with photograph corners, but they are much heavier than stamps alone and may cause the album leaves to come away from the binding, especially in peg-fitting albums, and if a large number are to be displayed it may be better to house them separately in a purpose-built cover or postcard album.

Controversy continues over the place of picture postcards in a philatelic collection. Normally a page from a properly-written up collection will contain only stamps and covers or cards showing the stamps in use – usually with scarce or unusual postal markings. In such cases the obverse (address and message side) of the postcard is shown. Some still argue that the reverse (picture) side has no place on an album page but in the more tolerant present climate of opinion it is becoming acceptable to include picture cards (or similar matter) where it has a direct and obvious relevance to the stamps/covers featured. For example a card showing a particular aircraft used to carry a specified mail for which stamps/postmarks were used would be considered relevant, a postcard showing a general view of a stamp-issuing territory would not—as it has no direct relevance to the stamps shown. However, these comments do not apply to thematic collections where the inclusion of postcards and other emphemera is almost a *sine qua non* of the collection. Even here discretion has to be exercised and the non-philatelic material shown should be closely related to the stamps. In both conventional and thematic collections the non-philatelic items shown should complement the stamps *not* overpower them. It is no good having a page comprising a large newscutting and a photograph with only one tiny stamp shown. In such instances the non-philatelic items would be best mounted on their own. Perhaps the simplest way for the novice to find out what is acceptable is to study some of the entries at a major local or national exhibition. Those exhibitors who receive awards have normally achieved the right balance.

In arranging stamps on a blank page, it is advisable to do some planning before the actual mounting begins. First of all, there is your heading, which in the majority of cases will be the name of a country. On the rest of the page, you have to place your stamps and whatever descriptive notes you are going to give. It is advisable to give some notes, otherwise your collection will mean very little to anyone who looks at it.

NORFOLK ISLAND

1966 Provisional Decimal Definitives

1960-2 Definitives surcharged with Decimal
Currency, in black on silver tablets
obliterating the old sterling value.

Issued:- February 14th 1966. Ptg. Typograph.

1c Small tablet.
$1 Large tablet.

Reprints - May 1966

1c Large tablet.
$1 Small tablet.

If the collection is an ordinary general display of the stamps of a country or group, you will only need a heading for each issue, giving the date, reason for issue, watermark and perforation (if your collection takes note of these varieties), and perhaps the names of the designer, engraver and printers, if known. Apart from such headings, all that will be needed is an occasional brief note to indicate some special variety. Where the position of a flaw, or other detail you want to show, is not easy to describe in writing, you can use paper arrows which can be bought quite cheaply and which have one end gummed to the album page, with the loose end overlapping the stamp and pointing to the spot you want to indicate. Some collectors like to draw a red frame line round any particularly rare stamp.

THE PALACE OF WESTMINSTER

The English Parliament dates back to the mid-13th century, having evolved from the earlier King's Council. The power of Parliament reached its peak following the temporary abolition of the monarchy in 1649. The Parliament buildings of the 17th century are shown in Hollar's print.

Following a fire in 1834 much of the Palace was rebuilt; the 19th century buildings have featured on many stamps including the 1946 Victory omnibus issue.

Statues of important characters in British history are sited or near the Palace; these include Richard I (near the Victoria Tower) and Sir Winston Churchill (in Parliament Square facing the Palace).

The British Parliament is often referred to as 'the Mother of Parliaments' as it has been the model for Parliaments in many Commonwealth countries. For this reason the Palace has featured on many stamps - sometimes with the local Parliament or symbol of their authority - for example a mace.

The Palace faces another of London's most famous buildings - Westminster Abbey, in the precincts of which lies St. Margaret's Church - known as the 'Church of the House of Commons' where special parliamentary services are held.

Written-up pages from 'country collection' (*Norfolk Island*) and 'thematic collection' (*The Palace of Westminster*)

In a highly specialised collection, it is often necessary to give very full notes, but even here the writing should be kept down to a minimum. A lot of description can be avoided by the use of enlarged sketches of details, which you can do yourself if you are clever with a pen, or small photographic enlargements of parts of the stamps can be mounted in the collection.

In a thematic collection it will be necessary to have a brief note below almost every stamp. Very great care is necessary here, or once again you will find your pages full of writing and with very few stamps on them. For example, if you are describing a stamp bearing a portrait of a famous author, you cannot give his whole life story in your album. His name, the date of his birth and death, and one or perhaps two of his principal works, might be mentioned, as it is necessary to maintain some kind of balance between stamps and writing, otherwise you will have an essay illustrated by a few stamps instead of a stamp collection enhanced by your notes.

Before mounting a page of stamps, therefore, you must decide what style of writing you will employ, how much you are going to write about the particular stamp or issue you are dealing with, and, bearing these facts in mind, how many stamps you are going to be able to get on the page.

If your album pages have a *quadrillé* background, you will very likely find that the central point of the page is marked by a thickening of two *quadrillé* lines at their junction, and the central horizontal and vertical lines of the background will be indicated at the edges of the sheet by being prolonged very slightly. As far as possible, the stamps on your finished page should balance evenly about the central point. You will naturally mount your stamps so that, in each row, there is the same number of stamps each side of the central vertical axis of your page, if there is an odd number of stamps in the row, the centre stamp will of course be placed on the centre line and the others spaced off from it at even distances on each side.

As regards the vertical arrangement, though you will get more stamps on to a page by putting the maximum number of stamps into each horizontal row, the result will be very ugly. It is better to vary the number, alternating between long and short rows, according to the number of stamps you have to get on the page you are dealing with.

In a general collection, the unit of arrangement will be a set or issue. You will have sets of varying length, some of which will go on a page and fill it comfortably, while others will probably go two to a page, or, if you collect both unused and used, a set can go on a page in both conditions. It is essential that the pages should not be overcrowded even though your stamps will take up more leaves when spaced out neatly.

It is a good idea to lay out your page before you do any hinging at all. Pencil dots may be used to indicate how much space will be occupied by your notes, experience will soon teach you how much space a note will take in your adopted style of writing and then the stamps can be laid on the page and moved about until the most attractive arrangement is arrived at. Do not, however, adopt any fantastic arrangements, laying out your stamps in crosses, circles or other mathematical figures. Such arrangements detract from the appearance of the stamps, and over-elaborate borders and scrolls, with which some artistically minded collectors adorn their albums, should also be avoided. The aim is to concentrate on the stamps and everything else, but notes, indicators or anything added to emphasis special items, must be subordinate.

There are various ways of actually putting your chosen wording onto the pages, and it really boils down to a matter of individual taste and preference. Many people have neat, efficient and perfectly legible handwriting, and this is really all that is needed for writing-up a stamp collection. Many others feel that their handwriting is so untidy that they have no choice but to type anything which they wish to produce in an attractive form.

There are several reasons why a high standard of everyday handwriting is not a prerequisite for being able to produce a neatly-written up collection. The printed squares on the pages of a blank album provide a useful visual frame on which to standardise the sizes of lettering used. In many cases, furthermore, only one or two lines of description are required and the writer does not have to produce large paragraphs of uniform writing. A good fountain-pen does not slide across a page so readily as a ballpoint or felt-tip and gives the writer more control over his lettering. With some careful thought and a good deal of practice on old discarded leaves, a neat writing-up style should be within the capability of practically every collector, even though he or she may not be able to master the skills of copperplate or italic scripts.

Typewriters can provide one solution to the problem of finding a neat and consistent way of writing-up a collection. Although some of the smaller portables do not have wide enough carriages to take some of the wider types of leaf and leaves with interleaving already attached cannot be used, most leaves will fit into most typewriters.

Whether writing-up is by hand or by typewriter, black ink or a black ribbon should be used. With the possible exception of a sparing use of red for initials and underlining, no other coloured inks or ribbons should be employed. Gaudy colours take the eye away from the items displayed and may clash with the colours of the stamps themselves.

CHAPTER EIGHTEEN
Ways of Collecting—Single Countries or Groups

Every collector comes, sooner or later, to a period when he feels that general collecting is too big a task for him to tackle, and that continuing to collect in this way will not, as far as he can see make much impression on those numerous gaps in his albums. He then looks round for some means of limiting his field, and thus intensifying his effort, and the result is usually a decision to take the stamps of a single geographical group, country or issue. Or he may take up a *thematic* collection.

Before starting to specialise in the stamps of a country, group or theme, the collector should have some idea of what specialisation really means. Many call themselves specialists from the moment they have taken the fateful decision to abandon their general collection, but no mere limitation of field can earn the title. The true specialist must study his stamps and try to add something to the sum of philatelic knowledge.

Here let me add that even when it is decided to collect only the stamps of a small section, it is very unwise to give up your general collection, at any rate to the extent of disposing of it. Keep it by you, and as you learn more about your pet issues, you will also find you are learning more about stamps in general, and will look at your old collection with a new interest and affection. It will be a bond of union between you and your fellow specialists when you visit the meetings of your philatelic society, and it will provide a nucleus for your further experiments in specialising when you have exhausted the delights of the country first chosen. Too many specialists tend to become narrow in their views and interests, and the possession and occasional examination of a general collection acts as a safeguard against carrying narrowness too far.

In any given field, an individual specialist may deal with only one or two particular aspects. Thus there may be several collectors, all specialists in the stamps of a certain country and all trying to make discoveries. One may be delving in the official archives to find out the history of the posts and postage stamps; another may be more interested in the production of the stamps themselves and in working out the settings of certain issues or overprints; while the third is passionately interested in the postmarks connected with the use of the stamps. If a group of friends can work in this way, each taking a section of the field and pooling information, much can be done, but even the lone student may do a great deal.

The preliminary to specialist study of stamps is to know what has already been learned by others. It is not very amusing to spend years elucidating problems by one's own unaided efforts and then to come proudly into the open with the results, only to find that someone had already made the same discoveries before one's own collection had even been begun. Most of the more important research work in connexion with stamps has been recorded either in published books, or in the pages of the philatelic journals. It is absolutely essential to start with a sound knowledge of what has been done before going on to independent study.

Another aid to the budding specialist is the examination of other collections. Many of the finest collections are displayed each year at one or other of the philatelic societies, and if you are able to find out where stamps you want to see are being shown, it should not be too difficult to see them, even if you are not a member of the particular society, as most societies welcome visitors. In this way, it may be possible to make the acquaintance of the leaders in your chosen field, as nothing brings collectors together like a common interest.

Having gained as much knowledge as possible, and perhaps been a little disheartened by the vision of other people's treasures, you can decide how far your own collection is to take you. It is certainly best to work by stages, concentrating on one issue or problem, and going as far as the available material allows before proceeding to the next group. The reader can decide for himself from the earlier chapters dealing with the printing and use of postage stamps how many aspects of philately he wishes to cover. He will gather from what has been said, that not only stamps, but knowledge, must be acquired. Very good work can be done in the direction of *historical* research (postal rates, etc.), with a minimum number of stamps, though technical research (plating, etc.) calls for as many stamps as it is possible to get, provided that they serve to add to the student's knowledge.

This brings us to the two essentials of a specialised collection. The first—which cannot be re-emphasised too often—is that the collector who claims the name of philatelist must study his stamps, even if it be but a single small problem in connexion with them. Hopefully he will, for the benefit of his fellow-philatelists, publish his results when he is satisfied that they are correct.

The second essential is that a specialised collection should contain only specimens which serve to elucidate the problems with which the collector is concerned. Other stamps whose place in the scheme of things has not been fully ascertained should also be retained. To fill a collection with repetitions of the same stamp, in the same state, which tell the student nothing, may be satisfactory to those who like their collections to illustrate the power of their purse but it is not philately. It is merely accumulating, and accumulating which prevents others from having their share of the available material and of partaking in philatelic research. Most readers of this book can find some stamp problem within their means and the scope of their powers to study, and those who have brought to a satisfactory conclusion even the smallest bit of philatelic research will testify to the mental stimulus and satisfaction which this branch of the hobby offers to all.

CHAPTER NINETEEN
Ways of Collecting—Thematics

The collecting of the stamps of a country in chronological order of issue is the earliest and most conventional form of the hobby, which has developed, in the case of some collectors, into intensified specialised study of the stamps of a certain country or issue.

The development of the pictorial stamp, and the tendency of our modern world to be more interested in life than in things, has given rise to a kind of collecting which disregards geographical and political boundaries, and groups stamps in relation to their design, inscriptions and associations. There is hardly a man or woman who can fail to find some subject illustrated by stamps, in which to interest themselves. Hence the great popularity of what is now known as thematic collecting.

Stamps featuring people and places of ancient times

Portraits and pictures on postage stamps can be used to tell the history of almost any country. Modern countries recall their ancient history—Rome reminds us of Romulus and Remus, Julius Caesar and Augustus; Egypt of Rameses, Cleopatra, and the builders of her ancient pyramids and temples; Persia of Darius, and Ethiopia of Solomon and the Queen of Sheba. The collector who sets out to form an historical collection of any kind will need to have a certain knowledge of his subject, based on a reading of something more than reference books. The necessary link between reading and postage stamps is supplied by stamp catalogues, for these give, in most cases the subjects of the stamp designs, without which the collector would be very much at sea. The educational advantages of stamp collecting are clearly recognised for in most schools it is now fostered instead of being frowned upon as it was in the past. Most schools have a stamp club and many teachers use stamps as an aid to instruction in subjects such as history, geography and even sometimes physics and chemistry.

The geographical side of the postage stamp is one which is stressed by many of the albums provided for the collector. There are pages for each country, and these are grouped in continents and the colonies or dependences of each country are grouped together.

Many collectors have produced most attractive and striking displays by grouping the stamps which depict places in various countries so that they illustrate a world tour. Such a stamp tour may be made extraordinarily interesting, if a proper sequence is observed, and the stamps themselves are accompanied by brief notes about the places depicted on them. These stamp views are not confined to famous buildings, statues and memorials, but include some of the world's most magnificent scenery, mountains, glaciers, waterfalls, rivers, lakes and seascapes, views beautiful in the miniature form in which they appear to the unaided eye, but often still more charming when seen under the magnifying glass.

A World Tour – stamps from Europe, the Mediterranean, the West Indies, the Far East, Australasia, Africa and the Americas

Once we are started on this world tour, there is no limit to the stamps which may be included. Many countries have used their stamps to show us something of the people who live there and of their life and work. In developing countries the inhabitants are seen doing simple tasks by hand, while on the stamps of modern industrialised states large factories and mills are pictured.

Stamps depicting scenes from every day life – fishing, agriculture and industry

Animals and birds are popular thematic subjects and have featured on numerous stamps

From the peoples of the world it is only a step to the birds and beasts, and a zoological collection is one of the most popular of the thematic groups. The fauna of the world have been so freely illustrated on stamps that a wonderful array can be got together, which will include many unusual and exotic species. The botanist, too, is liberally catered for. Even where the central design of a stamp does not show a tree, plant or flower, the artist will often use a spray or a flower to complete a design so that a hawk-like eye is needed if the full range of stamp botany is to be covered.

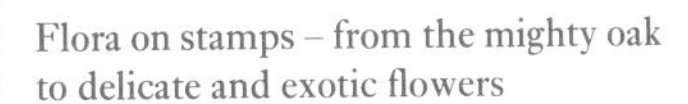
Flora on stamps – from the mighty oak to delicate and exotic flowers

A collection of map stamps can form a miniature atlas

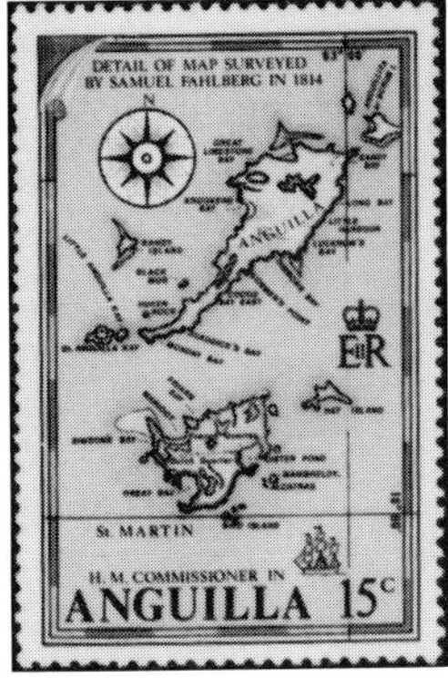

Ships – from native canoes to modern cargo vessels – stamps showing the development of the World's merchant marine

Transport by road and rail

Aircraft from biplanes to supersonic travel Concorde-style. Helicopters and Zeppelin balloons are also featured

When making his world tour, the collector will not be altogether unprovided with maps and charts, as were so many of the early explorers in whose tracks he must follow, for there are quite a few miniature maps on stamps. As for means of transport, he will find in the stamp album a range of vehicles sufficient to give him, in themselves, the subject for a collection. If he wishes to voyage on water, he has the choice of every type of vessel, from canoe and coracle, through sailing ships of all types, to the giant modern supertanker.

On land, he may go afoot, on horseback, in a litter, in wagons and carriages of all kinds, on motor-bike or by car or rail. In the air, there are aircraft of all kinds awaiting him, and balloons and airships differing from one another as widely as did the first dirigible gasbag of Santos Dumont from the *Graf Zeppelin*.

Our sections here overlap, for many stamps which find a place in a transport collection can also properly be included in an engineering collection. Stamp pictures include views of many famous canals, bridges, harbours, railways and aqueducts, while if we add the work of the builder to that of the engineer, there are cathedrals, government buildings, post offices, lighthouses, wireless stations and other erections. (It is quite an interesting study to take a cross-section of the world's stamps to show the various types of architecture, the modern buildings being contrasted with the ancient, and the civilised with the native huts and kraals which are also depicted on stamps.)

Cathedrals and public buildings have long featured on stamps, more recently bridges, harbours and lighthouses have also been depicted

The engineering section may also include a few stamp portraits of famous engineers, such as General Goethals, who was finally responsible for the completion of the Panama Canal. This mention of portrait stamps brings us to a wider subject: the men and women of the stamp album.

In days when kings and princes were more plentiful than they are today, the normal subject for a stamp design in a monarchical state was the ruler's portrait. The lead given by Britain may have had something to do with this, but the practice was more probably based on the association of stamps with coins. A portrait had the added advantage that any alteration by way of forgery changed the expression of the face, and such a change was more likely to be detected than any other, as men and women are accustomed to noticing variations in human expression.

If the royal portrait was not used, the arms of the country or reigning house were often taken as a suitable symbol, though frequently they are incorrectly represented on the stamps. Armorial and portrait stamps are still plentiful today but very few monarchs now figure on the world's issues. Occasionally a country forbade the appearance of its living rulers on its stamps. Chile, for example, would, for many years, have no portrait but that of Columbus on her stamps, while to this day only deceased presidents are portrayed on the stamps of the U.S.A.

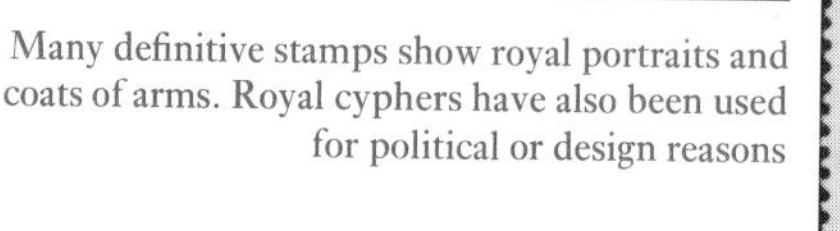

Many definitive stamps show royal portraits and coats of arms. Royal cyphers have also been used for political or design reasons

Portraits of heads of state obliterated – following their fall from power

Famous People – a huge thematic collection can be built up on this subject

It was natural vanity which made presidents of some small republics wish to record for posterity their portraits on the stamps of their country. And it was, with an equally natural feeling of pleasure that the successors of some of these short-lived presidents blotted out the stamp portraits of their predecessors. For example Shah Pahlavi of Iran on his accession, in 1925, instructed that the stamps then in use, which bore the portrait of his predecessor, should not pass through the post unless the likeness was thoroughly obliterated. Adhesive paper, burnt cork, and other materials were employed to obscure the portrait of the former Shah Ahmed Mirza. The Japanese blotted out the stamp portraits of Queen Wilhelmina of the Netherlands when they occupied the Dutch possessions in the East Indies.

With the coming of the commemorative stamp, it was natural that the honour of portrayal on stamps should be extended to famous figures of the past and, in some special cases, to living men. It thus became possible to form collections of stamp portraits illustrating various human activities, these being supplemented, in many cases, by pictorial stamps connected with their work. Most interesting of these are the explorers, whose portraits might well find a place in a geographical collection, though they form an equally suitable subject for a special display. Christopher Columbus is very popular with stamp designers, and his life and adventures have been the subject of numerous stamp issues. There is hardly an important incident in the life of the great discoverer which has not formed the subject of a stamp design. Captain Cook is another popular figure, while the name of Pizarro, Balboa, Magellan, Cabot, La Perouse and others give the album its flavour of adventure, which may be continued and expanded if the collector adds to his explorers the generals and admirals of the stamp world, and the many views of battles by land and sea, which are found on stamps. Many of the generals seem to be shown on stamps in a political capacity—for example, Ulysses Grant as a president of the U.S.A. (*1869–77*). Admirals include Nelson, Cochrane, who fought for Greece and Chile after falling foul of the British Admiralty, Sir Edward Codrington, who commanded the Allied fleets which destroyed the Turkish navy at Navarino, David Farragut, the first admiral of the U.S. Navy, and others.

Navigators and Explorers from the 16th to the 20th century

Admirals and Generals – a stamp from Antigua showing Viscount Nelson with his ship *Victory* and Sir Edward Codrington shown in the centre of a Greek commemorative stamp

Apart from these 'official' warriors, the stamp portrait gallery shows us a host of patriots of many nations who have fought for their countries' independence; in fact 'the story of liberty' would make a good subject for a stamp collection planned with a little imagination and knowledge, for there are not only the portrait stamps, but others which show declarations of independence, street fighting, formal battles, councils, meetings of conspirators, and all the usual paraphernalia of revolt. Two 'fighters for freedom' who have earned their places on hundreds of stamps which have been issued in their memory are President John F. Kennedy of the U.S.A. and Sir Winston Churchill.

There are also many thematic collections which may be formed in connexion with more peaceful pursuits. Literature, for example, is well represented by interesting commemorative stamps with which various countries have delighted to honour their famous sons. A case in point is Britain's celebrated writer and dramatist, William Shakespeare, whose 400th birth anniversary in 1964 was the occasion for stamp commemoratives by Britain and some of the Commonwealth territories as well as other countries in the world.

Eminent politicians of recent times – Sir Winston Churchill and President John F. Kennedy. Apart from royalty these two have probably featured on more stamps than any other celebrities

The Bard of Avon on British, Commonwealth and U.S. stamps

Julius Caesar appears on stamps of Italy, and Dante and Manzoni too, not to mention saints and apostles, who are portrayed for other reasons than that of authorship. St. Paul, too, will be found on the stamps of Malta. France gives us Pierre de Ronsard, Anatole France, Victor Hugo and others and also a picture of Daudet's mill; Germany honours Johann Wolfgang von Goethe, Friedrich von Schiller and Immanuel Kant; Spain Miguel de Cervantes; Hungary Sandor Petöfi and Maurus Jokai; Norway Henrik Ibsen and Bjørnstjerne Bjørnson, Denmark Hans Andersen; Fiume D'Annunzio; Portugal Luis De Camoes and Branco; Poland Henryk Sienkiewicz of *Quo Vadis?* fame; Russia Karl Marx, Maxim Gorky and Leo Tolstoy, as well as British writers Robert Burns, Daniel Defoe, Charles Dickens, Henry Fielding and George Bernard Shaw; Samoa Robert Louis Stevenson and Austria a whole series of authors, poets and playwrights, many little known outside that country.

The British P.O. has issued stamps depicting Charlotte and Emily Brontë, George Eliot (Mary Ann Evans) and Mrs Gaskell as well as issues featuring characters from the works of Charles Dickens, Beatrix Potter, Kenneth Grahame, A. A. Milne and Lewis Carroll (Charles Dodgson).

Prominent people of long ago – Dante, Julius Caesar and St Paul

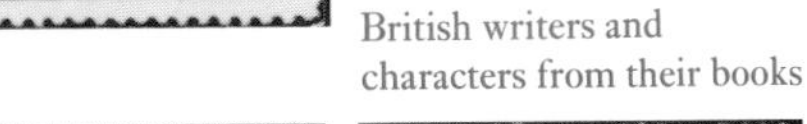

British writers and characters from their books

Artists and their works

There are, too, a number of authors who have appeared on stamps in other capacities; King James I and Francis Bacon on the Cabot series of Newfoundland, 'Carmen Sylva' of Roumania and Queen Marie, and quite a number of others. A literary collection might also be extended to include stamps depicting scenes and events which have been mentioned in famous works of fiction, and even occasionally shown on film.

The whole contents of the stamp album come within the realm of Art, for there are few stamps in the production of which some artist, however humble, has not collaborated. Quite a few stamp designs, particularly those devoted to historic scenes, and many portraits, are reproduced from paintings, and there are a number of stamp reproductions of really famous works of art. As examples, a fresco by Michelangelo is shown on stamps of Libya, paintings by Dyckmans and Raphael have found a place on stamps of the Saar, Rembrandt and some of his masterpieces appear on Dutch issues. Belgium has perpetuated designs by the famous war cartoonist Louis Raemaekers, while France has reproduced a wide range of famous paintings including a delicate work by Jean Honoré Fragonard. Collectors interested in art have made a considerable study of the story of the artists and engravers responsible for stamp designs and the subject is a fascinating one. Sculpture, good and bad, is plentiful in the pages of a stamp album. On the stamps of Greece there are beautiful reproductions of statues by Praxiteles, Peonias and other masters, and from them we can turn to conventional representations of modern warriors and politicians, or to the crude images of native ju-jus and idols.

Sculpture of all kinds

The orchestra on stamps

Music is very well represented on stamps. The stamp orchestra must be culled from many countries, and will be a varied one. Many musical instruments appear on stamps incidentally—and will take some searching for, often with a magnifying glass. When we think of composers, we naturally turn to the Austrian charity stamps of 1922, a wonderfully engraved series of portraits, which includes Haydn, Mozart, Beethoven, Schubert, Bruckner, Strauss and Hugo Wolf. Germany adds Bach, Handel and Wagner stamps. Poland has given us portraits of Paderewski and Chopin, the former in his political capacity, while Czechoslovakia has honoured Dvorák and Smetana. From France come stamps in memory of Berlioz and Debussy, from Russia Tchaikovsky. The U.S. Post Office issued five stamps depicting American composers in 1940, one of which featured John Philip Sousa. George Gershwin featured on one of the 'American Art Commemoration' stamps issued in 1973; the stamp featured a scene from the opera *Porgy and Bess*. Four famous conductors—Sir Henry Wood, Sir Thomas Beecham, Sir Malcolm Sargent and Sir John Barbirolli appeared on British stamps issued in 1980.

Famous composers – Debussy and Mozart

George Gershwin with characters Porgy and Bess

Famous scientists – Sir Isaac Newton and Lord Rutherford

The Space Age

The scientists and inventors might almost be grouped with our engineering section, already referred to above. Here we should find the astronomer Copernicus (Poland), the radio pioneer Popov (Russia), Volta (*after whom the volt is named*) and Galvani (Italy), Pasteur, Berthelot, Ampère and Daguerre (France) and many others.

Perhaps the most dramatic of modern scientific themes concerns space research. Astronauts, rockets, satellites and spaceships, all have appeared on stamps during the past few years.

The religions of the world also form the subject for an interesting thematic collection. The gods and goddesses of Greece and Rome will be found on numerous stamps, while Egypt has not altogether forgotten her deities when designing her stamps. Some of the Eastern religions are recalled by stamps of the Indian Native States, Japan and other countries, though sometimes the only reminder is a picture of a temple or shrine. Mythology, too, is the occasional subject of stamp designs, and legendary birds and beasts add variety to the album pages. Christianity has its representatives mainly in the pictured lives of the saints, St. Francis, St. Anthony, St. Benedict and others having been honoured with special series. Italy has given us stamps illustrating the ceremonies of the 'Holy Year', and there are numerous churches and cathedrals on stamps. The Maltese stamps showing the shipwreck of St. Paul have already been mentioned, and the stamp portrait of his host on that occasion, St. Publius, afterwards first Bishop of Malta, should not be overlooked on a 1s 6d stamp of 1938. Of equal interest is the $2\frac{1}{2}$ piastre stamp of the 1928 Jubilee issue of Cyprus, which reproduces a quaint old picture which shows the finding of the body of St. Barnabas. A number of scenes of biblical history may be found on stamps of Syria and the Lebanon, not to mention the views of the Holy Land which adorn the stamps of Israel, Jordan and Palestine.

Religious subjects

Heraldry – Channel Islands stamps are rich in heraldic designs

Students of heraldry will find it possible to form an extensive collection of stamps bearing arms, badges and devices, often more attractive to the eye than accurate to an extent which would satisfy the College of Arms but none the less interesting on that account. Coins too are reproduced on stamps, for example the current definitive stamps of Guernsey, and quite an attractive collection could be formed of 'numismatic philately'. Banknotes too have featured on stamps.

Numismatic philately – coins on stamps

Cricket – amateur and professional

1974 and 1978 World Cup football stamps

Athletics – Olympic and South Pacific Games

Skiing, Irish hurling and ice hockey

One collection which must not be overlooked is that of sports stamps. The craze for commemorating every event of importance has naturally been extended to include the various international Olympic meetings, and Greece, Holland, Belgium, Hungary, France, Bulgaria, Costa Rica, Cuba, Germany, U.S.A. and others have issued sets showing either the old Olympic Games of ancient Greece, or modern sportsmen of various kinds. Stamps commemorating football competitions are highly popular.

Most sports in fact are now represented on at least one stamp and some countries have issued stamps to commemorate particular sportsmen—for example 1981 Swedish stamps featured tennis star Bjorn Borg and skier Ingermar Stenmark.

Golf, sailing, cross-country, weight-lifting, motor cycling and horse racing

Famous Swedish sportsmen – Bjorn Borg (*tennis*) and Ingemar Stenmark (*skiing*)

Hands – at prayer, symbolic and at work

Like collectors who tend to follow a chronological sequence, the thematic collector will need to decide on some form of collecting policy by which to organise his collection. This will normally take place after he/she has accumulated a fairly considerable number of stamps and/or other philatelic items and arrives at the stage of contemplating mounting up. Margaret Moris, a leading thematic collector, suggested some answers to this problem in her book *Thematic Stamp Collecting*:

'What is it that turns this accumulation into a thematic collection? The answer is—*you*; your skill, judgment and taste; the way in which you link theme and philatelic information to your material; your selectivity; the way in which a thread appears to run through your collection.

Instead of just a hotch-potch of stamps you will want to try to find sensible and logical sub-divisions. Take, for example, a collection on HANDS. This could be divided into sections on Men's Hands, Women's Hands, Children's Hands, Hands of Famous People, Handshakes, Hands Holding or Brandishing Objects, Hands Performing Tasks (e.g. reading Braille, playing the piano), Stylised Hands . . . and so on. Use your imagination.

Consider, too, the wide theme of ARCHITECTURE and how it could be broken down. A few suggestions would be:

(*a*) Period—e.g. Classical, Gothic, Renaissance, Contemporary; (*b*) Function—cathedrals, palaces, dwelling houses; (*c*) Locality—European, Japanese, Indian; (*d*) Forms of construction—arches, domes, concrete structures; (*e*) Details—types of windows, doors, roofs, . . . and so on.

Sub-dividing your theme in this way has distinct advantages. If you are tackling a very large theme, you can build up only one section of it at a time if you wish (similar to a collector of G.B. trying to get a good representation of King George VI stamps before going on to Queen Elizabeth issues). Alternatively, if you are a bit short of time or cash, or if you do not want to be swamped by a very large theme, then a limitation of this kind can be a satisfactory compromise. For example, if you are interested in MAPS, you could consider restricting your collection to Antique Maps, or Town Plans.

However you collect, try to organise your material to some overall plan. This will not only help you by making you take a real grip of your topic, but will also make sense of your collection when you show it to other people.

Some themes lend themselves to logical treatment. If you collect anything relating to flora or fauna, you will find that the organisation into genus, family, species gives ready-made dividing lines. The same would be true of a collection on ART AND ARTISTS which could be organised according to the various schools of painting. Similarly in the case of a collection on AVIATION, you could have a thematic emphasis such as TYPES OF AIRCRAFT ON STAMP DESIGNS, or you could adopt the technique of the aero-philatelist and use fine, early flown covers to demonstrate THE MAILS BY AIR. However, if you decide on a more abstract theme, such as MORALITY, then you have to work out the logical sequence for yourself. For some themes, few guidelines are available. As with any other aspect of thematic collecting, you choose for yourself not only the theme but the degree of difficulty.'

As thematic collecting becomes more sophisticated (especially in the U.S.A.) so it will become more difficult to find a subject that has not been tackled before. Thus any one who wants to 'make his name' in forming a worth-while thematic collection on a new subject must be prepared for a lot of hard work and study—but the rewards will be great and the satisfaction achieved considerable. It is a tribute to the breadth of our hobby that there are very few branches of human interest and knowledge which cannot be in some way illustrated by postage stamps. By design, by association, by contrast, and by inscription, every stamp or group of stamps has its story to tell, and the collector who gets most fun out of the hobby is he, or she, who has the fullest appreciation of what lies behind the stamp and who does not merely treat it as just one more specimen to be added to a numerical score.

It is undoubtedly to the pictorial side of stamp-collecting, that the hobby owes so much of its present popularity. Cinema and television have accustomed millions of men, women and children to think in terms of pictures, and in the stamp album they find pictures which are alive with interest. The new issues of the world, as they come out from day to day, provide an international illustrated newspaper which cannot be beaten for scope and variety.

CHAPTER TWENTY
Aerophilately

The collecting of airmail stamps and covers has enjoyed a considerable vogue for many years. If mass enthusiasm has waned this is because now the bulk of overseas mail is carried by air and there is little 'pioneering' except perhaps in the introduction of new routes and the use of newer and faster jet aircraft. And while stamps are still issued inscribed 'Airmail' (or in the foreign equivalents), these are often part of a country's definitive issue and do not depict any particular aspect of aviation or the airmail services as the earlier issues did. Nevertheless many enthusiasts are still attracted to aerophilately, and this chapter is an acknowledgement of the fascination and romance of this branch of the hobby.

Air mail stamps

The air stamp is a fairly modern thing, for until mails were carried by air there was obviously no need for special stamps to frank them. On some of the pioneer balloon flights it was the practice to carry postcards of some special design, which were either posted on the arrival of the balloon at its destination, or were tossed overboard to be entrusted to the tender mercies of whoever picked them up. When the aeroplane began to be developed, aviation meetings and cross-country flights were organised, and on such occasions correspondence of a souvenir nature was often carried in the machines. Such correspondence might consist of special postcards or envelopes with distinctive designs, or ordinary letters and cards with a special postmark or handstamped design or inscription, the latter being described by collectors as 'cachets'. At some meetings special labels, looking as much like postage stamps as possible, were sold, and used to frank the cards, in fact some of these were postage stamps in a restricted sense, though they had only very limited franking power and rarely had any government authority behind them.

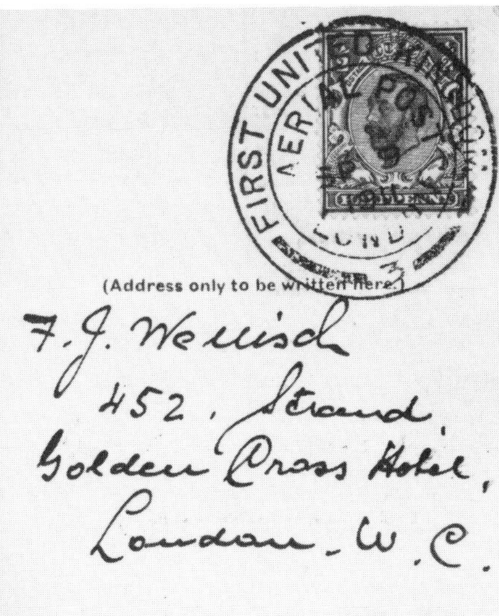

First official U.K. air post – from Hendon to Windsor in 1911

It was not until 1917 that the first official government air stamps were issued, when Italy applied special overprints to two of her 'express' stamps for use on correspondence on experimental flights between Rome and Turin and Naples and Palermo. Thenceforward, many of the important trial flights had their special stamps, issued under government auspices, and as regular air mail lines were established, some countries issued a series of special stamps for use in connexion with these services. The advantage of using distinctive stamps, in order that mail destined to be handled in a special way may quickly be identified, has already been noted.

The occasions for using air stamps range from some of the great historic transatlantic flights such as those of Hawker, De Pinedo, and Alcock, to the flights of modern jet aircraft. Their designs are as varied as the reasons for their existence. On some, the aerial character is indicated merely by an overprint, which may consist of words, or a device, such as an aeroplane propeller, or the machine itself. Of distinctive air mail designs, aeroplanes of all types, from the first Wright machine to the latest giant mail-carrier, are shown, sometimes 'in the blue' and on other stamps in flight over a particular town or stretch of country. For the rest, artists have vied with one another in an attempt to symbolise the speed of flight. Birds, winged beings, a winged posthorn, and a flight of arrows are typical designs. The faces of famous pioneers or pilots look out at us from the album page, and on some stamps there are maps of historic flights, one of the most interesting being Newfoundland's map of the North Atlantic showing the routes followed by those who had flown, or nearly flown that ocean at the time. There are also stamps commemorating record stratosphere flights.

'Hawker' air flight from Newfoundland to Britain, 1919

1919 Trans-atlantic and first England-Australia flights

1927 Lindbergh New York-Paris flight

Concorde – one of many stamps commemorating the starting of new routes (*Paris to Rio de Janeiro*)

Canadian 1924 authorised air service stamp

Unofficial air mail stamps

There are one or two countries, notably in South America, where the government has handed over the air services to a private company to develop and exploit, and where such companies have the right to issue air stamps backed by government authority. Such stamps are of almost as much importance as those issued by the national post offices and may well be collected. The 'S.C.A.D.T.A.' stamps of Colombia are examples, while Canada has permitted the issue of special stamps by companies carrying mail by air to outlying goldfields, etc. The collector who wishes to start an air collection will be well advised to begin by acquiring as many of the government air stamps as he can, supplementing them, if he wishes, by the stamps of authorised companies, such as those described above. Apart from the fact that this group of stamps is the most interesting, it has the added advantage that it is collected not only by those who take air stamps only, but also by collectors of stamps generally, and where the demand is, there also is the ultimate rise in value.

If he likes, he can continue further, and include labels and quasi-stamps of the early aviation meetings, rocket mails and others of similar kind. Many of these, though interesting as souvenirs of the early days of flying, were produced mainly with the object of making a profit out of collectors, and each philatelist will decide his own collecting policy in regard to them.

The same remark applies to 'air covers', a term which in its widest sense may be held to include any correspondence borne by air. In this section we have already referred to the various items carried on the early flights and at the early meetings. These may have been franked by special stamps, either governmental or private, or they may simply be distinguished by a pictorial device, by inscription descriptive of the occasion, or by handstamped cachets which also may be either inscriptions or of a pictorial nature. Then there are covers carried on the great historic flights, transatlantic, round the world, and so on. All of these have a great souvenir interest, but the most sought-after will normally be those of flights for which special government stamps were issued, for quantities of such stamps would naturally be small in most cases.

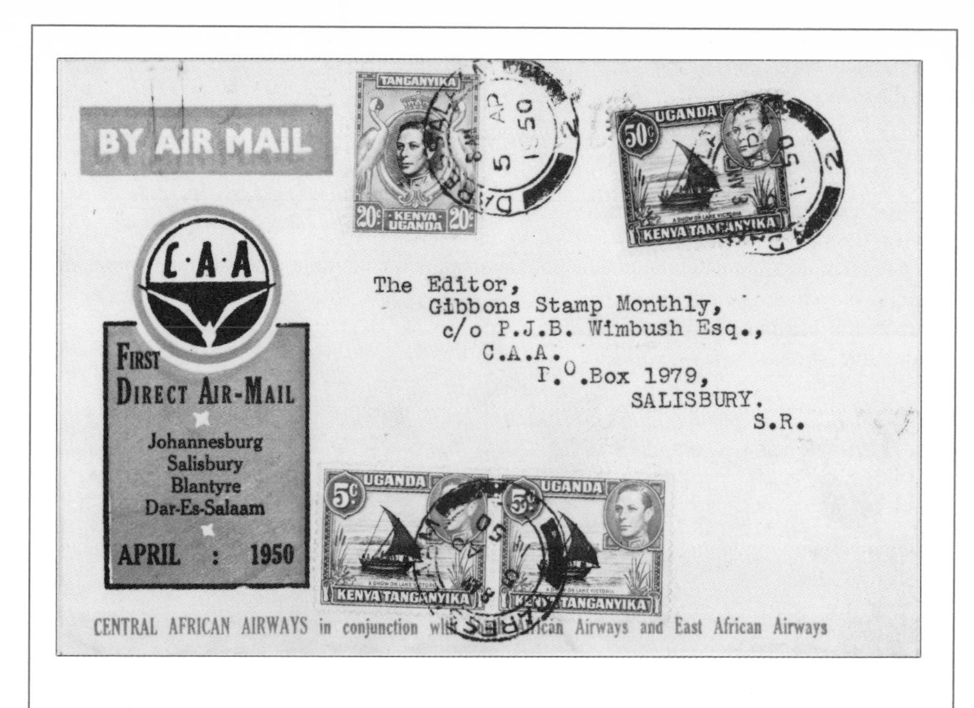

Souvenir cover carried on Johannesburg to Dar-es-Salaam and London to Tokyo flights (*1950 and 1959*)

It must frankly be admitted that there are a great number of air covers which would have had no reason for their existence, if there had been no collectors. The interest in 'first flight' covers—that is covers carried on the first flight over a new air route—at one time reached the proportions of a 'craze' with the most flimsy excuses used as a pretext for a flight, and every speculator tried to get exclusive batches of covers carried. Finally, there are the covers carried in the ordinary way of business on the established air mail routes. These have not the historic appeal of the world-famous flights, but they show the air mails doing their job, and there is no taint of the speculative about them. The best way to decide if an air cover should find a place in the album is to ask oneself whether the flight on which it was carried was of historic interest or whether the cover was carried by air in the ordinary course of post. If covers which satisfy neither of these conditions are included, it must only be because of the personal fancy of the owner of the collection.

Airmail etiquettes

Modern definitive air letter (*aerogramme*)

Modern commemorative air letter (*aerogramme*)

The aerophilatelist who is really bitten by the hobby does not stop short at stamps and covers. He studies the various types of cachet employed both on experimental flights, and on temporary and permanent air mail routes, and collects covers showing every variation in colour or detail. He has a collection of the adhesive labels—*etiquettes*—supplied at the post offices of various countries for affixing to envelopes to indicate that they are to be carried by air. If there are official types of air-post envelopes, airgraphs, or air letter forms (aerogrammes), he will want all these; while official notices and other documents in connexion with flights of all kinds will not come amiss to him. If a collection of this scope is formed on a definite historical plan, it can be made very interesting and instructive.

CHAPTER TWENTY-ONE
Postal History

The term 'Postal History' is perhaps ambiguous—the layman might assume it would be used to describe the history of postal services over the years. However, in the philatelic world the term is applied to covers, cards and other items bearing interesting postal markings and which thus tell something of postal services. Despite the misuse of the term, it is now in common use and it would be foolish to try to change it. The term 'postal historian' is applied not only to one who studies the history of the post but to a collector of covers, postmarks, etc. In this chapter the use of this term refers to a collector rather than a non-collector who is studying the postal service *per se*.

In the early days of philately, few collectors bothered to keep complete covers—the stamp was the important thing—and they were soaked off covers for mounting in albums. More recently interest has grown in keeping stamps on complete covers. This trend has had two causes—firstly the recognition that the stamp is just part of the story when one considers its use—as a receipt for the payment of a fee—in the postal service. One should also consider the item to be carried by the service (*i.e.* the cover) and any postal markings it receives. Indeed the story of a particular stamp can only be fully appreciated when one looks at the service to which it was put and the treatment (postmarking) it received. Secondly, the growing interest in the past has led many people to want to build up a collection of historically interesting items and collecting covers and postcards is a relatively cheap and easy way of doing so. Also they have the advantage of being fairly easy to store—unlike antiques, trade artifacts and the like—which require a lot of space—as well as dusting!

Some postal historians tend to regard only covers carried before the introduction of postage stamps in 1840 as worth collecting; others consider covers of any period to be of interest. If one accepts this— and there is no logical reason not to—then the collecting of postal history becomes an on-going process and one can even begin with present-day covers and work on. Modern postal history—for example postcoded covers, etc.—is fast becoming more popular and the studies now undertaken and published will be much appreciated by the collectors of the future. One should perhaps make one proviso about the collection of modern items—it should be remembered that postal history is really about the study of mail services and material which is collected and studied should have travelled through the mails as part of a normal service offered to the public. Thus items specially manufactured for philatelic consumption—such as first day covers—will not always be considered *bona fide* items for such a collection.

As with stamp collectors, each postal historian will decide exactly what he wants to collect, there being—fortunately—no hard and fast rules about what to collect. Some will try to build up a representative collection of covers from a particular country; carried by particular methods of mail transport (by air or rail); sent to or from particular persons or groups of people (*e.g.* Royal Households, Parliaments, Government Departments, famous people); sent during times of difficulty and disruption in the postal services (*e.g.* wars, postal strikes); sent by particular postal services (*e.g.* registered or express mail) or having suffered from accidents in the course of delivery (crash or wreck covers). We refer here to the collector of postal history items of a particular country as a 'national postal historian'.

Perhaps the most popular form of collecting is 'Local Postal History'—the collecting of material bearing the postal markings of a particular county, town or village. The collector of such material will be referred to as a 'local postal historian'. In a general work such as this it would be impossible to try to describe the postal history material that exists for each British county but a few comments on the types of markings found on mail from most parts of the country (with some local examples) might be of interest.

The postal service in England began in the 16th century with the setting up of a messenger service whereby the government in London could keep in touch with its officers in the provinces. One of the main reasons for this network of official messengers was to ensure news of any possible rebellion would reach London quickly and so instructions could be sent about what measures should be taken to safeguard the king's peace. The first 'Master of the Posts' Sir Brian Tuke (*d. 1545*) was appointed by Henry VIII in *c.* 1512. Copies of early letters carried by these messengers are today most rare—indeed relatively few exist outside national and local archives, museums and important private collections of manuscripts. No postal markings were used, any information as to the time of despatch or arrival or the route taken being gleaned from manuscript endorsements. By the end of the 16th century the service was fairly well established and a proclamation of 1591 made it necessary for all mail to be sent by the royal postal service. As well as a service within England and Wales, messengers carried letters abroad—under the control of an official entitled the 'Postmaster of England for Foreign Parts out of the King's Dominions'.

Charles I in 1635 confirmed the right of all citizens to use the Royal Mail but separated administration of the carriage of mail for ordinary folk from that of official government correspondence. By the 1630s the service was becoming more efficient and more letters from this period have survived. Much of the mail bore manuscript endorsements such as 'Haste, Haste, Post Haste' and on official mail postmasters were required to endorse the wrapper with details of the time the letter arrived at their office. The mail for the ordinary citizen was carried by postboys but the condition of the roads was so bad that the average rate of carriage was probably no more than three to four miles an hour. In 1657 Cromwell formally established the General Letter Office and this was confirmed by Charles II on his restoration in 1660. The 'Merry Monarch' appointed Colonel Sir Henry Bishop (*1605–91*) as Postmaster-General, a post he held for three years. Bishop was the first of 100 Postmasters-General, the office was abolished in 1969 when the Post Office became a public corporation rather than a government department. (The chief executive is now known as the Chairman of the Post Office and is appointed by the Secretary of State for Industry, the government minister ultimately in charge of the P.O.). Two stamps marking the tercentenary of the establishment of the General Letter Office were issued in July 1960 (*SG 619–620*).

Bishop is an important man as far as postal historians are concerned for it was he who introduced—in 1661—the first postmark, usually known as the 'Bishop Mark'. Bishop referred to these markings as 'stamps' which he ordered were to be put on all letters '. . . shewing the day of the moneth that every letter comes to this office, so that no letter Carryer may dare to detayne a letter from post to post, which before was usual'. The first Bishop Marks comprised small, circular handstamps, the circle divided into two with the month (*e.g.* NO for November) in the top section and the day of the month below.

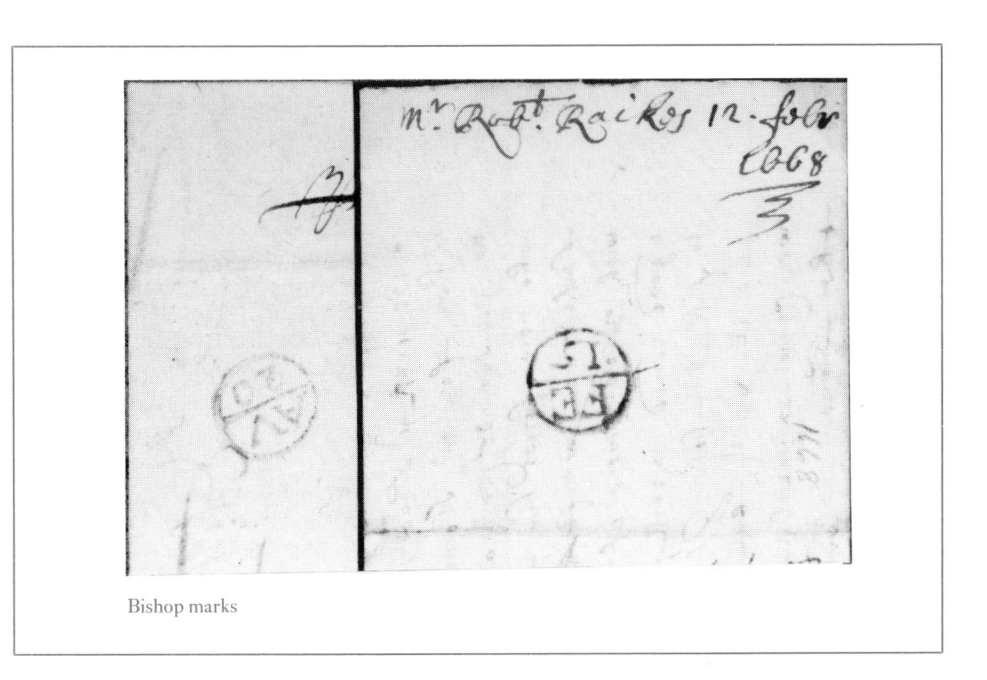

Bishop marks

These were first introduced at the Post Office in London and those used in the early years (1661–66) are now of considerable value. From 1713 larger size circles were introduced, these had the day in the top section with the month below and continued in use until the 1780s. Bishop Marks were introduced at post offices outside London from 1670 onwards—Dublin marks date from that year and marks were in use in Edinburgh by 1693. The Dublin mark consisted of two quite separate semi-circles, the Edinburgh marking was oval rather than circular. Marks of a more distinctive type were introduced from the 1690s—for example Bristol and Exeter used the date within the initials 'B' and 'E'. Later the circular markings were used at post offices in the Colonies (for example New York, 1758; Philadelphia, 1767; Boston, 1769; Albany and Charlestown, 1774; Calcutta, 1776). In addition one can find on letters from the late 17th century onwards a whole range of different 'Town Stamps'—some simply the name of the town in a straight line, others in two lines, convex or concave arc, horseshoe shape, etc. Straight line marks were introduced in Ireland in the late 1690s, in Scotland from the 1730s.

As well as markings used on the general mails, there are also to be found a great number of 'Local Post' markings used on mail sent within a specified area at a cheaper rate. In 1680 William Dockwra, a London merchant, and some business associates known as 'the Undertakers' established a local Penny Post in the city of London. This was suppressed two years later and replaced by an official service. Dockwra applied triangular markings to mail carried on his service, these are extremely rare. 'Government Dockwras'—similar markings used on the official service from 1682 to 1794 are more plentiful. Penny Posts for the delivery of local mails were permitted outside London from 1765 but such services do not appear to have become widespread until the 1790s. By 1840 there were some 2500 local Penny Posts in operation. Most of the markings used by these posts were simple rectangular or circular handstamps incorporating wording such as 'KELVEDEN/Penny Post'. For the most part these are still readily available on letters.

Government Dockwra postmark
Kelveden (*Essex*) Penny Post marking

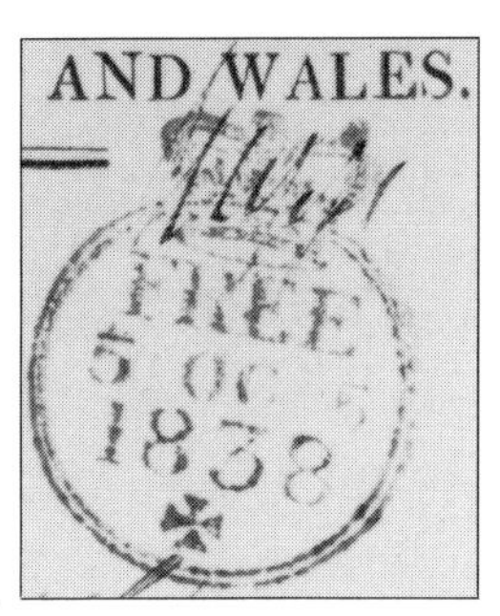

A 'Free' mark

Mention should be made here of one other group of pre-1840 markings—the so-called 'Free Franks' used on government mail. The earliest of these—simply the word 'FREE' within a circle, struck in red ink—were brought into use in 1764. Later a more elaborate mark was introduced comprising a circle topped by a crown and with the wording 'FREE' and the date. These were introduced in 1807 and continued in use until the 1860s when 'OFFICIAL PAID' handstamps were brought into use.

A uniform 4d Post was introduced on 5 December 1839 and operated for just over a month until the Penny Post came into being on 10 January 1840. In connexion with the 4d Post a number of handstamps simply inscribed '4' in a number of different typefaces were introduced at some 56 offices. These are rare. Similar handstamps were used at a far greater number of offices following the introduction of the Penny Post; these are worded '1', 'Paid/1', 'P1' or similar. These are normally found in red ink. For mail sent unpaid, 2d was charged and '2' stamps were used—usually in black but sometimes in blue or green. The use of the '1d' handstamps continued after the introduction of the postage stamp in May 1840. Usually these are found on letters in conjunction with the circular datestamps of the towns of despatch and arrival which are normally struck in black, on either the front or the back of the letter. Dated cancellations of this type were introduced in 1829.

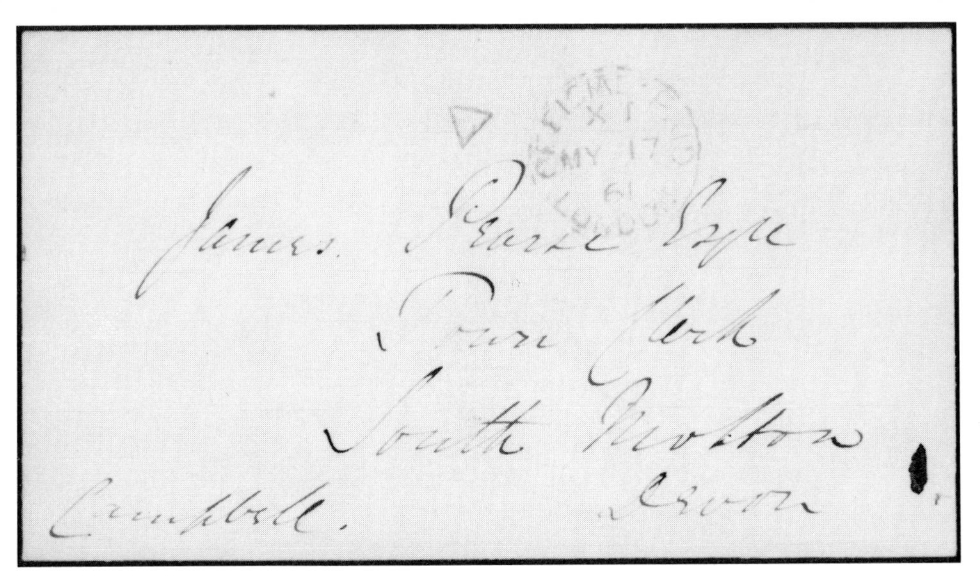

Early 'Official Paid' postmark

For some collectors, postal history ends in 1840—or in 1854 when the use of the '1d' handstamps finally ceased. For others it begins in 1840 with the cancellations used on postage stamps. The first cancellations were the famous 'Maltese Crosses'; these were undated and served only to cancel the stamp, datestamps were also applied to the letters to indicate despatch and arrival. Initially the Maltese Cross was struck in red on the Penny Black stamps, the following year the colour was changed to black and the penny stamp altered to red-brown. This resulted from the problem of stamps being reused—the red ink of the Maltese Cross cancel could be removed from the black stamp. Occasionally the Maltese Cross can be found in other colours—for example in yellow from Horsham, Sussex.

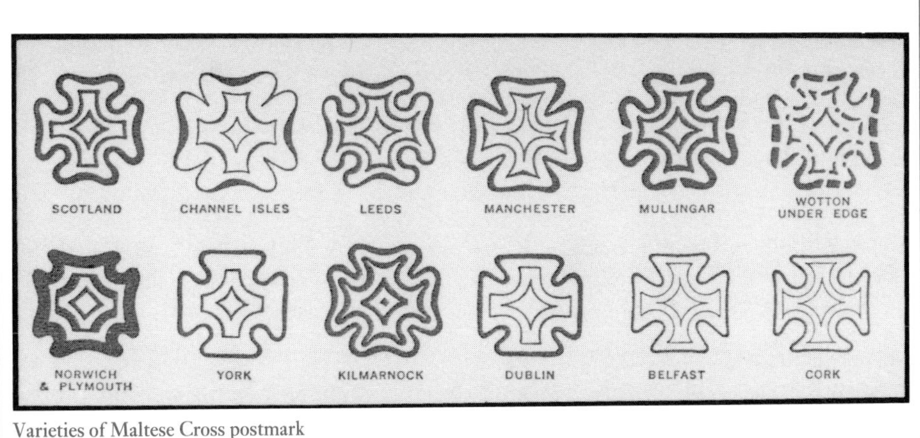

Varieties of Maltese Cross postmark

Edinburgh Duplex handstamp

Krag machine postmark

Although the Maltese Cross can be found in many variations, the basic design was not entirely satisfactory and the P.O. sought other forms of cancellation. In 1842 the town-dated postmarks were used to cancel stamps at certain towns in the South-West, for example Dorchester, Honiton, Lyme (Regis) and Totnes. Two years later the '1844 Type' cancellers were brought into general use—these comprised a number allocated to each office—set within a framework of bars; various types exist. The dated postmarks still had to be used as well so the process of cancelling the stamp and impressing the town's postmark remained a laborious job. In 1853 'duplex' postmarks were introduced—these served to cancel the stamp using a die of similar design to the '1844 type' and impress the town's postmark alongside. These continued in use until the 1890s (longer in some places) when the 'squared circle' handstamp began to be used. Single circle datestamps were used as backstamps from the 1850s and to cancel postage stamps from the 1880s. Double-circle cancels were introduced in 1883 and later variations of these two types of handstamp continue in use at some of the smaller post offices to the present day.

The use of machines for cancelling British stamps began experimentally in 1857 but their use did not become widespread outside London until after 1910. Three types of machine cancel are particularly well known—the Krag machine used from 1905 (with straight cancelling bars), the Universal machine used from 1910 (usually with wavy line bars) and the Hey-Dolphin machine in regular use from 1921 to 1933 (wavy line bars). Nowadays most mail is machine postmarked and the use of handstamps confined to cancelling the stamps on registered mail or counter work (certificates of posting, stamping pension books, etc.). The postal historian who includes modern handstamps may find some difficult to obtain on cover.

Early on it was realised that machine postmarking could be used for publicity purposes and in 1917 a slogan 'Buy War Bonds' replaced the wavy line portion in Krag machine postmarks. Many slogans were aimed at extolling the virtues of Post Office services ('Buy

Stamps in Books') or at encouraging customers 'To Post Early in the Day'. Occasionally a commemorative design was used—a Lover's Knot and the initials 'E' and 'P' being used at the time of the marriage of Princess Elizabeth to Philip Mountbatten in November 1947 and a 'God Save the Queen' slogan was used in Coronation Year (1953). Local postal historians will require specimens of these slogans used at post offices within their collecting area. In 1963 the P.O. agreed that holiday towns could advertise their amenities on slogan postmarks and the first to do so was Hastings with a slogan depicting 'Happy Harold the Saxon Warrior' and the wording 'We're ready for your invasion at Hastings'. Since then such slogans have been used at a considerable number of offices. Local events have also been publicised—for example the slogan 'Weymouth Carnival Wednesday 18th August' was used on all mail posted in the town between 3 and 16 August 1982. Local charities have been promoted, also local radio stations. Anniversaries of local significance have sometimes been commemorated—for example 'Fiftieth Anniversary of Southend Hospital 1932–1982' used from 26 July to 7 August 1982. Some of these slogans are in use for long periods of time—occasionally for as long as one year—others are used for only a few weeks or even days. Postal historians are advised to obtain copies at the time as they are not always easy to find later.

Parcel Post cancel and label

The British Post Office introduced the parcel post service in August 1883. Special handstamps have always been used on parcels. Initially the handstamps used to cancel adhesives were undated, circular and contained a design of horizontal or vertical bars. The large rectangular parcel post cancellations—still in use—were introduced from the late 1880s, their design has varied slightly over the years. In the early days of the service, the postage stamps were affixed to a special 'Parcel Post' label, which was then affixed to the parcel. More recently, the stamps have been affixed directly to the parcel but a small label bearing the counter datestamp of the office of despatch is sometimes affixed alongside. Parcel post postmarks and labels are an interesting field of study in their own right but few collectors will be brave enough to try to obtain all known examples. Local postal historians will, of course, confine themselves to the marks and labels used at offices within their district. Small packets often contain items of a fragile nature and uneven shape which cannot be fed through postmarking machines. Instead packet handstamps are used on these, the handstamps are normally made of rubber and are of larger size than the single-ring or double-ring metal datestamps. These were first introduced in the 1880s although not specifically for use on packets, this specialised use has come about in more recent times.

Packet handstamp

Oval registered post handstamp

Businesses who send large amounts of mail can hand in their letters or parcels at a post office unstamped together with the postage, the Post Office will then apply a red 'Postage Paid' postmark—either by hand or machine. Since 1968 these have been worded '1st Paid' or '2nd Paid' as appropriate. Very large mailings are marked 'R PAID' indicating rebate mail, the customer getting a substantial discount on the total postage bill. 'Paid' handstamps date back to the early years of the nineteenth century and were in regular use until 1852 (1855 in London). The prepayment of postage in cash (except for official mail) then ceased but was revived in 1857 and continues today. 'Paid' machine postmarks were introduced in 1902. These 'PAID' impressions should not be confused with 'Official Paid' postmarks (*see below*).

In addition to the handling of ordinary letters, cards and parcels, the P.O. also provide many other services and most of these offer something of interest to the local postal historian. Registered mail is always hand cancelled rather than machine postmarked and this is often the only way of acquiring a circular datestamp on an adhesive stamp. Some offices have special oval handstamps for use on registered mail and these oval cancellations are sometimes found on postage due covers. When mail is registered a small label bearing the name of the P.O. and a reference number is affixed to the cover. As these labels are unique to each office they have postal history significance and at least one sample from each office in your collecting area is worth obtaining. Variations will occur as the labels are reprinted but they remain the same basic design. There are a number of collectors who specialise in registration labels and try to acquire copies from all post offices—a tall order as there are over 20,000 in the British Isles, let alone overseas. As these labels are of dull appearance their popularity is limited and their value—once removed from cover—is minimal. The Recorded Delivery service was introduced in 1962 and the national postal historian will require copies of the certificates used and the labels affixed to mail. There have been several variations over the years, including ones printed in Welsh. However as the labels are not unique to particular post offices, they have considerably less appeal to the local postal historian.

Registration labels

Special Delivery and Express Post labels

Labels were affixed to mail sent by 'Express' or 'Special Delivery' service. These were abolished for inland mail in 1979 and replaced by a service known as 'Royal Mail Special Delivery'. Two different labels are affixed to each packet sent by this service and a certificate of posting issued to the sender. A similar label is affixed to mail sent by 'Swiftair', the equivalent service for mail addressed overseas. 'Expresspost' and 'Datapost' are designed more for the use of businesses than for the general public and so the labels used on packets sent by these services are not so often seen or widely known. Nevertheless the conscientious national postal historian should not overlook them.

Postal meter franking machines have been used since 1922; companies obtaining these machines from one of several manufacturers licensed by the P.O. Mail is fed through the machine and the correct postage amount printed on the cover in red. The design of the meter mark includes the name of the town, date of posting, postage and sometimes an advertising slogan for the company using the machine. The company takes the machine to the local post office for resetting as necessary and pays in advance for postage it is going to use. Meter marks are of relatively little interest unless a slogan is used which readily identifies the company concerned, although as each impression includes the reference number of the machine it is possible to identify the user even when no slogan is used.

Occasionally the advertising slogan is replaced by a commemorative design—for example Pitney-Bowes, one of the manufacturers of these machines, used attractive Shakespeare and Battle of Hastings anniversary designs on their own mail in 1964 and 1966 respectively. Mail from the Bristol City Council was meter-franked with a design commemorating the 600th anniversary of the city's charter in 1973. In recent years government departments have increasingly used meter franks and one can assemble an interesting display of these—National Gallery, Foreign Office, British Museum, National Railway Museum, etc.

Pitney-Bowes Battle of Hastings meter franking

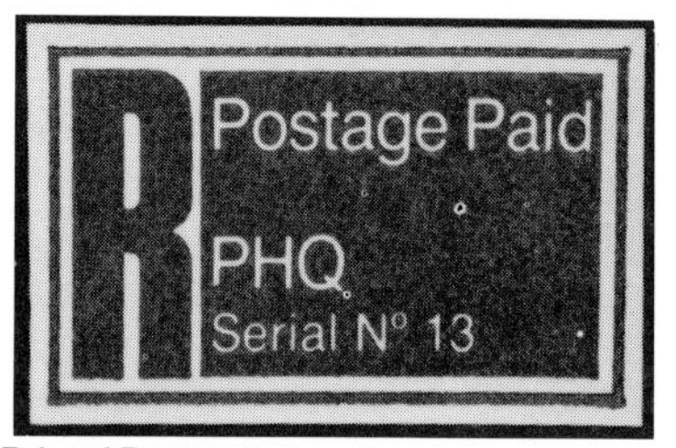

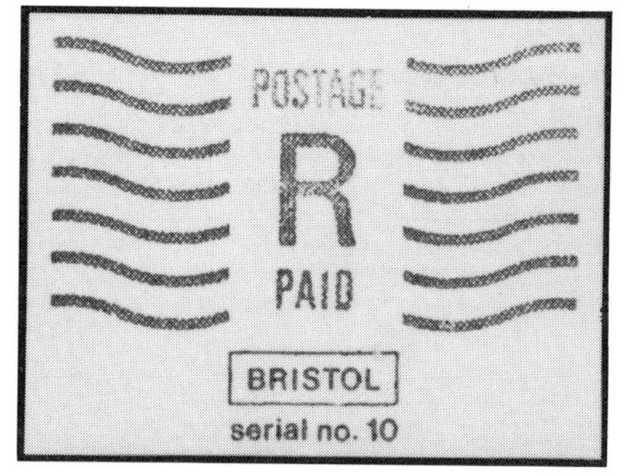

Printed Postage Impressions

Some large business houses send out advertising material in bulk—often these mailings run into many thousands of items—and it would be extremely time-consuming if each had to be franked with a postage stamp, meter mark or even 'Postage Paid' postmark. Thus in 1966 the P.O. introduced the 'Printed Postage Impression' (P.P.I.)—firms being permitted to print a postage paid design on their envelopes and pay the postage when the items are handed over to the P.O. The impression is normally of a standard design incorporating the name of the town, a licence number and a code indicating the type of postal service required—*e.g.* '1' = first class post, '2' = second class, 'P' = parcel post and 'R' = rebate mail (a reduced rate service when exceptionally large amounts of mail are handled in one go). The impressions are not cancelled by the P.O. as they cannot be reused. Local postal historians should keep specimens that come their way although it is perhaps not yet expected of them that they should make a positive effort to find copies. Where possible the impression should be kept on the entire cover as this will often have printed on it the name of the licensee. As these impressions are not postmarked, collectors should write the date of receipt in pencil on the back of the cover otherwise there will be no way of telling later when that particular impression was in use. These impressions are not unique to Britain and an interesting collection can be built up of those used in other countries.

Apart from postmarks used on routine mail, the local postal historian will want to include in his collection examples of postmarks used on special types of mail. Where the town lies on the coast, he may find that some mail receives a *Paquebot* postmark—these are used on mail handed in at a post office by members of ship's crew, the mail having been 'posted' on the high seas. Paquebot postmarks are not used so frequently now as in the past and some modern examples are extremely rare. Some post offices in major ports use a machine die inscribed 'PAQUEBOT' alongside the normal datestamp; smaller offices use handstamps which include the word 'Paquebot' in the inscription. In some offices normal datestamps are used to cancel the stamps and a cachet worded 'Paquebot' is applied alongside. Under the international regulations governing such mail, covers may be franked with the stamps of the country of embarkation of the ship, the country of destination or of the country under whose flag the ship sails. Thus stamps can be obtained 'used abroad'—for example mail posted on board cross-channel ferries franked with British stamps can receive French postmarks and vice-versa. Some Paquebot cancellations are used regularly and on considerable quantities of mail, others are used almost 'once in a blue moon' on a single piece or mere handful of mail. Needless to say the value of these postmarks ranges considerably—from a few pence to hundreds of pounds. Paquebot postmarks should not be confused with ship's cachets—these are held by the purser of nearly all vessels for use on documents of various kinds. Occasionally they are applied to covers and postcards—usually as a favour to philatelists, the mail is then posted at the next port of call and normally receives the standard rather than the Paquebot cancel. These cachets make interesting items—especially when found on picture postcards of the relevant ship—but they are not officially applied markings of a postal administration and consequently have less collector appeal and only modest value. Those used by British shipping companies usually include the ship's official registration number, gross tonnage and port of registration.

Paquebot postmark

Philatelic mail can be an interesting branch of postal history. Most offices have at some time used a special sponsored handstamp. Sometimes these commemorate some aspect of local history, others a special exhibition or similar event. Normally the handstamp will have been used for one day only and the number of items posted will vary from a few hundred to perhaps 5000. Occasionally, if the event commemorated is of more than local interest, the number of covers posted will be greater—for example 34,000 items of mail were posted in Canterbury on 29 May 1982 to receive a special handstamp marking the visit of Pope John Paul II to the city to take part in a special service at the Cathedral. Special handstamps have long been popular on the Continent, each month the French P.O. uses large numbers of them, often of very attractive designs; they are also frequently used by Scandinavian Post Offices and in the U.S.A. Mostly they are to be found on specially designed envelopes prepared by the sponsoring organisation but collectors can post their own (blank or designed) covers. Local postal historians should find little difficulty in obtaining copies of all such handstamps used in their area. Likewise, those interested in postmarks whose design features a particular theme, will find the number manageable. A complete one-country collection may (for some countries) now run into thousands of different impressions. However, these postmarks are normally available at very modest cost, thus any collector with the wish to complete a collection for his chosen country, could do so over a period of time without too great a strain on his resources.

Altrincham First Day of Issue handstamp and cachet

Irish First Day of Issue cachet

Since 1963 the British P.O. has provided 'First Day of Issue' postmarks at most major offices for use on first day covers of new stamps. A local postal historian will require a specimen of this handstamp used in his town on the date the first day posting facility was introduced there and specimens of any subsequent handstamps showing changes in design or wording. In some instances very few covers were posted on the first day of the service, for example only 486 covers were cancelled at Lerwick, Shetland when the philatelic box was first provided there on 22 July 1981. On one occasion a local Head Postmaster provided a special cachet to commemorate the introduction of his 'First Day of Issue' handstamp—this was used at Altrincham, Cheshire on 22 January 1975 and would be a vital item for a collector of Altrincham postal history. In Ireland a 'First Day of Issue' cachet worded 'Lá a Chéad Eisiúna', is normally applied alongside the stamps on first day covers, the stamps themselves being cancelled with ordinary datestamps (in Dublin and some other places proper 'First Day of Issue' postmarks are now used). In the U.S.A. a particular post office is designated as the 'First Day of Issue Office' for each new issue of stamps—

normally a place having a direct connexion with the subject of the issue. In Europe 'First Day of Issue' postmarks have been in use for many years, pictorial designs are frequently used and the standard of cancellation normally very high. However, European collectors favour unaddressed first day covers which, by definition, do not travel through the regular mails and consequently are not regarded by purist collectors as appropriate to a postal history (*even modern postal history*) collection.

Since 1972 pictorial handstamps have been used on mail posted at some British philatelic counters—these, too, are of interest to the local postal historian. Likewise tourist cachets—such as Land's End and John O'Groats—although not applied by the Post Office—may be included if they are in use within the postal district you are collecting. Some collectors regard such cachets as a specialist subject in their own right and an engaging collection of them can be built up. However, much patience is required as many are rarely seen. There are at least 80 different Land's End cachets, some of which are hard to find as they were in use for only a short time.

Broadstairs station postmark

Having looked at material of interest to the local postal historian we now turn our attention to certain other Postal History collecting subjects. Railway covers are very popular. There are three main types of covers sought by the railway postal historian—(1) bearing handstamps used at post offices sited on or close to railway stations, (2) T(ravelling) P(ost) O(ffice) handstamps and (3) covers carried by the railway letter service. In the 19th century post offices were located on many railway stations in Britain so that mail could quickly be processed and forwarded by rail to its destination. A few such offices still operate but most have closed, including those on main London stations—the last to close was that at Waterloo station in March 1977. Some still operate at locations near a station and this fact is attested in the wording of the handstamps used—for example 'Anerley, near Station, London SE20' or 'Silvertown, near Station, London E16'. The first British T.P.O.s were introduced in the 1850s and there are still a number in operation. Special handstamps are applied to mail posted in the box on the side of the T.P.O. carriage or in special 'Late Posting Boxes' on the stations. These handstamps are inscribed with the name of the T.P.O. and the word 'Up' or 'Down' depending on the direction the service is operating. Until 1976 all mail posted on these travelling post offices had to bear additional postage stamps to prepay a 'Late Fee', this no longer applies but letters despatched by T.P.O. must be sent by the first class inland post. Finally we come to railway letters. This service is explained in Chapter 12, suffice here to say that collectors of railway postal history will want a few examples of such items in their collections and local postal historians would do well to have an example from their local station.

Covers sent from royal residences and government departments are popular. From 1840 until 1901 mail sent from royal homes bore postage stamps in the normal way although Queen Victoria wrote 'The Queen' in the bottom left hand corner of envelopes containing her personal correspondence. Needless to say these are scarce. Edward VII restored the privilege of free postage for the Royal Household and envelopes sent by him or his senior staff were given a small circular 'franking stamp' (cachet) bearing the royal cypher. 'Official Paid' handstamps in red ink were applied by the Post Office. The royal franking stamps have been used by subsequent sovereigns and are generally fairly easy to obtain—except the one used during the short reign of Edward VIII. That used by George VI exists in two forms—inscribed 'GRI' (George Rex Imperator—King, Emperor) or, from 1946 'GR'.

Other cachets are applied by the staffs of various departments within the Royal Household—Privy Purse, Master of the Horse, etc. As these are used on quite large amounts of mail and as the recipients tend to keep them, they are not uncommon and can normally be obtained surprisingly cheaply. Collectors not infrequently write to Buckingham Palace for specimens of these cachets but such requests are not normally met. Registered mail sent from royal residences is franked with postage stamps and these are cancelled with circular handstamps inscribed 'Buckingham Palace', 'Windsor Castle', 'Balmoral Castle', 'Holyrood Palace' or 'Sandringham House, Norfolk'. These handstamps are not used very frequently and covers bearing them are normally quite scarce. Red 'Official Paid' handstamps are used on ordinary mail and are inscribed only with the town name—London SW (Buckingham Palace), Windsor, Ballater (Balmoral), Edinburgh (Holyrood) or King's Lynn (Sandringham). Normally these are found on covers with the royal cypher frank and are not rare.

Mail from Parliament bearing postage stamps receives one of three postmarks—a 'House of Commons' machine cancel or 'House of Commons' or 'House of Lords' handstamps. Most of the mail, however, is unstamped and receives a red 'Official Paid House of Commons' or 'Official Paid House of Lords' handstamp. Some cachets are still applied prior to posting—Black Rod, Speaker, Lord Great Chamberlain, etc. Those currently in use are fairly easy to obtain, earlier versions are not. Franks or official cachets inscribed with the name of the department have been used at many government offices since at least the 1860s. Prior to this mail was signed by a senior official to indicate that it should go free of postage. Some officials had metal handstamps of their signatures made to prevent them getting writers' cramp. Today the only such 'signature stamp' in use is that of the Government Chief Whip in the House of Lords.

'Official Paid' handstamps were introduced from the 1860s—struck in red and an interesting display of the various types used over the years can be made. Initially these were used only at London offices but with the spread of the civil service to other places these postmarks can now be found for most cities and large towns. They are closely akin to the 'Paid' postmarks already mentioned. Until recently vast amounts of government mail were despatched in envelopes bearing an 'Official Paid' device (printed design) in the top right hand corner. This was introduced in *c.* 1904 and at least three different designs were used. In 1980 it was decided to phase out the use of such envelopes and correspondence is now sent in envelopes bearing either a meter mark or printed postage impression (*see above*). A few departments have returned to the use of postage stamps which are cancelled in the normal way.

Interesting government covers can be obtained from other countries. Some Commonwealth governments still apply official cachets to their mail, for example the Prime Minister's Office in New Zealand and the Governors' Offices in Gibraltar and the Bahamas.

Official cachet of the Postmaster of Anguilla

Most government departments in the Republic of Ireland still apply cachets—featuring the Irish harp as a central motif. Many postal authorities apply cachets of some description to their mail. Even postal authority envelopes bearing 'Official Paid' designs can make an interesting study—for example the variations in the 'coat of arms' design on mail from Guernsey P.O. or the pictorial designs on the Isle of Man Philatelic Bureau envelopes.

The national postal historian should not ignore changes in the basic postal rates—nowadays often all too frequent—and should endeavour to obtain covers bearing each rate. For example since the two-tier postal service was introduced in Britain in September 1968, the postal rate has been increased on a number of occasions and a complete collection of covers for each of the two basic rates would be a telling testimony to modern inflation. Nor should one ignore postal notices and information leaflets and any collector mounting modern covers showing postal rate increases could well include some of the leaflets issued by the P.O. giving details of the new rates. Leaflets about other postal services—registration, special delivery, etc. should also be retained—even if not mounted on the album page.

In recent years collectors have begun to save covers associated with postal mechanisation. In Britain the first experiments took place at Brighton in the 1930s using machines known as 'Transorma' which printed small red codes on to envelopes. Since the mid-1960s phosphor dots (almost colourless or since 1976 in blue) have been applied to mail code-sorted at mechanised sorting offices. These were first used experimentally at Luton in the late 1950s and these early covers are scarce and eagerly sought by those interested in postal mechanisation. A local postal historian will want covers coded at his local office. Those used with postcode dots on the first day of use of the machinery will often be scarce as all too frequently little warning was given for collectors to prepare covers. Akin to the mechanised sorting of mail using postcodes is the segregating of mail into first and second class using the phosphor bands on the stamps (see Chapter 6). When the mail has been sorted it is postmarked and the A.L.F. ('Automatic Letter Facer) machines have their own identifiable postmarks. The first machine was introduced at Southampton P.O. in December 1957 and mail received a postmark inscribed 'Southampton' at top and 'S' below. Mail processed by the normal machinery received other alphabetical codings. Later the 'S' machine was replaced by one with a 'T' postmark. Copies of the 'Remember to Use the Postcode' slogan and other relevant postmarks should also be included in a study of postal mechanisation material.

In this chapter we have looked chiefly at some of the many different postal markings found on mail handled by the British Post Office. Most other countries operate similar services (*e.g.* registration, official paid mail, etc.) to those provided in Britain and the postal markings are often surprisingly similar—but of course inscribed in a different language.

As with stamp collectors, some postal history collectors arrange their collections on thematic or 'cross frontier' lines—specialising in mail carried by ship, plane, sent during times of war, etc. We cannot hope to cover all the different themes in any detail here so will confine ourselves to a few general, but hopefully helpful, comments.

Aerophilately has been discussed in Chapter 20. Whilst some collectors confine their interest to unused or used examples of air post stamps, the more imaginative collector will seek covers carried on first or special flights, or covers bearing special postmarks or cachets. In ancient times pigeons were used to carry letters and these messengers of the air were extensively used to carry correspondence in and out of Paris during the siege of 1870–71. Mail was also carried by balloon. A regular pigeon post operated in New Zealand from Auckland to the Great Barrier Island from 1896 to 1908. The letters so carried were written on tissue paper. Special stamps for this service were in use from 1898 to 1908.

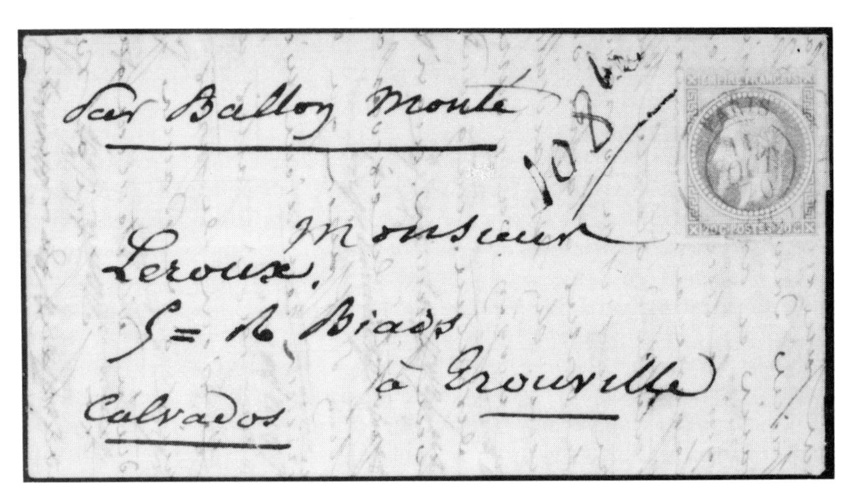

Paris Ballon Monté cover (*October 1870*)

The earliest carriage of mail by aeroplane took place at demonstration meetings—most of the mail comprised souvenir postcards which were given a variety of cachets and labels. The postage stamps on these cards were normally cancelled with ordinary, operational postmarks. In India special airmail flights took place in 1911 and mail carried on these flights was given a special postmark. The fiftieth anniversary of these flights was commemorated by special stamps in February 1961—these depicted the 1911 plane and the 'Aerial Post' cancellation. Similar special flights also took place during 1911 in Italy and the U.S.A. The first regular air mail services in the U.S.A. was inaugurated in 1918 (Washington to New York via Philadelphia). A special 24c airmail stamp depicting the biplane used was issued. The initial flight did not go smoothly but did prove the worth of carrying mail by air and after the war a considerable network of internal air route services was developed. The first regular airmail service in Europe—between Berlin and Weimar—started in February 1919. Also in 1919 an airmail service was introduced in Colombia, South America. There were two major air companies carrying mail—the *Compania Colombiana de Navegacion Aerea* (C.C. de N.A.) and the *Sociedad-Colombo-Alemana De Transportes Aereos* (S.C.A.D.T.A.). Both issued airmail stamps and these used on cover—alongside postage stamps—are desirable items.

The first trans-Atlantic flight from Newfoundland in May 1919 gave rise to a special overprint on the Newfoundland 3c definitive stamp. Only 95 of these stamps were used on letters. The plane—piloted by a 30-year old Australian Harry George Hawker with Lt. Commander Kenneth Mackenzie Grieve—came down in the sea and the two airmen had to be rescued by a Danish ship. The mail was recovered although it was damaged by sea water. Various other Newfoundland stamps were overprinted for later airmail flights but 'the Hawker' remains the most sought-after. By the 1930s regular airmail services were operated to many parts of the world. Some mail was automatically carried by air without any additional charge—for example the Empire Air Mail Scheme of 1937–39 by which all first class mail between Britain and the Empire countries was sent by air or 'all up' as it was popularly known. Few postal historians can hope to acquire some of the great rarities such as 'the Hawker' on cover but many of the first flight covers from the 1930s and 1940s can still be found priced at a few pounds each. Those on which the postage stamp is cancelled with a special postmark as opposed to an ordinary one are normally of greater interest and will probably command a slightly higher price. Some of the specially designed covers are in themselves collectable—depicting aircraft of the period, route maps, etc. In recent times special postmarks have been used, and commemorative covers produced, in connexion with the first commercial flights of Concorde on various routes. As these have been prepared in large numbers they will never achieve the same rarity as the early flight covers but will no doubt still be sought after by future generations of postal historians.

In Britain an appreciable amount of first class inland mail is now carried by air rather than by road or rail. However no special postal markings are used to denote the method of carriage. Only 'airway letters' carried by British Airways as agents for the Post Office bear special airmail stamps and markings. Details of the airway letter service are given in Chapter 12. A collection of covers carried on each of the various internal routes makes an interesting display. The local postal historian will require covers sent by this service from any airports in his area.

Many collectors find fascination in the postal history of war time. Some of the most interesting markings are to be found on covers sent from soldiers engaged in the Egyptian Campaign, the Occupation of Sudan, the Boer War and the First World War. Following the murder of Europeans in Alexandria in 1882 a British Expeditionary Force was despatched to Egypt and Field Post Office services were provided. Two postmarks were supplied to the F.P.O.—one single ring datestamp worded 'BRITISH ARMY POST OFFICE/EGYPT' and a 'killer' inscribed 'B.A./E.'. The killer was only occasionally used and then not usually to cancel adhesives. As a result of the assassination of General Gordon at Khartoum a combined British and Indian force was despatched to the Sudan in 1885. Handstamps similar to those used in the Egyptian campaign were provided.

The Boer War of October 1899—May 1902 is of considerable interest to postal history collectors—a wide variety of cancellations, censor marks, prisoner of war mails, etc. being used. The Army Postal Service established its headquarters at Cape Town from which control was exercised over some 71 stationary, field and railway travelling post offices—all using distinctive postmarks. These postmarks come in circular, rectangular and octagonal shapes. Perhaps the most common are double ring datestamps inscribed 'FIELD POST OFFICE/BRITISH ARMY SOUTH AFRICA' or FIELD POST OFFICE/BRITISH ARMY S.AFRICA'.

The expertise and organisation acquired during the Boer War was put to good use during the First World War. Some 300 staff were employed in the Army Postal Service—mail was sent from London to the Base Army P.O.s—at Boulogne, Calais, Le Havre and Rouen and from there to post offices at Divisional Headquarters and finally to the Unit Field

P.O.s for delivery to front-line troops. This postal service for the 'Tommies' was described in the book *Arms and the Men* (by Ian Hay) as 'one of the unadvertised marvels of the war'. Cancellations—single or double-circle—were inscribed 'ARMY BASE POST OFFICE', 'ARMY POST OFFICE' or 'FIELD POST OFFICE'. Each postmark included a coding indicating the location of the office concerned. From 1916, following fears that the postmark codes could be used by the enemy to ascertain exact military formations, the postmarks were changed round between army units every three months to conceal information concerning locations.

As well as postmarks used at Army bases overseas during both war and peace time, an interesting collection can be made of the cancellations used at Army bases at home (*e.g.* Bisley Camp, Woking or Shorncliffe Camp, Folkestone). In recent years the Forces Postal Service has become aware of philatelic interest and specially designed handstamps have been used to commemorate military anniversaries, tattoos and the like. During both World Wars mails were liable to inspection by the censor and various cachets were applied to show that mail had been examined. These markings were struck in various inks and a colourful display of them can be arranged.

Army Post Office postmarks

Even during hostilities, governments have realised the importance of allowing servicemen to receive and send mail—subject of course to the need to safeguard strategic details which could be of value to the enemy. Covers can be found showing evidence of internatonal co-operation in the delivery of mail—for example during the Boxer Rebellion of June 1900–September 1901. As the Chinese government incited violence against foreigners in their country, troops from a number of countries were sent to China as a sort of 'peace-keeping force'. Mail franked with stamps of more than one country and cancelled with respective Field Post Office postmarks can be found (*e.g.* Indian and German stamps on one cover). Indian stamps were overprinted 'C.E.F.' (China Expeditionary Force) for use on mail sent during the Boxer Rebellion.

Mail from prisoner of war camps makes a fascinating area of study. During the Napoleonic Wars, French prisoners were provided with letter sheets to write to their families; during the Franco-Prussian War (1870–71) and the First World War the Red Cross was instrumental in aiding prisoners to write home using special cards—often showing views of the camp or the prisoners during work or recreation periods. Prisoners in German camps during the Second World War were given Prisoner of War Post Cards (*Kriegsgefangenenpost*), these were printed in two parts—the first for the use of the prisoner, the second for the reply from his family.

During the Falklands Campaign (April–June 1982), mail from members of the British 'Task Force' received a plethora of cancellations and markings. Most mail from men aboard Royal Navy and requisitioned Merchant Navy vessels received at least one cachet worded with name of the ship and on arrival in London passed through the Inland Section of the Mount Pleasant P.O. receiving a 'MARITIME MAIL' handstamp or machine postmark. Mail sent by troops landed on the islands was given Field Post Office cancellations—numbers 941 and 141. Postal services for the civilian population were of course severely disrupted—covers exist bearing Falkland stamps left uncancelled but with an Argentine 'MALVINAS' cachet alongside; others have Argentinian stamps cancelled with this cachet. Mail services were quickly restored after the reintroduction of British control on 15 June 1982 and covers bearing Falkland stamps cancelled shortly after the resumption of postal services are also of interest.

Falklands Campaign cover (*1982*)

Mail is sometimes delayed and/or damaged by accidents—air crashes and less frequently by shipwrecks. Mail recovered from these accidents is usually given a special cachet to indicate the reason for the delay or damage. Such items are usually of limited number and keenly sought. Mail carried on the liner *Empress of India* lost off the coast of Canada in 1914 was not recovered until some years later—the covers, then in a rather dilapidated condition, were given a cachet worded 'Recovered by divers from the wreck of S.S. *Empress of India*'. Covers recovered from the ill-fated Aer Lingus aircraft St. Kevin on a flight from Sweden to Dublin in 1952 were given a label explaining their unhappy journey. Less dramatic accidents also occur—mail is destroyed or damaged by fires in letter boxes or sorting offices or is sometimes eaten by snails or similar creatures which somehow get into letter boxes. Damaged mail of this sort is normally delivered with some endorsement explaining the reason for damage. Sometimes a specially printed label is affixed, the reason being completed in manuscript. A small percentage of mail is damaged by modern high-speed letter sorting machinery and again these are normally given the explanatory label. They are of interest to collectors of postal mechanisation material as well as to collectors of damaged mail.

Wreck Cover – Saved from the Colombo (*1862*)

Label used on mail damaged in sorting machinery

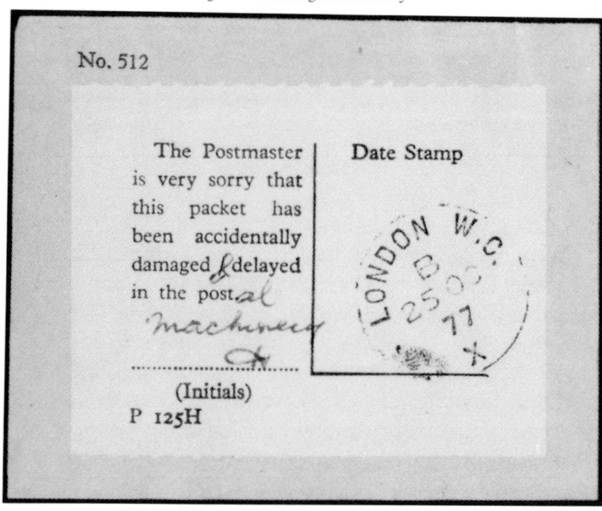

No. 512

The Postmaster is very sorry that this packet has been accidentally damaged & delayed in the postal machinery

Date Stamp

LONDON W.C.
B
77

(Initials)

P 125H

Postage Due covers can be the subject of a worthwhile collection—and such covers have particular appeal if they have travelled across national frontiers. As long ago as 1875 the Universal Postal Union agreed that there should be a uniform postal rate for mail weighing up to 15 grammes (25 centimes, 2½d or 5c U.S.). Understamped mail was to be given a marking 'T' (*Taxe*) to indicate that postage due should be collected. On arrival in the country of destination, the Post Office would affix postage due stamps or apply cachets or manuscript endorsements to indicate the exact amount to be collected.

Since 1967 by international agreement mail has been marked in the country of posting with an indicator of how much postage due is to be collected. For example where the postal rate was 40 units and only 30 units of postage had been affixed, the deficiency of 10 units was doubled and the indicator of postage due shown as $\frac{20}{40}$. The post office of delivery would then multiply their basic international postage rate by this indicator. Since 1976 the postage due has been indicated by the exact amount of the deficiency—in the example above, $\frac{10}{40}$. A standard surcharge is also levied. For British mail a standard double-deficiency system still applies. An interesting development in the field of British postage due took place in 1969 when Guernsey and Jersey took over responsibility for their own postal services. Many letters and cards bearing Channel Island stamps are posted at Weymouth (the port for the C.I.) and as C.I. stamps are no longer valid on the mainland a special cachet was produced for use on such mail—it is worded 'CHANNEL ISLANDS STAMPS NOT VALID'. British postage due stamps are affixed at the office of delivery. Care is normally taken to ensure the C.I. stamps are not cancelled with the 'Weymouth, Dorset' postmark.

Postage Due cover with Channel Islands stamps posted in Weymouth

'Stamps' issued from vending machines could become a postal history collecting area in the forseeable future. In recent years postal rates have increased quite considerably in most countries. One of the problems caused by this was the difficulty of providing the necessary stamps for stamp vending machines outside post offices. The British P.O. tried to solve the problem by introducing multi-value strips of stamps instead of single values in machines from 1969. However by 1978 the postal rate had increased to such a level that this was difficult to maintain. Booklets of stamps are now dispensed. Some other countries have introduced machines which print on to adhesive paper a 'stamp' of the required value. These are affixed to mail and cancelled in the usual way. Such stamps—referred to in the *Stanley Gibbons Catalogue* as 'Machine Labels' are sometimes called 'Automat stamps'. Amongst the countries using them are Brazil, Belgium, Finland, West Germany, Norway, Portugal and Switzerland. The West German machines were introduced in January 1981 and initially 14 different values could be printed—ranging from 10 to 280pf. These stamps are recorded but not listed and priced in the Gibbons Catalogue. However, they may well prove popular with collectors in the long-term—both unused and used on cover. Postal history collectors would be well advised to obtain specimens of each value used on cover—particularly covers postmarked during the early days of usage. Some collectors might regard these stamps as 'cinderella'—this would be a pity as they perform exactly the same function as ordinary postage stamps and are issued by the official postal authority. To give them second class status would be illogical especially as in time they may well be used to the same extent as traditional stamps.

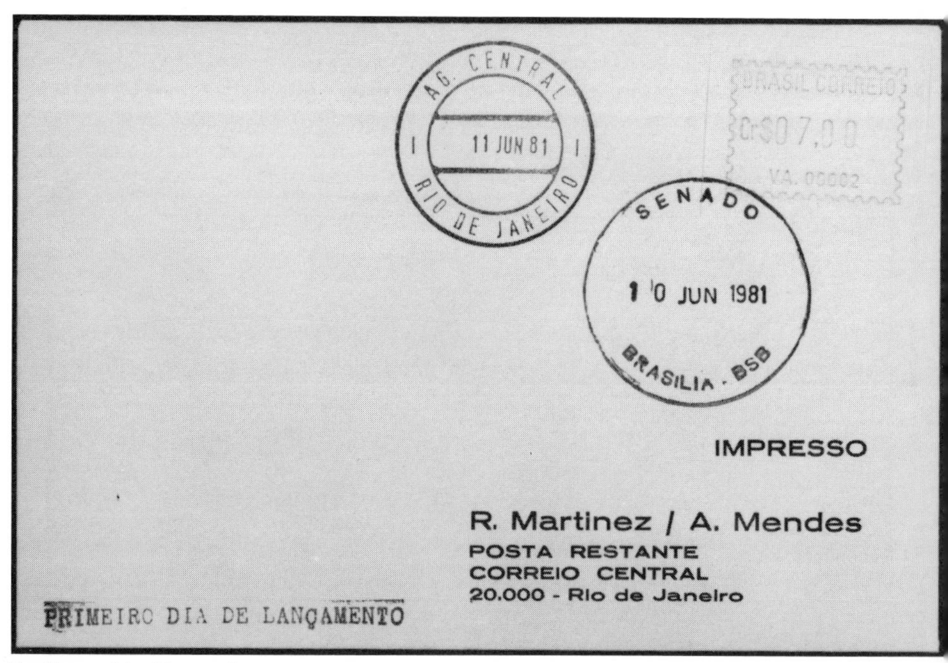

Vending machine 'Automat' stamp

Some collectors like illustrated covers. These were quite plentiful in the 19th century as many designers and artists produced covers taking off the famous but much maligned Mulready envelope. Many of these covers were 'one-off', hand-drawn and painted. As well as the individually prepared covers, several printers produced covers of a decorative nature—including Valentines of Dundee who produced envelopes depicting the evils of drink as part of a nationwide temperance movement. Space was provided in the top right-hand corner for the postage stamp and in the centre of the design for the address. Pictorial envelopes were extremely popular in the U.S.A.—in the 1850s covers were printed extolling the virtues of 'cheap inland and ocean postage', and many were produced during the Civil War. Some Confederate postmasters produced their own stamps and postal stationery. Even now some artists like to prepare individual covers either for use as first day covers with new stamps or simply as works of art to impress and please their correspondents. Such material is not vital to the study and documentation of postal services but few collectors would turn away any such items they come across which please them and which are reasonably priced.

Illustrated cover

This leads us to picture postcards. Collecting postcards for the picture side is now a respectable hobby in its own right but is quite separate from both stamp and postal history collecting. Having said that, there are of course collectors who are both philatelists/postal historians and deltiologists (postcard collectors) *per se*. However the picture side of postcards can be a useful adjunct for the postal historian and can be used—where relevant—to illustrate facets of postal history—local post offices, old mail trains, vans, mail ships, etc. However the inclusion of postcards on the album page should be discriminatory—especially if the pages are to form an entry at a major stamp exhibition. Few judges will take kindly to an exhibit overcrowded with picture postcards however unusual, beautiful or interesting they might be. Nevertheless the postal historian would be wise to obtain relevant cards he finds in stamp or postcard dealers stocks and to keep these in his reference files along with postal notices, leaflets, newspaper cuttings and the like. Only the most significant of these should find their way onto the album page. Likewise modern postcards issued by Post Offices or philatelic societies depicting old postmarks, letter boxes and mail transport are worth obtaining but not usually worthy of inclusion in the postal history collection itself.

Post card of London's Chief Post Office (*1915*)

Finally a few words about caring for and buying postal history material. Many of the early letters will now be in a somewhat fragile state and care should be taken when handling these. In particular it is advisable not to try to store them in cover albums as taking them in and out of the transparent pockets may well cause damage—this is less likely with modern material (*e.g.* first day covers) which are made from more robust paper. The covers should be mounted on good quality album pages using large size photograph corners or large transparent mounts (produced for mounting blocks of stamps). Where the cover is grubby, dirt can be removed by careful cleaning with a very soft white rubber, artist's putty rubber or even a piece of dry white bread. Never use a coloured rubber or a white one which has hardened with age. Often an envelope will have been less than carefully opened and the opened edge will be rough—this can be trimmed using sharp scissors but otherwise the cover should not be cut in any way. A tear in the cover should be repaired by pasting a small piece of paper across the back of the tear. Never use Sellotape or similar substances which may well discolour and damage the paper of the envelope. Creased covers can be pressed carefully using a hot iron over blotting paper. Many old covers will now be in a less than immaculate condition and collectors should not be unduly fussy. Always choose the best covers you can afford but as long as the postal markings are clear and complete, the condition of the remainder of the cover is of less importance. Badly torn and unreasonably grubby covers should be avoided unless the postal markings on them are exceptionally rare or the cover is required as a spacefiller until a better specimen is available.

The better stamp and postal history dealers will have considerable experience in acquiring stocks and will price their material according to the scarcity of the postal markings and the condition of the cover. Other dealers will be less knowledgeable and the collector who 'knows his stuff' can still pick up bargains in postal history—more so than in stamps. Often a cover will have been priced almost entirely on the catalogue value of the stamp rather than on the postal markings and it may well be that these are of greater significance and value than the stamp. Quite often one can find interesting postmarks on the back of old picture postcards. All too frequently postcard dealers price the item solely on the interest of the picture side, ignoring or insufficiently considering the philatelic interest of the stamp and postmark. Thus a collector is likely to find more bargains in the stocks of postcard rather than stamp or postal history dealers.

In this chapter we have looked, albeit briefly, at some of the many and varied facets of postal history collecting. Many of the early items can now only be obtained from dealers and in auction, but much interesting postal history material probably remains in drawers, cupboards, attics, etc. still to be discovered. Useful items may well be found in your own mail and it is as well to examine this carefully. Many good items of postal history end up in waste-paper baskets. Look out for good examples of postcoded mail, postmark errors (inverted dates, etc.) and keep any attractive looking registered envelopes, or covers bearing postage due stamps. Postal history collecting is fun and can be economical—an important factor for those whose depth of pocket does not match their instincts for research or wish to build up a different, interesting and worthwhile collection.

CHAPTER TWENTY-TWO
The Stamp Market

In the early days of the hobby, the collector who paid a few pence for a postage stamp was considered a lunatic by his friends. Even to collect stamps at all was considered, if not insane, then at least not quite respectable, and even today something of this atmosphere hangs about philately, and men and women with no other crimes on their conscience sometimes hide from their friends the fact that they collect stamps, as if it were an unforgivable sin. Nowadays there is such a general demand for stamps that most stamps have a cash value, and this value, generally speaking, will increase as the number of collectors and hence the demand for stamps grows.

A stamp auction in progress

Though stamp values as a whole increase steadily, the value of an individual stamp will fluctuate, according to the conditions under which it has to be disposed of. A dealer who has a large stock of a stamp will not pay the same price for extra supplies as he might if he were short of it. A collector who is specially interested in the stamps of a certain country will perhaps pay more for a particular variety than one who is less keen. The issues of a country or group will be more in demand in one part of the world than in another, and will consequently fetch higher prices there.

Fortunately, in stamps, there is no chain of central 'stock exchanges' which can give numerical expression to the world demand (or lack of it) for a particular stamp. The best guides to comparative values are the prices in the leading stamp catalogues, but these prices do not represent what his stamps are worth to the collector. They may be the selling prices of the dealer who publishes the catalogue, and represent his own ideas, based on a wide experience, and on the facility or difficulty with which he sells or is able to buy stamps on the basis of his prices.

Even the prices given in the stamp catalogue may not be fixed. The dealer may secure a temporary supply of a stamp cheaply. He knows the supply will not last long, so there is no object in lowering the catalogue price. He therefore makes an offer of the stamp at a reduced price, for a short period. He probably also allows a discount off his catalogue price to regular customers, and this rate may vary according to the popularity of particular stamps at a particular period, for certain stamps have their fashionable periods, and their periods of neglect.

The method by which stamps are sold also affects their price to the collector, for the sum charged includes not only the original cost of the stamp to the dealer, but the cost of stocking and selling the stamp (rent, salaries, taxes, advertising, etc.) plus a small profit. In other words, the collector is paying for service as well as for the stamp.

Now if stamps are ordered singly from the catalogue, the dealer has to take the order, and go from book to book, or from box to box, picking out each of the stamps one by one, putting them in a book, pricing them, adding up the value and so on; quite a lot of work which, when the stamps are very cheap ones, it does not in fact pay him to do. If, however, he can pick, say, one hundred cheap stamps of which he has plenty of stock, and make them up into packets of '100 different', the work involved is much less, and those stamps will cost the collector proportionately less.

In the case of rarer stamps, the purchaser is getting more stamp value and less service value, and is therefore getting more for his money. This is obvious, for directly he has bought a stamp, the part of its cost which represents dealer service and profit disappear so far as he is concerned, and he can get for it only its value as a stamp, *i.e.* what he is able to re-sell it for.

How can the would-be vendor of stamps (the private owner) find out their value, then? The catalogue will tell him whether he has any rare items, but the inexperienced must be careful that they are reading the catalogue correctly, for slight differences may make a variation of pounds in the value, and although the human tendency is to take the highest price as the correct one, the odds are naturally in favour of the stamp being the commoner, cheaper one. Then, too, allowance has to be made for stamps not in fine condition, which often have only the merest fraction of the value of perfect specimens. Your catalogue may give some indication of the range of value in the connexion. Finally, in old collections particularly, some of the stamps which seem to be rare and valuable could be forgeries, so that the owner is greatly misled as to the value of the collection as a whole.

One way a collector can find out the value of his stamps is to have them valued by a reliable stamp valuer. Certain of the big firms are licensed valuers, and will carry out the work for a moderate fee (although in the case of small collections the fee could be more than the collection is worth). A dealer will normally be willing to make you an offer for your stamps and if the dealer is a reliable one, the offer will be a fair one. Do not, however, think that you can necessarily get a figure from him, and then go somewhere else to see if you can get more. He is not going to allow his offer to be made a basis for his competitors to bid on, and you may be politely told that you must accept or reject it and that the offer is withdrawn directly the stamps leave his premises.

Therefore, if you want to sell stamps, find a dealer whose reputation stands high, and put yourself in his hands. You will find that in this way you will get a fair price, or, if your stamps do not interest the firm you have selected, you may get some helpful advice as to the best means of disposing of them elsewhere.

association with the local printers W Brendon and Son, who had previously printed the medicine-bottle labels for William Gibbons.
In 1874 Gibbons took the bold step of moving to London, and dealt from his private house in the residential area of Clapham

Common until, to the obvious relief of his neighbours, he found a shop and accommodation at 8 Gower Street, Bloomsbury. Stanley traded successfully for the next fifteen years until, at the age of 50, he decided to retire to his villa at Twickenham and travel the world so well known to him from postage stamps.

When the news of Gibbons' impending retirement reached the ears of Charles J Phillips, a civil servant and a spare-time stamp dealer, he offered to purchase the entire business. Following an appraisal of Gibbons' vast stock of stamps, the offer was accepted at £25,000, and the business was turned into a private limited company – 'Stanley Gibbons Limited' – in July 1890.

The Monthly Journal, a house magazine and forerunner of *Gibbons Stamp Monthly*, was published as a link between the new firm and its

customers. In 1893, new shop premises were acquired at 391 Strand, an address which was to become as famous to philatelists as the name of its occupants.

...up ... ..e Royal Wedding, ...s consolidated its retail and rare stamp operations in the old 'Romano' site at 399-401 Strand, opening one of the largest and most attractive stamp shops in the world, whilst retaining the prestigious Stamp Gallery where many famous collectors have exhibited.

Today the shop, the company, and the quality of its products, live up to the 125 years of tradition and service started in 1856 by Edward Stanley Gibbons.

Pages from the £4 Stanley Gibbons stamp booklet showing the old 391 and new 399 Strand shops

A good deal has already been said in previous chapters about the need for care in buying stamps, and emphasis has been laid on the fact that stamps which look the cheapest are often very dear. You want, for your money, genuine stamps with a guarantee behind them, and stamps in the right condition for the price you are paying. It is poor satisfaction to get stamps at say a half of catalogue price if they are in such condition that they are not worth a quarter.

It is also necessary to consider the service you are receiving from the particular dealer from whom you are buying, for you have to pay for this as well as the stamps. This is best judged, in stamp business, by the quality and scope of the approval selections sent out by a particular firm, and by the proportion of your 'wants' than can be supplied at any given time. A firm which is able to let you have extensive and valuable selections of stamps to look at will naturally have to keep more capital locked up than one which can only send out small selections, and capital costs money in interest. On your part, the bigger selections give you a better chance of making a purchase of satisfactory specimens, while you gain valuable experience from seeing so many stamps, even if you are not able to buy them all. It is an obvious convenience to you to be able to get a large proportion of your want list filled from one firm and at one time, but here again such service calls for the holding of a large stock.

Now to the vexed question of making money from stamps not as a dealer but as a collector. Many collectors seem to think that it is only necessary to spend a sum of money on stamps in order to be able to sell them at a profit in a comparatively short period. There could be no greater fallacy. It is definitely possible to make money by stamp-collecting (though this may seem out-of-place when we consider that we are discussing what is primarily an amateur hobby), but it can only be made by investing money in stamps *with knowledge and sound judgment*, or by luck, or by spending a considerable sum spread over a wide field, and leaving time and the general upward tendency of stamp values, to produce an ultimate profit.

There is much to be learned by looking at the values of stamps issued in the early days. It will be seen that many which were common 70 or 80 years ago, are still common today. It is obvious then, that many low value new issues of today, which are printed in much larger quantities than those of earlier days, will be likely to remain common till long after the readers of this volume are dead. They will get scarcer and scarcer, owing to loss and wastage, but this increased scarcity will not show itself materially in the value of the individual common stamp, but only in wholesale prices. We can therefore rule out common stamps as a likely source of profit.

In stamps of medium price, there will be some that will almost certainly rise fairly rapidly in value, but who is to say which they are? Long experience or intensive study may enable a collector to say that certain moderately priced stamps are much scarcer than they appear, and he may be able to secure some of them and make an eventual profit, but this is not collecting. The man who tries to 'find the winners' by buying all the medium-priced stamps of a certain group will find that his gains on those that rise will be lessened by the loss on those that stand still, for obviously one cannot sell a stamp back to a dealer for what one gave for it, unless his selling price has risen in the meantime.

Except for an occasional speculation in a stamp which one thinks will rise rapidly in value, there is no great fortune to be made out of medium-priced stamps, though a collection of these will nearly always show a better return than one of common stamps. Even then it is doubtful if a real profit will be shown, if the compound interest value of the capital invested be reckoned.

Speculation in stamps, usually in new issues which happen to be printed in limited quantities, is a favourite pursuit with some folk, but even those who know most of the game rarely make a profit when their transactions are regarded as a whole, the gain on one deal being swallowed up by the losses on others. It is just as hard to pick winners in stamps as it is on the Turf or the Stock Exchange. Dealers in stamps should know what they are about, and those who have been most successful were not the ones who bought stamps and held them for a rise, but *those who never refused a profit*, however small.

Ruling out the common and medium stamps, we are left with rarities. Here there is a more promising field for investment. For most rare stamps the demand is greater than the supply and, generally speaking, prices rise more rapidly than they do in the lower priced groups. Scarce stamps, in fine condition, are undoubtedly the best philatelic investment, and many wealthy men have put large sums of money into such property. Not all have made a profit, but the majority will be able to say that they have more to show for their money than they would have had if it had been put into stocks and shares and other more conventional forms of investment.

The collector of limited means cannot hope to buy many fine and rare stamps, and, from the investment point of view, even if he does, he may select some which do not rise in value. Is there any way by which he can hope to profit? 'Money breeds money' in stamps as in most other departments of live, but there is another thing which produces money and that is hard work. The collector with a small purse, who will take up a country not in too keen demand at the moment, who will study its stamps intensively, make them his pet subject, know where to find the bargains, and when to avoid pitfalls, and who will do judicious propaganda work on behalf of its stamps by writing in the philatelic press concerning his discoveries, will, in many cases, find that he can sell his collection eventually at a profit. Not in all cases, for interest in a particular country may be so 'dead' that nothing will revive it within a single lifetime, but it is a fact that, apart from the wealthy buyers of philatelic gems, the keenest students of stamps have been the most fortunate financially. As philatelic study is open to all, there is thus hope for every collector.

Profits are sometimes made by collectors who take up a new stamp-issuing country from the start, and follow its stamps closely. If a 'boom' starts, as happened in the case of Israel and the United Nations, quick profits may be made, but only by those who pick the right country (a matter of instinct or luck) and who sell out in time, for a boom is inevitably followed by a decline in interest.

The best attitude for the average collector to take up in regard to the financial aspect of philately is to remember always that he is spending money on an intensely interesting hobby. He is getting more than his money's worth out of it in enjoyment alone (few who have collected stamps will deny this) and thus when he sells his collection, if he ever does, any money he obtains for it is clear profit, even if it does not represent the whole of his outlay. To collect solely with the idea of making money is to place oneself outside the circle of stamp lovers, but to build up a collection with a real love for stamps and with a determination to study them and find out more about them than has yet been known, is the likeliest way to eventual profit.

CHAPTER TWENTY-THREE
The Stamp World

The stamp world which this chapter will describe is one into which the majority of collectors unfortunately never enter, a small inner circle which is to some extent organised in societies or groups. Beyond this is an intermediate group—or series of groups—of collectors whose only link is that they read the same stamp magazine, while beyond them again is the great army of stamp collectors, the people who collect because they love the hobby, but who do not regularly see a stamp magazine nor ever contemplate joining a stamp club or philatelic society. Though the members of the inner and intermediate circles do much good work for philately—by study, writing and propaganda—it is the outer ring, the host of ordinary, unorganised, unlinked collectors, which is the backbone of the hobby.

The germ of the present-day philatelic society will be found in the informal open-air meetings for the exchange of stamps, which took place in several European capitals in the early days of the hobby. Birchin Lane, near the Mansion House, was the rendezvous in London until the police asked philately to 'move on'. It did move on, and the consequence was the formation of societies or clubs of enthusiastic collectors for social intercourse, exchange of information and stamps, and the general cultivation of the hobby. Paris led the way in about 1865, but its first society did not have a long life, nor did the first New York Society, which followed it in 1867, fare any better, though its successor, the modern Collectors' Club, ranks very high today.

Britain, a little late in the field, as she often is, was able to build on a firmer foundation, and the London Philatelic Society (now the Royal Philatelic Society), which was born in 1869, is still alive and flourishing and numbers among its past presidents King George V. There are other societies of various grades and sizes, scattered throughout England and the civilised world. Some of them cater for the young collector, while others are more concerned with advanced students of stamps. They hold regular meetings, at which the members, or invited guests, show and describe their collections. Papers are read on various topics, or lectures are given on matters of interest. Some societies have their own library, of which the wiser members make full use, while nearly all have a section through which stamps may be sold through the post, members having stamps for disposal contributing priced books of stamps to a circulating packet. The society usually takes a percentage on the turnover for its general funds.

It has become the practice of late years in many countries for delegates from the various philatelic societies to meet in congress each year. At such gatherings, matters of moment in connexion with the hobby are discussed in papers read before the meetings and are then debated. Practical results do not always follow from these congresses, they provide an opportunity for collectors from different parts of the country to meet socially and to widen their philatelic horizon.

Philatelic societies can be divided into three main groups: Countrywide Societies; Local Societies and Specialist Societies. The majority of those currently operating are listed—under these three headings—in The British Philatelic Federation's *Yearbook and Philatelic Societies' Directory* which is published each January and is a recommended book for the library of the aspiring philatelist.

British Philatelic Federation Yearbook and Philatelic Societies' Directory – an essential reference book for all serious collectors

This is not the place for a detailed account of the history and activities of each society but a few words about the oldest and most prestigious will not be out of place. The premier British society is the Royal Philatelic Society which was founded as the London Philatelic Society of London in 1869. Today it has a membership of about 1500 and operates from its headquarters at 41 Devonshire Place, London W1. Membership is open to all collectors who are not full-time philatelists (*i.e.* employed by a company dealing in stamps).

New members have to be sponsored by two existing members. Those who are active in the society will normally after a number of years membership be elected a 'fellow' of the society and so be entitled to put the coveted initials *F.R.P.S.L.* after their name. The ultimate accolade in British philately is perhaps election as the Society's President. Nearly all the most distinguished British philatelists have held this office—George V as Prince of Wales (1896–1910), Sir Edward Bacon (1917–23), Sir John Wilson (1934–40, 1949–50) and R. A. G. Lee (1975–77). The Society publishes *The London Philatelist* six times a year, the major journal for detailed research articles. The Patron of the Society is, of course, H.M. The Queen who attended the centenary celebrations in 1969 and who toured the London 1980 International Stamp Exhibition attended by some of the Society's chief officers.

The National Philatelic Society was founded—as the Junior Philatelic Society—in 1899, its founder being the prolific philatelic writer Frederick J. Melville (*1882–1940*). Meetings are held regularly in London and members are sent a quarterly journal *The Stamp Lover*. The Society has an impressive library, second only to that of the Royal Philatelic Society. Members may borrow books by personal application or by post. The Society—in conjunction with the Philatelic Traders Society—organises one of London's two annual exhibitions—STAMPEX—held in February or March.

The British Philatelic Federation was formed—as the British Philatelic Association in 1926 and in 1976 joined forces with the Philatelic Congress of G.B. (formed 1909) to form the present organisation. It has over 800 collector members and about 300 members of the stamp trade. It published a journal *Philately* until 1981, since when—in conjunction with a commercial publishing company—it has produced a fortnightly newspaper *Stamp & Postal History News*.

The second group listed in the B.P.F. *Yearbook* are the local societies—over 450 of these were listed in the 1983 edition. Many of these have a long and distinguished history—30 date back to before 1920. The longest established is the Plymouth Philatelic Society founded in 1876. New societies are still being set up which is always a good sign of a healthy and prospering hobby.

It is not a difficult matter to form a philatelic society or stamp club. The first essential is an extremely energetic person, very keen on the hobby, to act as secretary. Around him he should gather a small nucleus of equally enthusiastic collectors. These may meet at first in one another's houses, at not too frequent intervals; possibly once a fortnight, while the first glow of pride in the society is still there, and later, when things settle down, once a month. The early meetings should consist simply of an informal interchange of experiences and a similarly informal inspection of the collections of members, with, of course, keen discussions as to the best method of promoting and developing the society.

The next step, after the first nucleus has attracted to itself a rather larger membership, is to find a more permanent meeting-place. In most cases philatelic societies hold their meetings in a room at the local library or institute, and usually manage to secure the additional privilege of a lock-up cupboard for such catalogues and books as the club library may contain. In such surroundings, the meetings will become more formal, but always some portion of the time should be given up to informal chat. A programme will be drafted, and here the first great difficulty will be encountered.

In a modern stamp circle, particularly if the members are adults, most of them will be specialists, collecting different countries or groups, and if they are anything like the average collector, they will find very little to interest them in the stamps owned by their fellow members. The keen secretary will do all in his or her power to promote mutual interest and his programme must include, in addition to formal displays of members' collections, talks on general topics interesting to all, debates, film shows, competitions and anything he can think of to brighten the evenings. Film strips, with accompanying lectures for reading, can be borrowed for a small fee, and some of these lectures are suitable for recruiting purposes, that is to say they can be delivered publicly in a hall hired for the purpose to an audience drawn there by advertising or by the persuasion of members of the stamp club, in the hope of converting some to an appreciation of stamp collecting.

On all these matters and in connexion with the building up of a section for the exchange of stamps, the budding secretary will be able to take advantage of the experience of other secretaries in charge of established societies, most of whom will be willing to pass on their knowledge. It is essential, however, that he should avoid copying the defects of other organisations, especially if moribund through lack of imagination.

The outstanding drawbacks to many philatelic meetings are: unpunctual starting, uncomfortable quarters, too much unnecessary talk from the officials, and above all (owing to the fact that so many collectors specialise in the stamps of one group or country) displays and talks which appeal to very few persons in each audience. Unpunctual starting can be overcome by choosing a time for meetings which is convenient for the majority of members, electing a chairman and secretary who can be there punctually, and making it quite clear that meetings are going to start at the appointed hour and not later. Uncomfortable meeting-places cannot always be avoided, but even the worst of those bleak rooms at public libraries and institutes, where so many stamp meetings are held, can be improved for the occasion with a little thought and care, especially in regard to lighting. The formal business of the meetings should be cut down to the absolute minimum. Officials should be trained to avoid long speeches when introducing or thanking the speaker of the evening, and so should those members who propose and second the vote of thanks.

The main object of a stamp meeting is to see stamps or talk about them and as far as possible to interest all the members all the time, not a few of the members some of the time. If the programme is of interest to the majority of members at every meeting, the success of the society is assured. Looking at the programmes of the philatelic societies in Great Britain, as a whole, one is struck by the fact that the majority of the meetings are occupied with papers and displays dealing with a single country. Only a genius can make a specialised paper on one country interesting to people who do not collect its stamps, and so varied are the interests of collectors that, out of any audience, it is pretty certain that at least 80 per cent will have no interest in a particular specialised display. Obviously, therefore, specialised displays of a single country are *the worst possible fare to put before philatelic meetings*. Displays by those public-spirited 'leading philatelists' who visit so many societies each season, are even worse, if over-indulged in, for, even where the papers read are not above the heads of the audiences, the stamps shown are often so magnificent and plentiful that they dishearten the average collector. Better by far to have two or four shorter displays in an evening, or even a series of ten-minute papers and displays. In this way variety is secured and the interest of members retained.

If a display is properly arranged and written-up, there is really no need for a lot of talk about it, all that is necessary being a few introductory remarks after which the members present can ask questions while the stamps are being viewed. It is a good idea, if feasible, to lay the display out before the meeting is formally opened, so that those present may gain a general idea of what is going to be shown. Where conditions permit, it is a good plan to have at least one entirely informal meeting each season, the members gathering round and handing round a couple of pages from their collections. There are sure to be items which will arouse discussion and members who would not speak at a formal meeting will be tempted to give their views in conversation.

Do not think that because the members of a society are nearly all specialists, they will not be interested in meetings of a more elementary nature. Talks dealing with the designs of stamps, if interesting, will always hold an audience, while competitions calling on members to identify parts of stamp designs, or to say which country issued a stamp with a certain inscription, have proved very popular. Competitions of this kind, if they have to be based on hand-drawn pictures of bits of stamps, are rather hard to organise, but if a film or slide projector is used, any competition can be run at a comparatively low cost. An over-head projector (epidiascope) is even better, for then no films or slides are needed, the stamps themselves being placed in the instrument and reflected on to the screen, but the hire of an epidiascope is fairly costly. Many schools have them, however, and can probably be induced to lend them.

One meeting a year should be reserved for a film show of a popular nature, and if this is made an open meeting and held in a fairly large hall to which the public is invited, early in the season, it could prove a good means of obtaining recruits for any philatelic society. Another way of building up a reserve of collectors for future membership is to hold a meeting aimed specifically at the junior members at least once a season. They will, of course, also be invited to the film show. Joint meetings with neighbouring societies will provide a means of widening interest and making new contacts, while some societies find at least one purely social evening per season a valuable help in creating and fostering good-fellowship.

Debates on philatelic topics of general interest will often provide good fun, especially if they are not made too formal. A conversational atmosphere is best if you wish to have the majority of those present taking part. An evening of impromptu talks will prove very interesting if it is understood that anyone who is called upon to speak must do so. The best method of selecting speakers is for those present to draw slips of paper out of a hat, each member having to deal in a five minutes' talk with the subject written on the slip. The subjects must, of course, be of a general nature, such as 'My Favourite Stamp Designs', or 'Why I like (or dislike) Commemoratives'.

Members who take an interest in philatelic history or in the by-ways of philately may usually be relied upon to fill a whole evening, for they are generally people who look at the hobby from a wider angle than your 'one-country' man. A 'ladies' night', with displays and talks by lady members and with a lady 'chairman', will furnish a welcome change if a society has enough members of the fair sex.

Informality and ingenuity are the keys to interest. When that august body, the Royal Philatelic Society, started meetings which it described by the title of 'Tea, Toast and Talk' no doubt many grey hairs stood on end, but these informal gatherings proved most enjoyable. Ingenuity in devising programmes need not become eccentricity, but a committee whose members have a wide knowledge of the many interesting aspects of our hobby, should be able to arrange competitions, surprise evenings, and other novelties in almost endless variety.

The collector who joins a philatelic society after collecting for some time 'in the wilderness', will be surprised to find how much pleasure it can add to the hobby, while his knowledge and experience will be greatly increased when he meets other collectors. He will also be able to widen his human horizon and to appreciate the value of the philatelic bond, for in the stamp clubs he will find men and women of all classes, united in the pursuit and study of philatelic material of all kinds.

Most of the comments above have been concerned with the local philatelic society or stamp club which exists in most towns and which usually has 50–100 members. In addition there are a number of specialist societies which are not locally based and have members scattered throughout the British Isles, often throughout the world. These concentrate on particular types of stamps—either the stamps of a particular country or group of countries, stamps of a particular kind (*e.g.* airmails) or stamps of a certain theme. Most of these publish a regular journal of some kind which is the main 'contact' between members, especially those in the more far-flung places. Some of these societies hold meetings (usually in London), others are purely postal. When meetings are held they are often only attended by a small minority of the society members, hence the publication of a regular journal is perhaps their major function and the one on which the success of the society will largely depend. In addition to the journal, some societies operate exchange or sales packets and organise periodic auctions and produce learned monographs based on the research of an individual member or group of members. A full listing of these societies appears as Section 2 (*Specialist Societies and Study Circles in the United Kingdom*) in the *B.P.F. Yearbook and Philatelic Societies' Directory*. A list of the more important ones is given below:

American Stamp Club of Great Britain
Austrian Stamp Club of Great Britain
Belgian Study Circle
Belgian Congo Study Circle
British Association of Palestine-Israel Philatelists
British Society of Australian Philately
British Society of Russian Philately
British West Africa Study Circle
British West Indies Study Circle
Canadian Philatelic Society of Great Britain
China Philatelic Society of London
Cyprus Study Circle
Czechoslovak Philatelic Society of Great Britain
Egypt Study Circle
Ethiopian Collectors Club
France and Colonies Philatelic Society
Germany and Colonies Philatelic Society
Great Britain Philatelic Society
Hellenic Philatelic Society of Great Britain (Greece)
Helvetia Study Circle (Switzerland)
Hong Kong Study Circle
India Study Circle
Indian Ocean Study Circle
International Society for Japanese Philately
Iran Philatelic Study Circle
Irish Philatelic Circle
Italy and Colonies Study Circle
Magyar Philatelic Society
Malaya Study Group
Malta Study Circle
Netherlands Philatelic Circle
New Zealand Society of Great Britain
Oriental Philatelic Association of London
Pacific Islands Study Circle
Polish Philatelic Society of London
Rhodesian Study Circle
Sarawak Specialists Society

Scandinavia Philatelic Society
South African Collectors Society
Spanish Philatelic Society
Thailand Philatelic Society
Transvaal Study Circle

Societies catering for collectors of postmarks and postal history include:

British Airmail Society
British Postmark Society
Forces Postal History Society
The Postal History Society
The Precancel Stamp Society (G.B.)
Society of Postal Historians
T.P.O. and Seapost Society

Societies catering for thematic collectors are typified by:

Guild of St Gabriel (*Religion on Stamps*)
Philatelic Music Circle (*Music on Stamps*)
Scout Stamps Collectors Club
Ship Stamp Society

Subscriptions are often no more than £5 per year, which most members count a small price to pay for the facilities afforded.

The Minister of Posts (*Christopher Chataway*) opening 'Philympia' – London's international stamp exhibition, 1970

The leading philatelic societies of the world have been and remain the prime movers behind stamp exhibitions. Some of these are merely local shows, organised by a single society, but they have a good effect in promoting interest in philately and attracting recruits. The earliest philatelic exhibitions were probably similar—very different from the great international exhibitions of the present day, in which collectors from all parts of the world display their collections in the hope of winning medals or trophies, and where stamps to the value of several million pounds may be displayed under one roof. These exhibitions draw visitors from all over the globe, and provide opportunities for discussion in the international sphere, such as the congress offers in national circles. Occasionally an exhibition is staged by a stamp dealer. In 1956 Stanley Gibbons commemorated their centenary with a splendid exhibition at the Waldorf Hotel in London, and in 1965 they held a much bigger exhibition at the Royal Festival Hall, London for the centenary of the Gibbons catalogue. At this magnificent show were displayed some of the world's rarest stamps, including the unique British Guiana One Cent black on magenta of 1856.

Today the cost of staging a major international stamp exhibition is considerable and many postal administrations help offset the cost with funds raised from the sale of stamps to philatelists. In February 1981 the British Post Office set up a British Philatelic Trust to administer money raised by the sale of miniature sheets in 1978, 1979 and 1980. The Trust is advised by the British Philatelic Council on which sit representatives of the major philatelic societies, the Philatelic Traders Society, the National Postal Museum, and the philatelic press. The main aim of the Trust is to provide financial support for philatelic exhibitions, as well as the granting of aid to 'activities . . . concerned with philately and postal history, including the financing of seminars, lectures and other educational and cultural activities' and 'the promotion of approved research and study'.

From the philatelic societies has also sprung the idea of honouring those who have done good work for the hobby, either by study, by writing, or in any other way. The British Philatelic Federation is responsible for the Roll of Distinguished Philatelists, which includes the names of leading collectors of many nations, headed by that of King George V. This Roll was inaugurated at the Philatelic Congress of Great Britain meeting in Harrogate in 1921, when the names of 40 eminent philatelists were inscribed. By 1982 over 200 names had been added—including that of Stanley Phillips (1937). The Collectors' Club of New York has a similar Roll of Honour. Awards are also given by some philatelic societies for good work done by their members, either in the field of philatelic research or for their efforts in the running of the society.

CHAPTER TWENTY-FOUR
Famous Collectors and Collections

It is no easy matter, to get together a collection of stamps which will bring fame to its owner. There are a few who have done it by taking up one of the more unusual themes or methods of collecting. There are quite a number who have achieved the same object by studying intensively the stamps of a single country until they have entered the ranks of the recognised authorities on those issues. Those who now rise to the philatelic heights in the realm of *general* collecting, must have the purse of Croesus and the energy of Hercules.

Among the early British collectors several names stand out. Sir Daniel Cooper (*1821–1902*), one of the founders of the London Philatelic Society, was a very active collector in the 1860s and 1870s but afterwards sold his collection to another famous pioneer, Judge Frederick Adolphus Philbrick (*1835–1910*). When the latter, in his turn, sold his stamps to M. Philippe la Rénotière of Paris, they included practically all the great rarities of those days, and in some cases quite a number of each.

M. la Rénotière (*1848–1917*) is better known to collectors of the present day by the name of Ferrary. He was a very eccentric man who spent a fortune in stamps. A lover of England and a resident of France, he was technically of Austrian nationality, and after his death his wonderful collection was sold at auction on the instructions of the French Government, realising the immense sum of over £400,000. Ferrary was a somewhat bizarre character—he wore a white yachting cap and was always very mysterious concerning the movements of supposed enemies who, he thought, were on his track. He visited stamp dealers with his pockets full of British banknotes, which he exchanged, in solid rolls, for the stamps accumulated for him in the intervals between his visits. To his intimates he announced his intention to visit them by telegrams which always ended with the words 'Affectionate shake hands' for his knowledge of English was not as complete as his collection of stamps.

James Ludovic Lindsay, 26th Earl of Crawford (*1847–1913*) was a greater collector than Ferrary, for he studied stamps intensively, and his albums included every sort of document which could in any way throw light on the stamps and their production and history. His collections of the stamps of Great Britain and the U.S.A. were a revelation of what could be achieved by scientific study.

Another very large general collection which brought fame to its owner was that formed by Henry J. Duveen (*1856–1919*), a member of the famous family of art experts. His collections were disposed of after his death, and brought in a sum which was probably second only to that realised by the sale of the Ferrary collection.

M. la Rénotière – usually known as Ferrary

James Ludovic Lindsay, 26th Earl of Crawford

A book could be filled with descriptions of the pioneer and famous collectors and their stamps, but we must confine ourselves to a few more examples. First among these was King George V, whose place in the front rank of philatelists was due, not to his high position, but to his personal keenness and the fact that his wonderful collections of the stamps of the British Commonwealth fully entitled him to the honour. When Alfred, Duke of Edinburgh (*1844–1900, second son of Queen Victoria*) opened the big London Stamp Exhibition in 1890, he remarked that his nephew, Prince George (later George V), was then starting from Chatham in command of the *Thrush*. As he too was a stamp collector, the Duke hoped his nephew would be bringing back many fine specimens from the countries visited during his cruise.

Alfred, Duke of Edinburgh, second son of Queen Victoria

King George V

King George started collecting when he was a midshipman in the *Bacchante* and was mainly interested in the stamps of the British Commonwealth, though he received many gifts of stamps from foreign countries. At his death his collection filled several hundred volumes and was housed in a special room at Buckingham Palace. In 1893, as Prince of Wales, he became Hon. Vice-President of the London (now the Royal) Philatelic Society, and when he married in the same year the Society gave him a present of more than 1000 scarce and interesting stamps for his collection. He was also an exhibitor at a display of West Indian stamps organised by the Society. Three years later he became President of the Society and took the chair at meetings on at least two occasions. It was due to his initiative that in November 1906 the London Philatelic Society was granted the privilege of using the word 'Royal' in its title. After his accession, King George became Patron of the R.P.S. and each season of the Society still opens with a display of part of the Royal Collection.

King George V also allowed his name to be placed at the head of the Roll of Distinguished Philatelists, which is now under the control of the British Philatelic Federation, and inclusion on which is a coveted international honour. The King's many opportunities for travel enabled him to build up his remarkable collection in a way which every collector must envy, while few can emulate it. It is probably the finest general collection of British Commonwealth stamps in the world, for while his displays of some countries could be beaten by those who had devoted their energy and fortune to a single group, his collection was an all-round one, sane in plan and balanced in contents. Though the King devoted a great deal of time and personal attention to his stamps, his field was so vast, and the correspondence which he received from all parts of the world so voluminous, that he always had to employ the services of an expert curator known as the keeper of the Royal Collection. The first was J. A. Tilleard (*1850–1913*) who was followed by Sir Edward Denny Bacon (*1860–1938*) whose work was rewarded by a knighthood in 1932.

Bacon was succeeded by Sir John Wilson Bt. (*1898–1975*) who remained keeper until 1969 when he relinquished the post. The current holder of the title is John B. Marriott, MVO, RDP, FRPSL, an expert of wide knowledge and sound philatelic judgement.

Among the outstanding sections of the collection are the stamps of Great Britain, Mauritius (which includes both the 1d and 2d 'Post Office' rarities), British Guiana and the West Indies, but no section of the Commonwealth's stamps is poorly represented.

Many people have suggested that perhaps philately was just a formal hobby, so far as King George V was concerned, but this was far from the truth. He was intensely keen on his stamps, indeed on the stamps of the British Commonwealth wherever they might be found, and he used to reserve as much time as he could from his official duties for the study of his collection and discussions with other philatelists. He said once that he did not think he would ever have been able to stand the strain of the First World War had it not been for the relaxation he obtained from stamp collecting, and his personal interest in the hobby was again shown during Silver Jubilee week, in 1935, at a time when the King must have been subjected to great emotional and physical strain. He did not get many moments to himself during that momentous week, but during one brief period of leisure he drove to the headquarters of the Royal Philatelic Society to inspect an exhibition of the finest stamps owned by members of the Society, which had been assembled as a tribute to their Royal patron, an exhibition which, for quality and interest, has never been surpassed.

King George VI maintained his father's collection and formed a separate collection of the issues of his own reign, which is housed in special blue albums to distinguish it from his father's famous red volumes. He gave an interview to a popular illustrated weekly and was photographed while inspecting some of his stamps. Nowadays H.M. The Queen maintains the collections, and has her own special albums for the stamps of her reign.

Members of several European royal families, including the Belgian and Italian and King Carol II of Rumania (*1893–1953*), were stamp collectors, though not on the same scale as George V, or King Fuad of Egypt (*d. 1936*). The latter had a magnificent collection, particularly of the stamps of his own country. Several of the Indian princes were also keen collectors.

Royal stamp collectors – King Carol II of Rumania and King Fuad of Egypt; President Franklin Delano Roosevelt, America's most famous philatelist

The Duke of Windsor (*1894–1972*) was also at one time a general collector, though it is doubtful if the hobby ever really gripped him after he had passed the schoolboy stage.

When we turn to the U.S.A. we think of another philatelist—head of state—President Franklin D. Roosevelt (*1882–1945*), who was a keen collector on general lines. His collection, which included many interesting gifts from foreign states and rulers, was sold after his death and realised a very large sum.

Arthur Hind (*1856–1933*) had a world-famous collection, which was dispersed at auction in New York and London in 1934 and 1935, many of his rarities fetching high prices. He will be chiefly remembered as the owner of the world's most valuable single stamp, the One Cent British Guiana of 1856, for which he paid over £7000 at the sale of the Ferrary collection.

To bring together a comprehensive general collection at the present day is work for a millionaire and even a successful collection of a single big country may cost the owner thousands of pounds. In its higher ranks, therefore, stamp collecting is becoming more and more the hobby of the rich, and particularly of wealthy professional and business men. Such is the elasticity of the pursuit, however, that it is still possible for the collector with little to spend to gain a measure of fame by studying the stamps of one of the (philatelically) smaller countries, and there is the joy of collecting and of competing for the possession of the less valuable stamps.

CHAPTER TWENTY-FIVE
Stamp Literature

It is not surprising that a hobby so varied and complex as stamp-collecting should require a literature of its own, but it is one of the most curious characteristics of stamp collectors generally that they do not, to any great extent, avail themselves of existing literature. Some may have an introductory primer to the hobby; many possess a stamp catalogue of some kind, but more rarely do we find collectors who have troubled to acquire the books and magazines which will help them to study their stamps in the light of the knowledge already acquired by other collectors. It is as if a student tried to pass an important examination by the light of his own unaided research, and without the use of a single text-book.

The earliest contribution to the philatelic library came from France, in September 1861, where a Strasbourg printer, M. Berger-Levrault, produced for private circulation a small list of the existing postage stamps. In December of the same year this was followed by the Potiquet Catalogue, while the following year, 1862, witnessed the appearance of two English stamp catalogues, that of Mount Brown, which listed 1200 different stamps and the Booty Catalogue, which mentioned 1100.

In September 1862, came the first stamp magazine, the *Monthly Intelligencer*, a Birmingham publication, which was not exclusively philatelic, followed, after a short interval, by the *Stamp-Collector's Monthly Advertiser* and the *Stamp-Collector's Magazine*. The latter had quite a long and useful life. Though albums hardly find a place in the stamp library, it is worth noting that the first stamp album also saw the light in 1862, and again the honour goes to France, for this was the famous Lallier album. The first Gibbons album—the *Improved*—appeared in the 1870s.

The modern stamp library is divided into three sections, catalogues, books and magazines. Of these, the catalogues are the most important. No serious collector should be without an up-to-date stamp catalogue. It is true that some stamp albums include what may appear to be the equivalent of a catalogue, facing the squares for the stamps, but this gives nothing like the amount of information included in a stamp catalogue.

In choosing a stamp catalogue, the collector should be guided by the scope of the collection he intends to form; thus the very young beginner will naturally require an elementary catalogue, but the enthusiast who wants to grow in knowledge as his collection grows in size, will buy a catalogue which seems a little beyond him at first sight, for from such a catalogue he will be always learning something new.

On the bookshelf of the advanced collector you will probably find a whole battery of catalogues, together with some more highly specialised catalogues of the stamps of a single country or group. These specialised catalogues of which a large number exist, cannot be disregarded by the serious collector, who will find a knowledge of some of the principal foreign languages necessary for their use, as many of them are published abroad.

The main British catalogue is published by Stanley Gibbons—a brief history of which is given below. Other countries have their own national catalogues—*Yvert* in France, *Michel* in West Germany, *Scott* and *Minkus* in the U.S.A.

The first Gibbons catalogue consisted of a penny price list issued in November 1865. These price lists were issued at monthly intervals for the next 14 years. The early issues are very rare—only two copies are known of the first edition (one in the British Library). The earliest copy in the Company's possession is dated May 1869. From 1879 the monthly price lists gave way to a more elaborate, virtually annual catalogue with illustrations. The first edition comprises 100 pages and over 1500 illustrations. Each stamp was numbered—but unlike today—the numbers progressed through all countries—so the last stamp for Canada (172) was followed by the first for the Cape of Good Hope (173). The price was one shilling. By the eighth edition (1888) the book had increased to 228 pages and 2800 illustrations. The tenth edition (1895–6) listed postal stationery in addition to stamps. Over 6000 illustrations were included—the cost 3s 6d. With the next edition separate volumes were published for *Empire* and *Foreign* stamps. This continued until the 1940s when the *Foreign* section was further split into *Europe* and *Rest of the World* volumes (the latter published in six separate sections). The ever-increasing number of new stamps has meant that successive Catalogue Editors have needed to rethink catalogue policy from time to time to ensure it contains as much up-to-date information as possible and is produced and sold at a cost reasonable to collectors' pockets. As an experiment the foreign listings were published in 12 sections in 1971 but this did not prove universally popular and the foreign catalogue was reconstituted as *Europe* (3 volumes) and *Overseas* (4 volumes), published 1972–75. In 1979–81 the foreign catalogue was again reconstituted in 21 parts—based on collecting areas—rather than on alphabetical or political units—this arrangement has met with general collector approval.

In addition to the standard catalogue (now Parts 1–22), Gibbons also produce a *Great Britain Specialised Catalogue*—in four volumes—*1* Queen Victoria (first published 1963), *2* Four Kings (Edward VII–George VI) (1967), *3* Elizabeth II Pre-decimal Issues (1970) and *4* Elizabeth II Decimal Issues (1976). A *Channel Islands Specialised Catalogue* was added to the range in 1979. A catalogue of the stamps of George VI was published in 1949, later this included the stamps of Elizabeth II and was retitled *Two Reigns Catalogue*. This continued until 1964, being replaced in the following year by the *Elizabethan Specialised Catalogue* which was highly acclaimed. A checklist of British stamps—*Collect British Stamps* was published in 1967 and is now published twice a year (Summer & Winter). This is a simplified listing of all issues—each stamp illustrated in colour. Over 2½ million copies have been sold. Similar checklists—*Collect Channel Islands Stamps* and *Collect Isle of Man Stamps* were introduced in 1972 and 1976 respectively.

One of the most popular of the Gibbons range is the *Stamps of the World* catalogue—this was first published in 1934 as the *Simplified Catalogue* and listed some 50,000 stamps. Publication of this continued as a single volume until 1982 by when it listed over 216,000 stamps and had no fewer than 48,000 illustrations. New stamps were being added at the rate of 6000 each year (2000 new illustrations). From the 1983 edition, the catalogue was split into two—Volume 1 covering countries A–J, Volume 2 K–Z. These list all basic stamps issued since 1840; varieties of watermark, perforation, shades etc. are not included.

Initially the catalogue was edited by Stanley Gibbons himself. Since his retirement in 1890 there have been six editors: Charles Phillips (1890–1922), Stanley Phillips (1922–54), Frederick Wall (1954–66), Rex Phillips (1966–76), James Negus (1977–81) and Stanley Zimmerman (since 1981). Each has made innovations and improvements, whilst continuing the standard format of the catalogue which has stood the test of time so well. The regular monthly supplement to the standard catalogue forms one of the most popular features in Stanley Gibbons magazine *Stamp Monthly*.

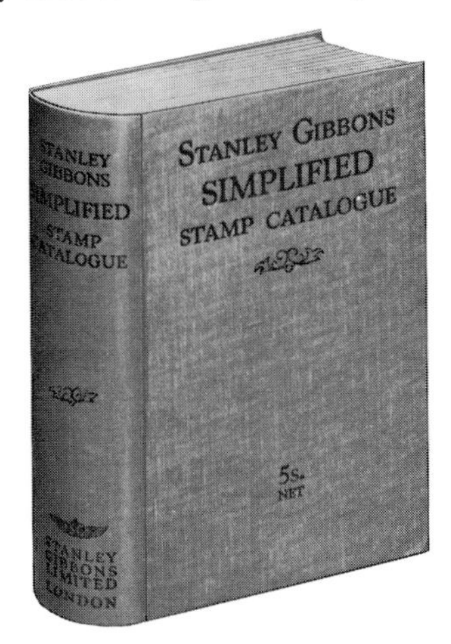

Stanley Gibbons Simplified Catalogue, 1934

Stanley Phillips – author of this book and Editor of the Stanley Gibbons Catalogue, 1923–54

There is an extraordinarily wide range of books for the stamp collector to choose from, though owing to the international nature of the hobby, he will perhaps find that some of those he most wished to read are written in a foreign language. Reference works include bibliographies, glossaries and catalogues of all kinds.

Guides to the hobby range from the elementary primer to the technical or semi-technical work dealing with stamp production and advanced philatelic study generally. There are also books about stamp designs and the historical and pictorial aspects of the hobby.

Finally we come to the so-called 'handbooks'; these are books relating to the stamps of a single country of issue, and cover a very wide range. Some of them are quite elementary in character, and form excellent guides to a collector taking up the stamps of a particular country for the first time. Others—the monographs published by the learned philatelic societies, are detailed, almost academic studies, in which the authors endeavour to include everything that is known about the stamps of the country they are dealing with. Many result from years of painstaking study.

The keen collector is strongly advised not to neglect the help which he can obtain from books. It is true that, in many directions, experience will prove his best guide, but if he relies on that alone, he will waste many years acquiring knowledge which others have already put on record in print. The beginner will want his general guide to the hobby and, above all, his catalogue. When the next stage is reached, and he looks about for a limited field on which to concentrate his efforts, the elementary books about the stamps of various countries will provide him with an excellent means of testing the comparative merits of those which he is considering, before he makes his selection. Finally, when he has decided to specialise in the stamps of a definite country or group, the very first thing he should do is to read and study everything that has been written in the philatelic press and in books, on that particular subject, unless indeed, he is fortunate enough to find that it has been the subject of a recent authoritative book, in which case the earlier press references can perhaps be disregarded.

The great thing is to know what others have done and discovered in connexion with particular stamps, and then the collector can proceed from that point, either adding to, or correcting, previous discoveries in the light of his own experience.

As the ordinary bookshop does not cater for the stamp collector, beyond the provision of one or two general works on the hobby, the reader who wants to know what literature exists in connexion with his particular subject should write to one of the dealers in philatelic literature, who will advise him. Apart from books still current, there will probably be some out-of-print works which he will need, while back numbers of various stamp magazines will also be necessary to complete his information in many cases.

Gibbons *Stamp Monthly*: the special issue for the 1980 London International Stamp Exhibition

Stamp magazines may be grouped in two classes—those published by philatelic societies and issued to their members (sometimes on sale to non-members) and the commercial magazines sold through stamp shops, newsagents and also available on postal subscription direct from the publishers. In Great Britain the most prestigious of the society publications is *The London Philatelist*, the journal of the Royal Philatelic Society (published six times a year). As might be expected its contents are of an advanced nature. Its opposite number in the U.S.A. is the *Collectors' Club Philatelist*, the organ of the Collectors' Club of New York (published quarterly). In Britain the second major society—the National Philatelic Society—has published a quarterly journal *The Stamp Lover* since 1908. This has had mixed fortunes but in recent times has undergone something of a face-lift and is now a most informative and readable magazine. The American equivalent of the National is the American Philatelic Society which publishes an impressive monthly *The American Philatelist*. Its articles—mostly concerning American stamps and postal history—are often based on the results of detailed research work.

Amongst the other more important society journals are *The G.B. Journal* (G.B. Philatelic Society), *Austria* (Austrian Stamp Club of G.B.), *BAPIP Bulletin* (British Association of Palestine-Israel Philatelists), *British Journal of Russian Philately*, *The British Postmark*

Society Quarterly Bulletin, *The Cinderella Philatelist* (Cinderella Stamp Club), *Germania* (German & Colonies Philatelic Society), *India Post* (Indian Study Circle), *Journal of Chinese Philately* (China Philatelic Society of London), *Maple Leaves* (Canadian Philatelic Society of G.B.), *Stamps of Hungary* (Magyar Philatelic Society of G.B.) and *The Springbok* (South African Collectors Society). Most of the above are printed and illustrated rather than of the duplicated newsletter format. However, one should never judge a philatelic society journal solely by its appearance for many of the simple, economically produced journals contain a wealth of useful information written by leading authorities which is not published elsewhere.

Turning now to the commercial magazines, a few are still produced by stamp dealers, the most eminent of which is Gibbons *Stamp Monthly* which has a history dating back to 1890 making it the longest running commercial journal (it has appeared under various titles, originally the *Stanley Gibbons Monthly Journal*). Amongst its most popular and best known features are the supplements to the Gibbons Catalogue, 'Through the Magnifying Glass' (a look at varieties sent in by readers), 'Panorama' (a guide to new issues) and 'An Issue is Born' (giving details of how a particular issue was designed). *The Philatelist & Philatelic Journal of Great Britain* is published six times a year by Robson Lowe Ltd of London and usually contains fairly specialised articles and extensive book reviews. (*The Philatelist* was first published in 1937, the *Philatelic Journal of Great Britain* in 1891; the two magazines merged in 1981). *The Aero-Field*—published since 1928—is produced by Francis J. Field Ltd of Sutton Coldfield, West Midlands and is the specialist magazine dealing with aero-philately. Other commercial magazines are the so-called 'independent journals' not published by companies dealing in stamps but by commercial publishing houses. The longest-running of these is *Stamp Collecting*—a weekly which first appeared in 1913. Its sister publication *Philatelic Magazine* (monthly, formerly fortnightly) dates from 1911 (including its forerunner *Philatelic Circular*). *Stamp Magazine* began life in 1933 and tends to cater for the younger philatelist and the new-issue collector. The most recent additions to the range of magazines available are the monthlies *Stamps* (1980), *Foreign Stamps* (1982) and the fortnightly *Stamp & Postal History News* (1981).

The British Post Office has since 1963 published its own monthly magazine *The Philatelic Bulletin* which of course restricts itself to the stamps and postal history of Great Britain. The magazine includes details of forthcoming issues as well as short but significant articles on earlier stamps and postal history including features on the treasures of the National Postal Museum. For postmark collectors the P.O. produces a fortnightly guide to forthcoming postmarks (handstamps and slogans)—*The Postmark Bulletin*. Both are available on subscription from the P.O. Philatelic Bureau and *The Philatelic Bulletin* is also sold at philatelic counters. For the young collector the P.O. runs an informal club—the Stamp Bug Club (started 1980) which has its own colourful magazine *Stamp Bug News*. This does a lot to interest youngsters and gives useful advice and hints on stamp collecting as well as details of new British issues.

It cannot be urged too strongly upon the collector that money spent on catalogues, magazines and books, is not wasted. Presumably he wishes to do something more than merely to *collect*, and would clothe the dry bones of his stamps with a garment of fact, even if he has no ambition to be a searcher after new knowledge. It is absolutely certain that money spent on the proper kind of helpful reading matter will repay itself in interest and encouragement a hundred times over. Knowledge is power in stamp-collecting as in everything else and, though we are not discussing here the monetary aspects of the hobby, it is most certainly the man who studies his stamps in the light of published information, who makes the most of them in the end.

Conclusion

The writer who, with a full knowledge of and love for the hobby of stamp-collecting, attempts to bring within the covers of a single volume a description of its many attractions, must inevitably be depressed with a sense of the hopelessness of his task. There is so much to be said that a library would not suffice to tell the story, and even if the writer were granted unlimited time and space, and could find readers willing to follow him, he might well miss conveying some of the charm of this pursuit—the sudden unexpected sidelights on history, the glimpses of human nature, the peeps into the storehouse of general knowledge.

Some attempt must be made, however, to sum up the many-sided appeal of a hobby about which so much has been and could still be written, even though cold print can never do justice to the feelings of the enthusiast. Even the most sceptical reader must surely admit that stamp collecting has 'something in it'—or why this great army of collectors, this world-wide press and trade organisation, these accepted monetary values?

What that 'something' is we must leave the reader to find out, either from what he has already learned from this volume, or from the experiments he may base upon what he has read, and certainly experiment will be a better introduction than all the writing in the world.

It may be that you—the reader—will collect, just because the collecting mania has bitten you. If so, it is unlikely that you will stay at the elementary stage of collecting. Sooner or later curiosity will grip you. You will want to know the meaning of this design, the circumstances under which that stamp was issued, why this overprint was applied, or how such a variation in printing occurred. Once this curiosity is aroused your permanent enjoyment of the hobby is assured, for arousing and satisfaction of curiosity is one of philately's attractions. Once you realise what lies behind the humble postage stamp, it cannot fail to interest you in one way or another and what that way shall be will be decided by the bent of your own mind.

There is no doubt that the stamp collector who exercises this curiosity in the right way will eventually find himself the possessor of much knowledge of a practical kind, which will broaden his horizon and may prove of considerable value in the ordinary give-and-take of life. No one, in these days, takes pride in ignorance, and if even the time devoted to a hobby may be regarded as educationally spent, the pursuit of that hobby is in keeping with the spirit of the age.

What of its practical advantages? Nerve-strain is perhaps the greatest evil from which we suffer at the present day, and doctors generally are in agreement in telling us that the best remedy is to switch the mind, in leisure hours, from the ruts along which it moves in the course of the daily task, and that an absorbing hobby provides the best alternative to work. When we ask 'What hobby?' we find, marvellous to relate, that the doctors take their own prescription, and that the hobby they favour above all is stamp-collecting.

Why they, and other busy professional and commercial men, choose this in preference to other hobbies, is easily discovered. Apart from its attractions as having a mental and not a purely mechanical appeal, it is a hobby which can be taken up at odd moments, which need not necessarily occupy much space, which does not require a complicated apparatus, which is clean and can have a social aspect as well if so desired.

Owing to their world-wide distribution, it is possible to collect stamps in almost any place on the globe. Their small size and light weight also make it easy to send stamps for exchange or sale through the post, so that collectors in out-of-the-way places are still able to keep up their hobby. Another advantage arises from the fact that the average value of postage stamps is less than that of many other things which are collected. The stamp collector is thus able to add continually to his treasures, while some other collectors can only make an occasional purchase after long intervals of 'saving-up'. Nor is it necessary to spend large sums in order to obtain the maximum of pleasure from the hobby. The school boy with his pence probably can have as much pleasure as the millionaire who spends thousands of pounds on a single stamp.

While many collectors carry on the hobby in lonely isolation, it can be made the basis of pleasant social relationships, either by correspondence or by personal touch through philatelic societies and clubs, which abound in most parts of the globe. For many individuals, the hobby has proved a godsend. It can be pursued just as easily in the sick-room as at the outposts of civilisation. It can help the sufferer to forget pain as it helps the exile to bear his loneliness.

Thus men, women and children of all nationalities, classes and types of mind, are united in the pursuit of the postage stamp and in love of this leading universal hobby. The best that the author can wish his readers is that they are sharing or may soon come to share in the pleasures offered by it.

Index